THE ANSWER!

THE ANSW

VOLUME 1

STORY BY

DENNIS HOPELESS
and MIKE NORTON

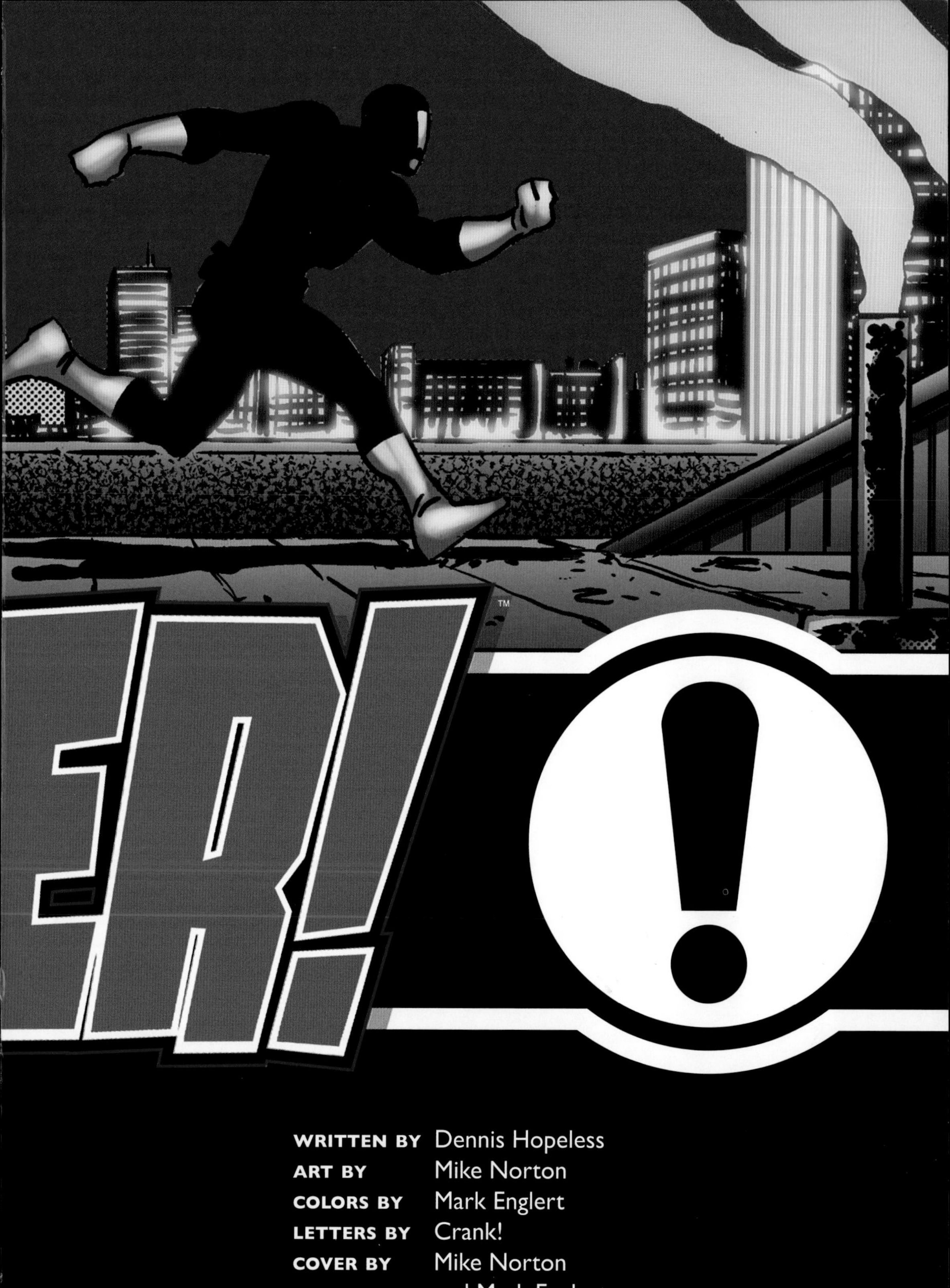
ER!

WRITTEN BY Dennis Hopeless
ART BY Mike Norton
COLORS BY Mark Englert
LETTERS BY Crank!
COVER BY Mike Norton

PRESIDENT AND PUBLISHER
Mike Richardson

DESIGNER
Adam Grano

DIGITAL PRODUCTION
Christianne Goudreau

ASSISTANT EDITOR
Everett Patterson

EDITOR
Patrick Thorpe

Special thanks to Annie Gullion.

This volume collects issues #1 through #4 of Dark Horse Comics' miniseries *The Answer!*

Published by
Dark Horse Books
A division of Dark Horse Comics, Inc.
10956 SE Main Street
Milwaukie, OR 97222

DarkHorse.com

To find a comics shop in your area, call the Comic Shop Locator Service
toll-free at (888) 266-4226. International Licensing: (503) 905-2377.

First edition: October 2013
ISBN 978-1-61655-197-1

Printed in China

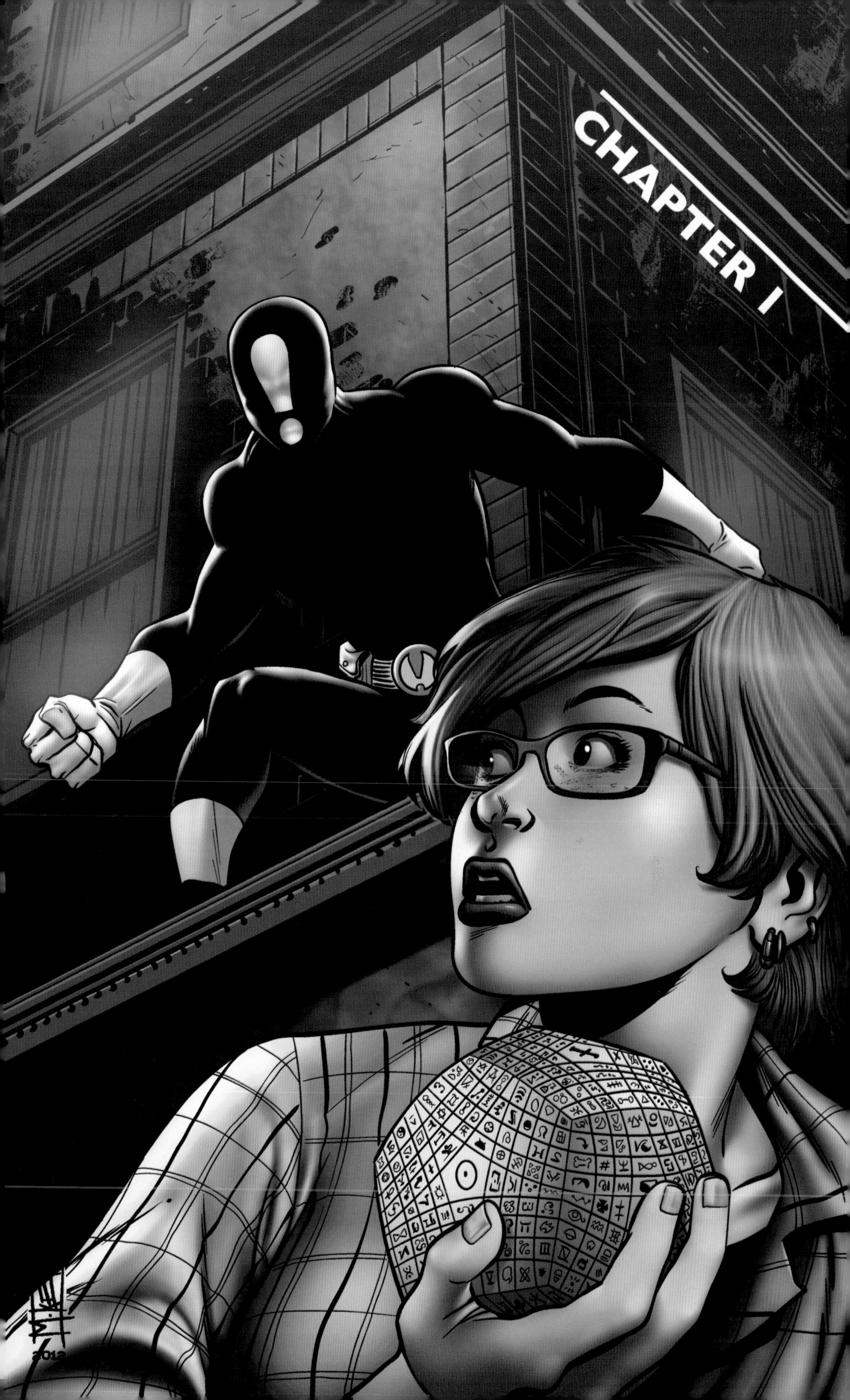
CHAPTER I

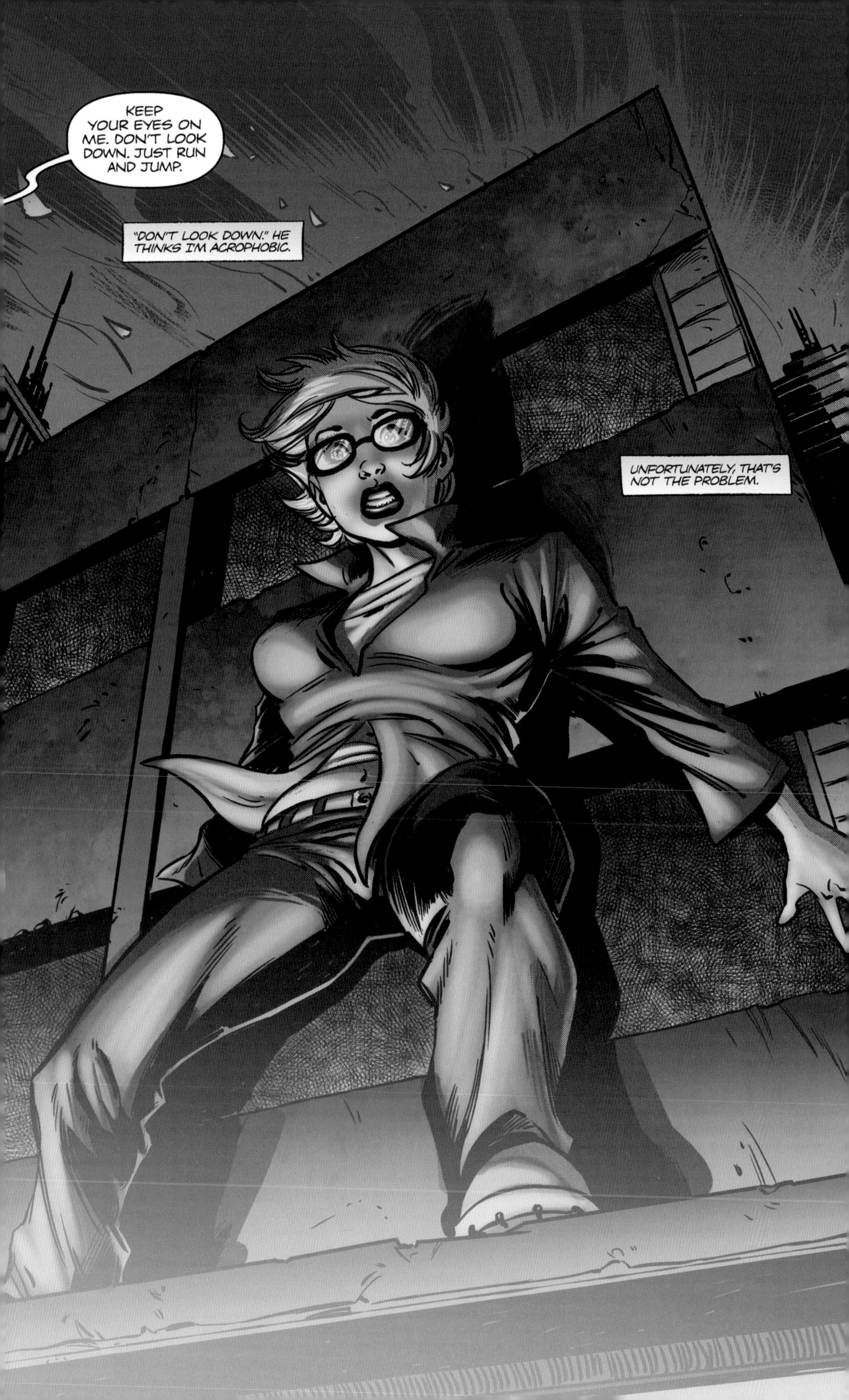
KEEP YOUR EYES ON ME. DON'T LOOK DOWN. JUST RUN AND JUMP.
"DON'T LOOK DOWN." HE THINKS I'M ACROPHOBIC.
UNFORTUNATELY, THAT'S NOT THE PROBLEM.

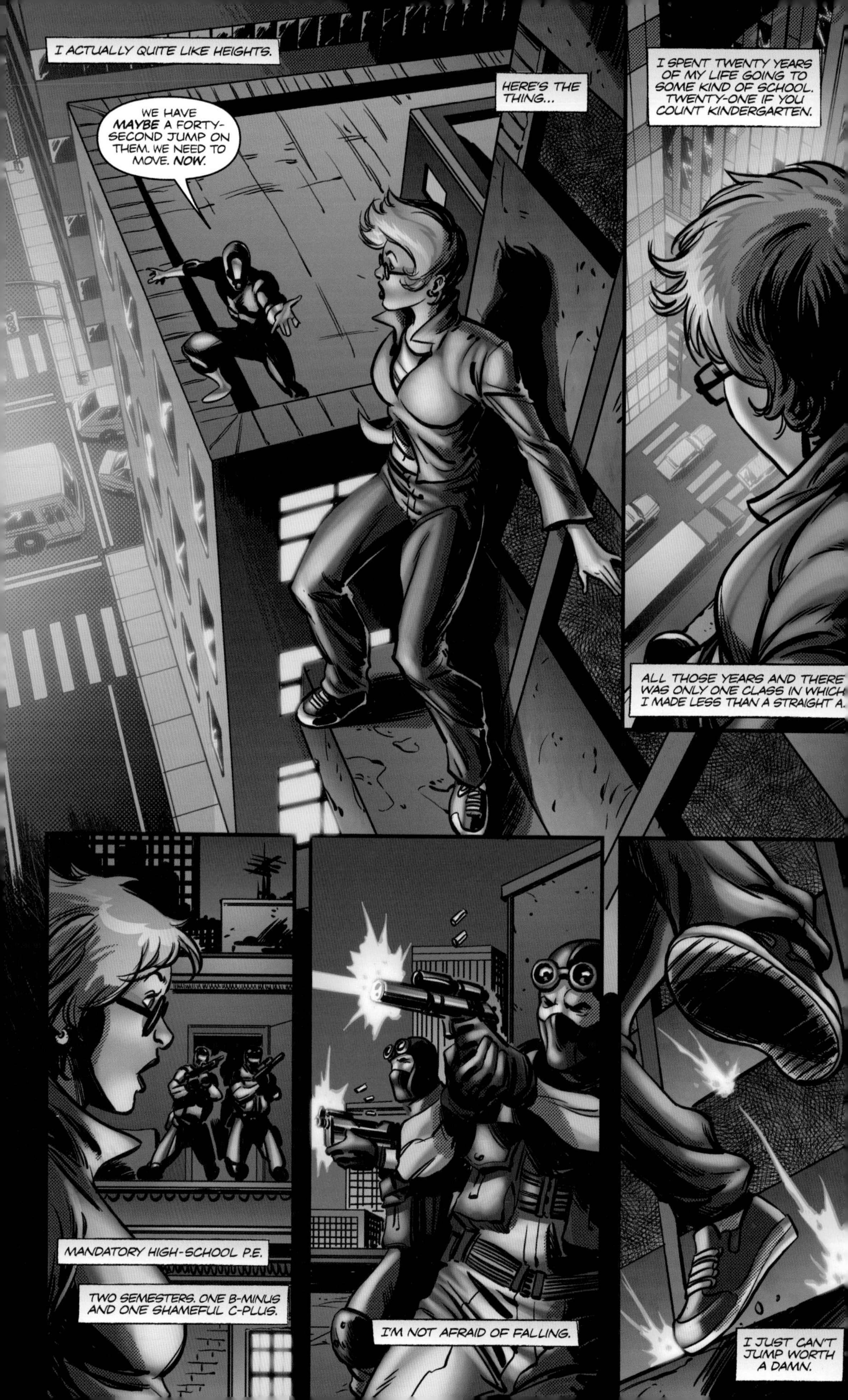
I ACTUALLY QUITE LIKE HEIGHTS.
WE HAVE MAYBE A FORTY-SECOND JUMP ON THEM. WE NEED TO MOVE. NOW.
HERE'S THE THING...
I SPENT TWENTY YEARS OF MY LIFE GOING TO SOME KIND OF SCHOOL. TWENTY-ONE IF YOU COUNT KINDERGARTEN.
ALL THOSE YEARS AND THERE WAS ONLY ONE CLASS IN WHICH I MADE LESS THAN A STRAIGHT A.
MANDATORY HIGH-SCHOOL P.E.
TWO SEMESTERS. ONE B-MINUS AND ONE SHAMEFUL C-PLUS.
I'M NOT AFRAID OF FALLING.
I JUST CAN'T JUMP WORTH A DAMN.

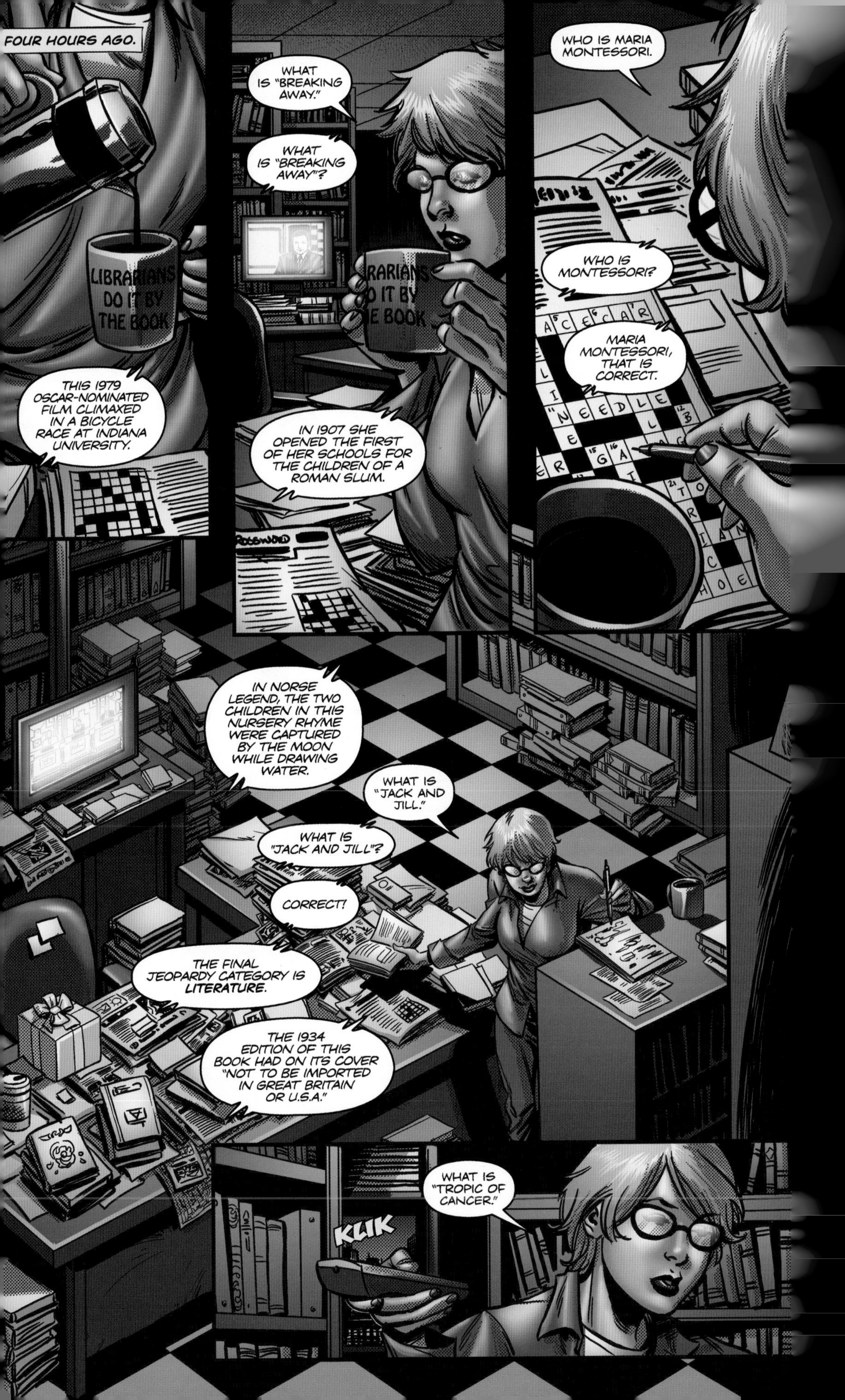
FOUR HOURS AGO.
THIS 1979 OSCAR-NOMINATED FILM CLIMAXED IN A BICYCLE RACE AT INDIANA UNIVERSITY.
LIBRARIANS DO IT BY THE BOOK
WHAT IS "BREAKING AWAY."
WHAT IS "BREAKING AWAY"?
IN 1907 SHE OPENED THE FIRST OF HER SCHOOLS FOR THE CHILDREN OF A ROMAN SLUM.
WHO IS MARIA MONTESSORI.
WHO IS MONTESSORI?
MARIA MONTESSORI, THAT IS CORRECT.
IN NORSE LEGEND, THE TWO CHILDREN IN THIS NURSERY RHYME WERE CAPTURED BY THE MOON WHILE DRAWING WATER.
WHAT IS "JACK AND JILL."
WHAT IS "JACK AND JILL"?
CORRECT!
THE FINAL JEOPARDY CATEGORY IS LITERATURE.
THE 1934 EDITION OF THIS BOOK HAD ON ITS COVER "NOT TO BE IMPORTED IN GREAT BRITAIN OR U.S.A."
WHAT IS "TROPIC OF CANCER."
KLIK

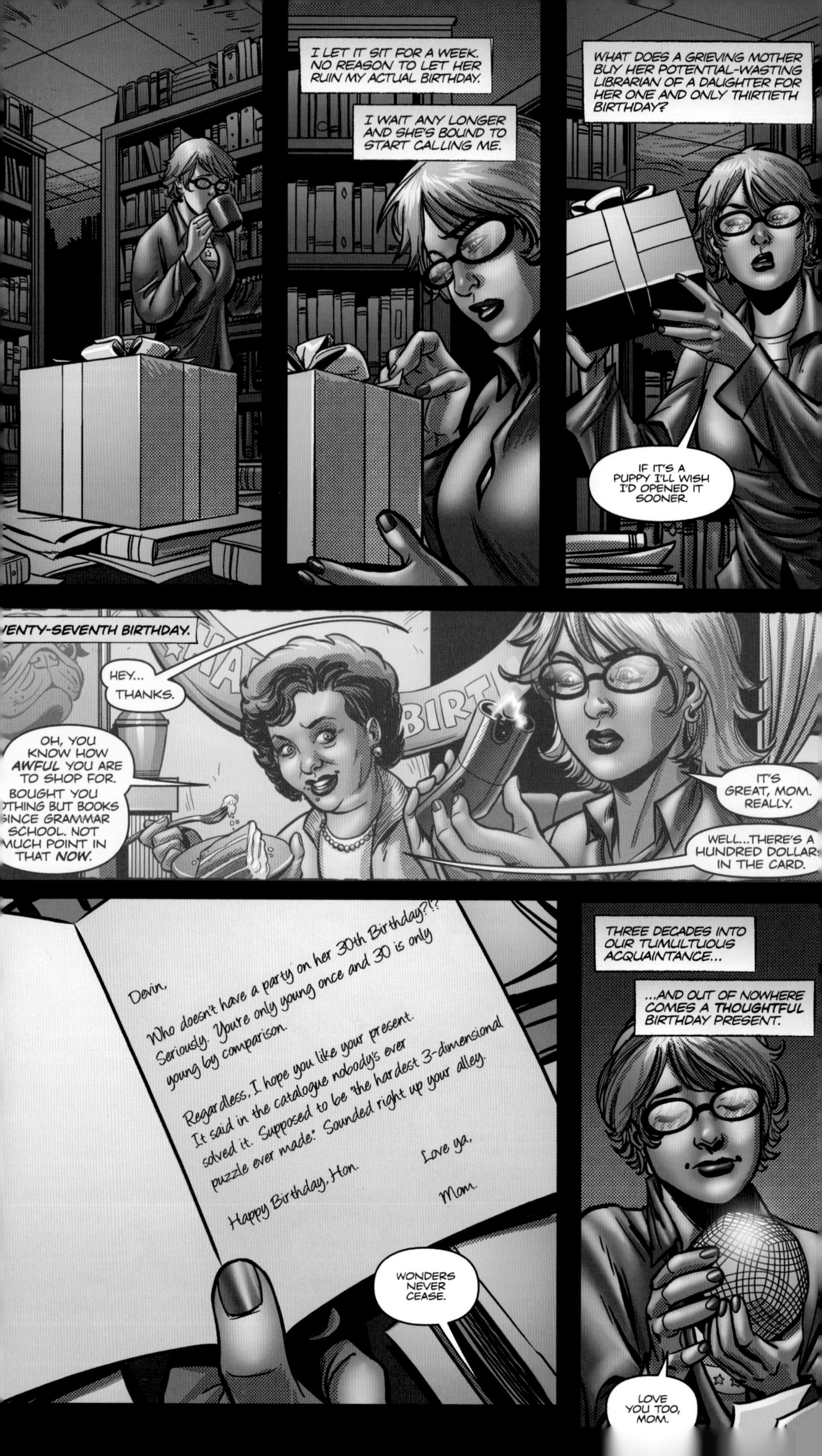
I LET IT SIT FOR A WEEK. NO REASON TO LET HER RUIN MY ACTUAL BIRTHDAY.
I WAIT ANY LONGER AND SHE'S BOUND TO START CALLING ME.
WHAT DOES A GRIEVING MOTHER BUY HER POTENTIAL-WASTING LIBRARIAN OF A DAUGHTER FOR HER ONE AND ONLY THIRTIETH BIRTHDAY?
IF IT'S A PUPPY I'LL WISH I'D OPENED IT SOONER.
ENTY-SEVENTH BIRTHDAY.
HEY... THANKS.
OH, YOU KNOW HOW **AWFUL** YOU ARE TO SHOP FOR. BOUGHT YOU OTHING BUT BOOKS SINCE GRAMMAR SCHOOL. NOT MUCH POINT IN THAT **NOW**.
IT'S GREAT, MOM. REALLY.
WELL...THERE'S A HUNDRED DOLLAR IN THE CARD.
Devin,
Who doesn't have a party on her 30th Birthday?!? Seriously. You're only young once and 30 is only young by comparison.
Regardless, I hope you like your present. It said in the catalogue nobody's ever solved it. Supposed to be "the hardest 3-dimensional puzzle ever made." Sounded right up your alley.
Happy Birthday, Hon.
Love ya,
Mom.
WONDERS NEVER CEASE.
THREE DECADES INTO OUR TUMULTUOUS ACQUAINTANCE...
...AND OUT OF NOWHERE COMES A **THOUGHTFUL** BIRTHDAY PRESENT.
LOVE YOU TOO, MOM.

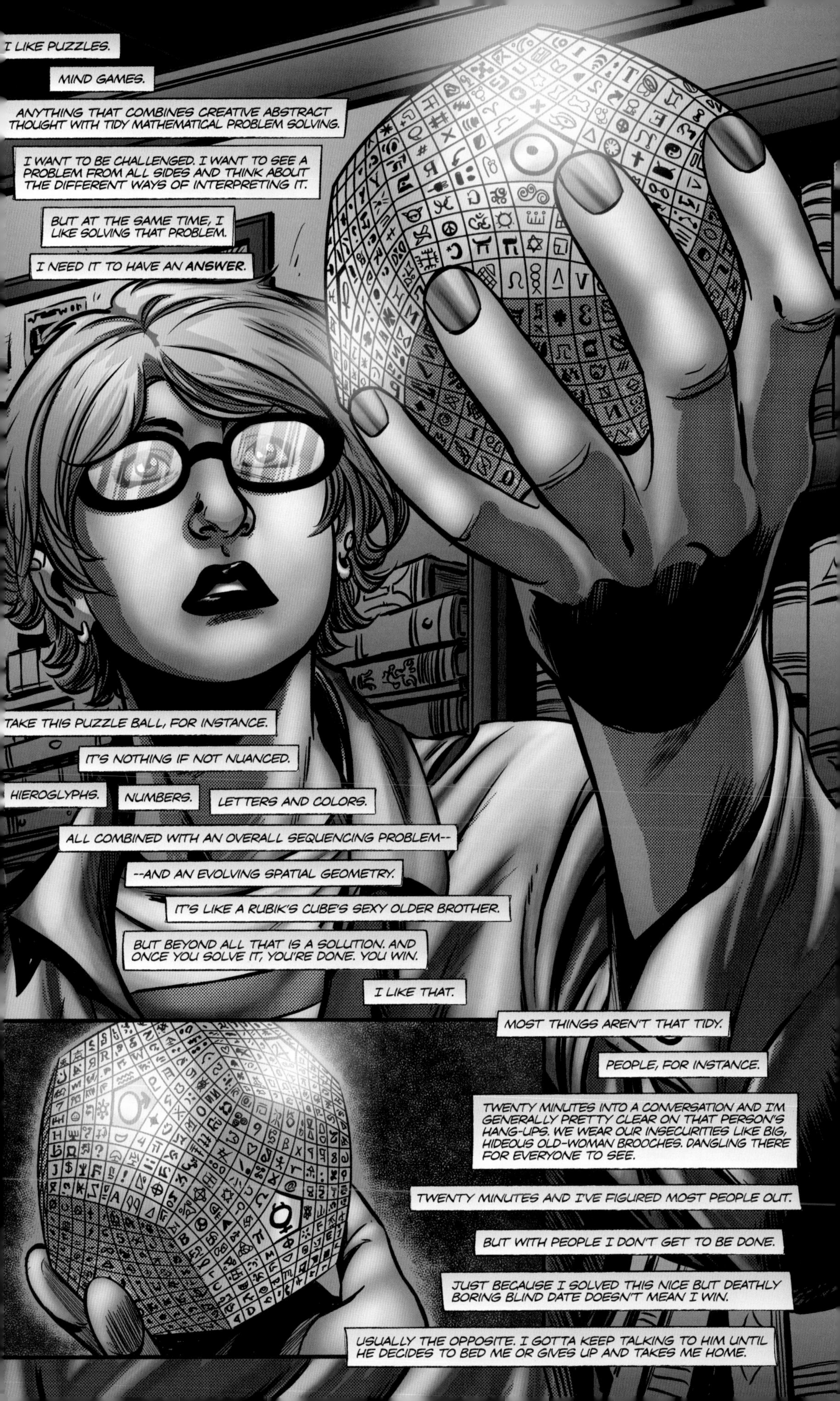

I LIKE PUZZLES.
MIND GAMES.
ANYTHING THAT COMBINES CREATIVE ABSTRACT THOUGHT WITH TIDY MATHEMATICAL PROBLEM SOLVING.
I WANT TO BE CHALLENGED. I WANT TO SEE A PROBLEM FROM ALL SIDES AND THINK ABOUT THE DIFFERENT WAYS OF INTERPRETING IT.
BUT AT THE SAME TIME, I LIKE SOLVING THAT PROBLEM.
I NEED IT TO HAVE AN ANSWER.
TAKE THIS PUZZLE BALL, FOR INSTANCE.
IT'S NOTHING IF NOT NUANCED.
HIEROGLYPHS.
NUMBERS.
LETTERS AND COLORS.
ALL COMBINED WITH AN OVERALL SEQUENCING PROBLEM--
--AND AN EVOLVING SPATIAL GEOMETRY.
IT'S LIKE A RUBIK'S CUBE'S SEXY OLDER BROTHER.
BUT BEYOND ALL THAT IS A SOLUTION. AND ONCE YOU SOLVE IT, YOU'RE DONE. YOU WIN.
I LIKE THAT.
MOST THINGS AREN'T THAT TIDY.
PEOPLE, FOR INSTANCE.
TWENTY MINUTES INTO A CONVERSATION AND I'M GENERALLY PRETTY CLEAR ON THAT PERSON'S HANG-UPS. WE WEAR OUR INSECURITIES LIKE BIG, HIDEOUS OLD-WOMAN BROOCHES. DANGLING THERE FOR EVERYONE TO SEE.
TWENTY MINUTES AND I'VE FIGURED MOST PEOPLE OUT.
BUT WITH PEOPLE I DON'T GET TO BE DONE.
JUST BECAUSE I SOLVED THIS NICE BUT DEATHLY BORING BLIND DATE DOESN'T MEAN I WIN.
USUALLY THE OPPOSITE. I GOTTA KEEP TALKING TO HIM UNTIL HE DECIDES TO BED ME OR GIVES UP AND TAKES ME HOME.

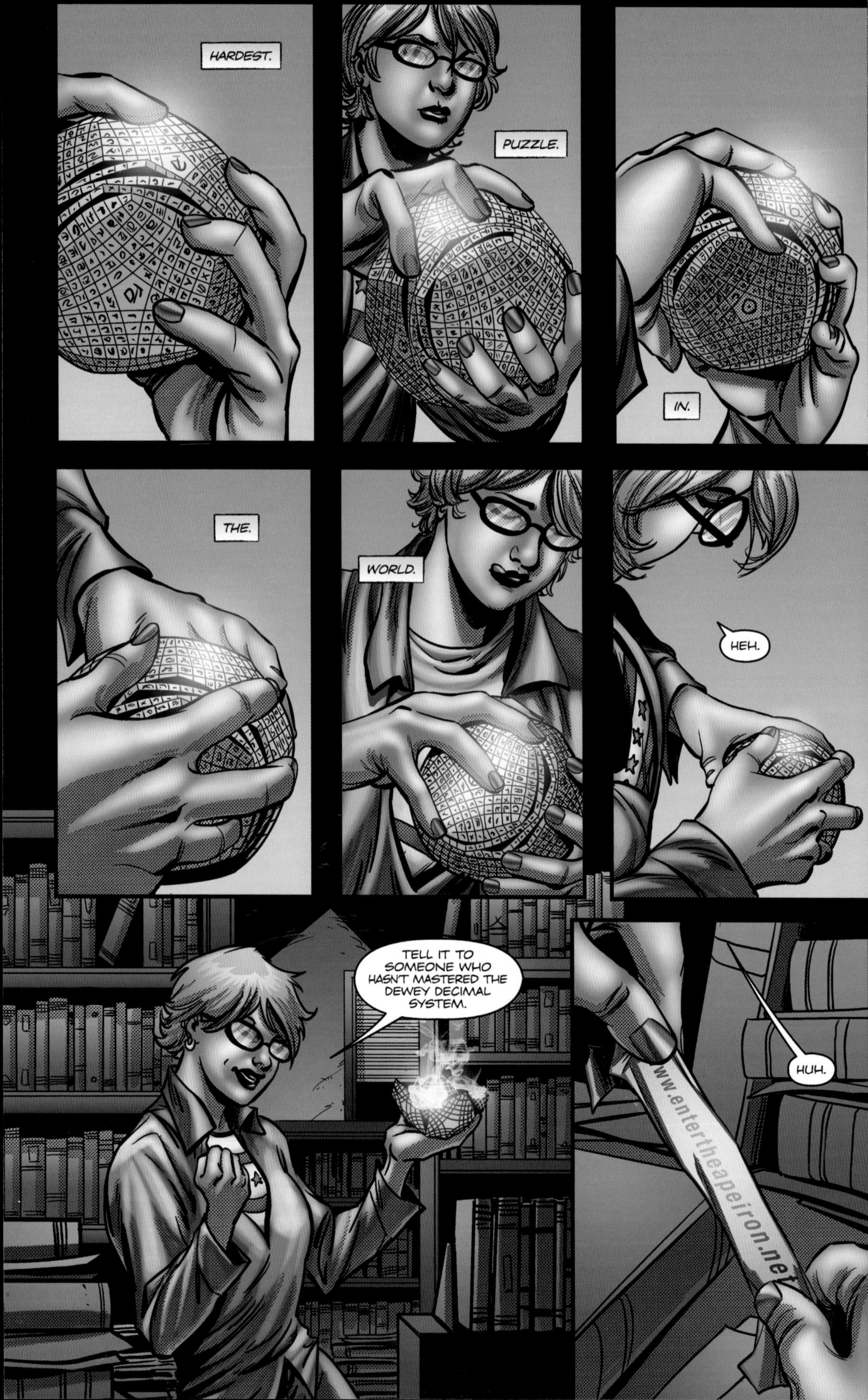
HARDEST.
PUZZLE.
IN.
THE.
WORLD.
HEH.
TELL IT TO SOMEONE WHO HASN'T MASTERED THE DEWEY DECIMAL SYSTEM.
www.entertheapeiron.net
HUH.

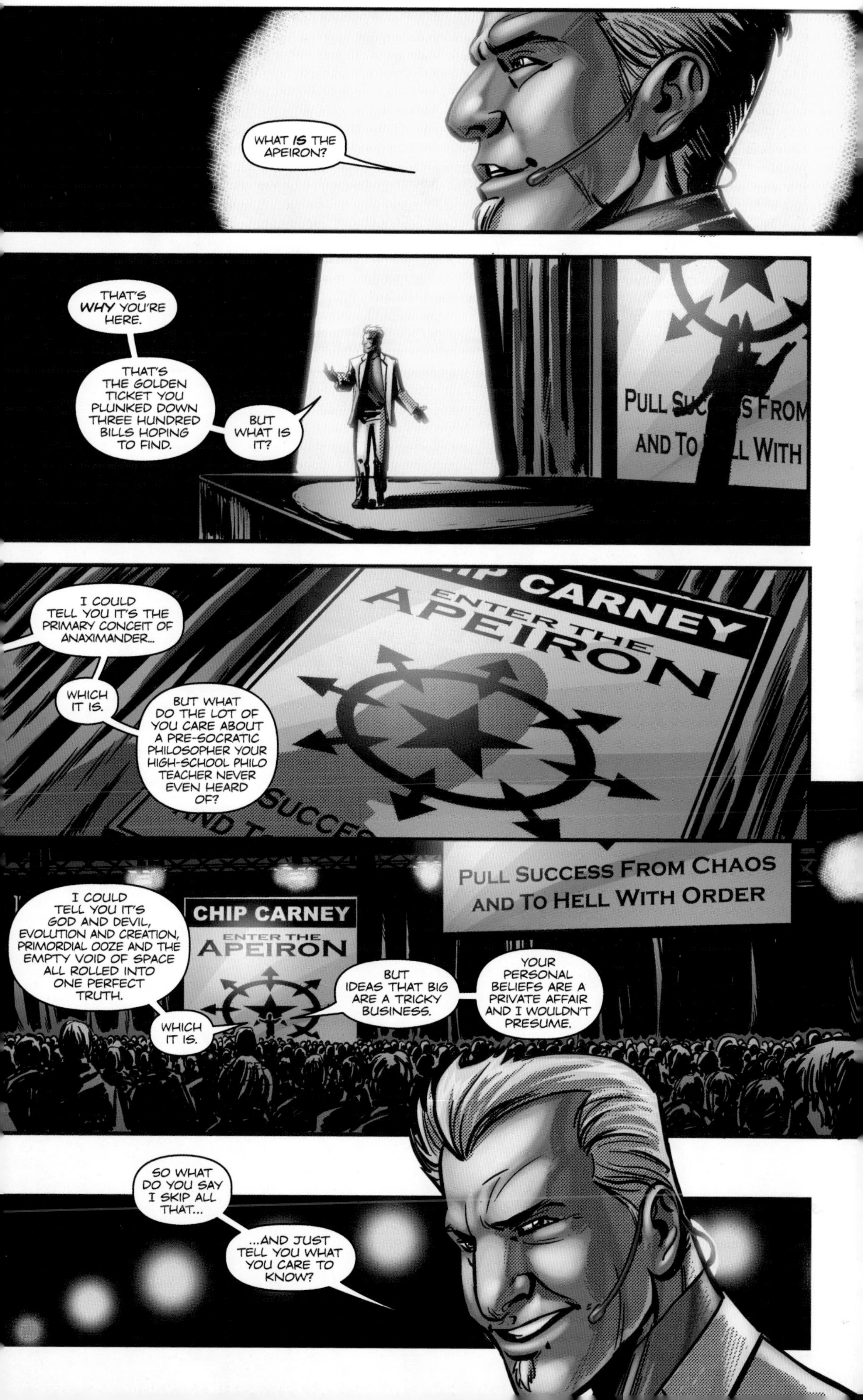

WHAT *IS* THE APEIRON?
THAT'S *WHY* YOU'RE HERE.
THAT'S THE GOLDEN TICKET YOU PLUNKED DOWN THREE HUNDRED BILLS HOPING TO FIND.
BUT WHAT IS IT?
CHIP CARNEY
ENTER THE APEIRON
I COULD TELL YOU IT'S THE PRIMARY CONCEIT OF ANAXIMANDER...
WHICH IT IS.
BUT WHAT DO THE LOT OF YOU CARE ABOUT A PRE-SOCRATIC PHILOSOPHER YOUR HIGH-SCHOOL PHILO TEACHER NEVER EVEN HEARD OF?
PULL SUCCESS FROM CHAOS AND TO HELL WITH ORDER
CHIP CARNEY
ENTER THE APEIRON
I COULD TELL YOU IT'S GOD AND DEVIL, EVOLUTION AND CREATION, PRIMORDIAL OOZE AND THE EMPTY VOID OF SPACE ALL ROLLED INTO ONE PERFECT TRUTH.
WHICH IT IS.
BUT IDEAS THAT BIG ARE A TRICKY BUSINESS.
YOUR PERSONAL BELIEFS ARE A PRIVATE AFFAIR AND I WOULDN'T PRESUME.
SO WHAT DO YOU SAY I SKIP ALL THAT...
...AND JUST TELL YOU WHAT YOU CARE TO KNOW?

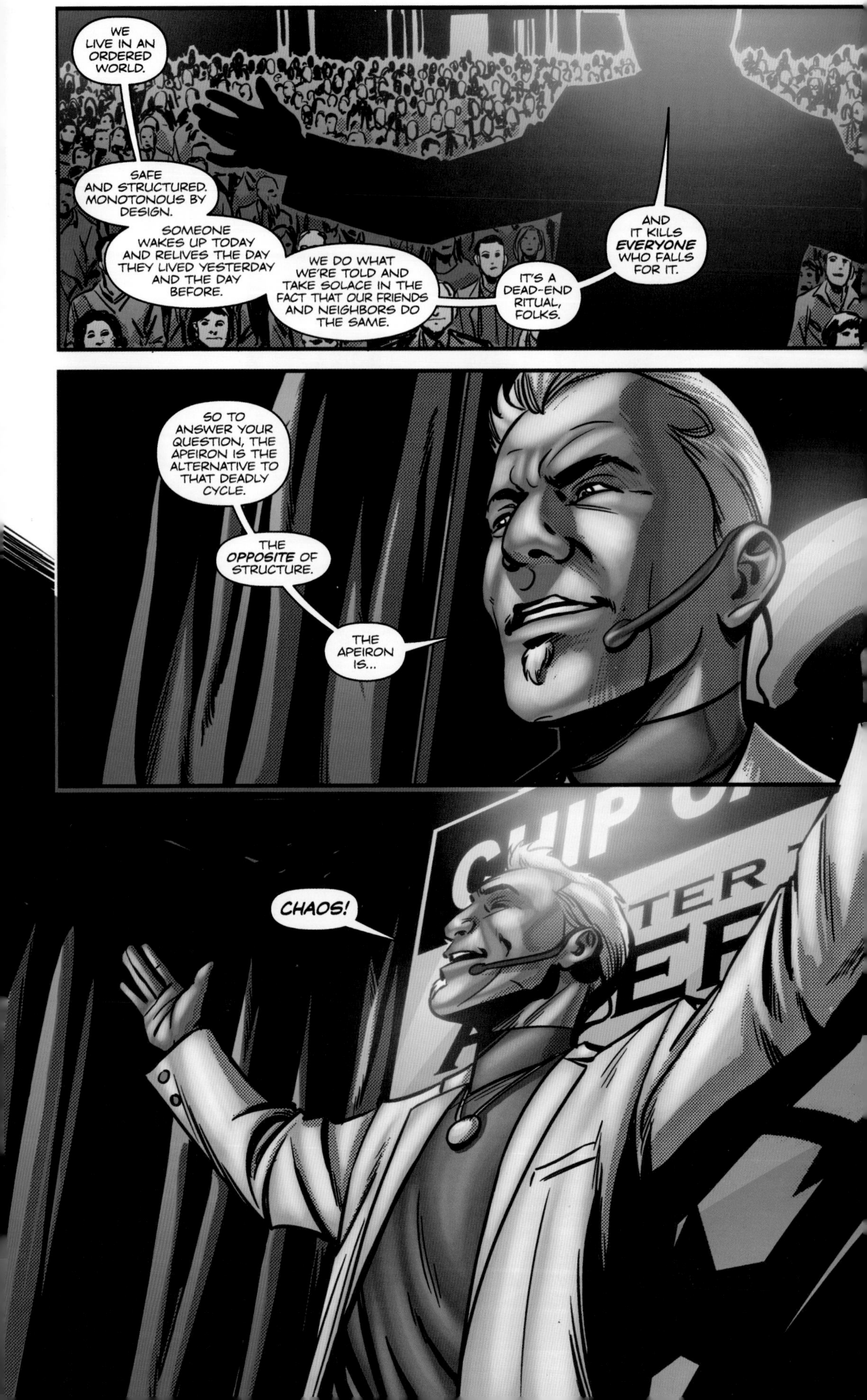
WE LIVE IN AN ORDERED WORLD.
SAFE AND STRUCTURED. MONOTONOUS BY DESIGN.
SOMEONE WAKES UP TODAY AND RELIVES THE DAY THEY LIVED YESTERDAY AND THE DAY BEFORE.
WE DO WHAT WE'RE TOLD AND TAKE SOLACE IN THE FACT THAT OUR FRIENDS AND NEIGHBORS DO THE SAME.
IT'S A DEAD-END RITUAL, FOLKS.
AND IT KILLS *EVERYONE* WHO FALLS FOR IT.
SO TO ANSWER YOUR QUESTION, THE APEIRON IS THE ALTERNATIVE TO THAT DEADLY CYCLE.
THE *OPPOSITE* OF STRUCTURE.
THE APEIRON IS...
CHAOS!
CHIP O
TER
EE

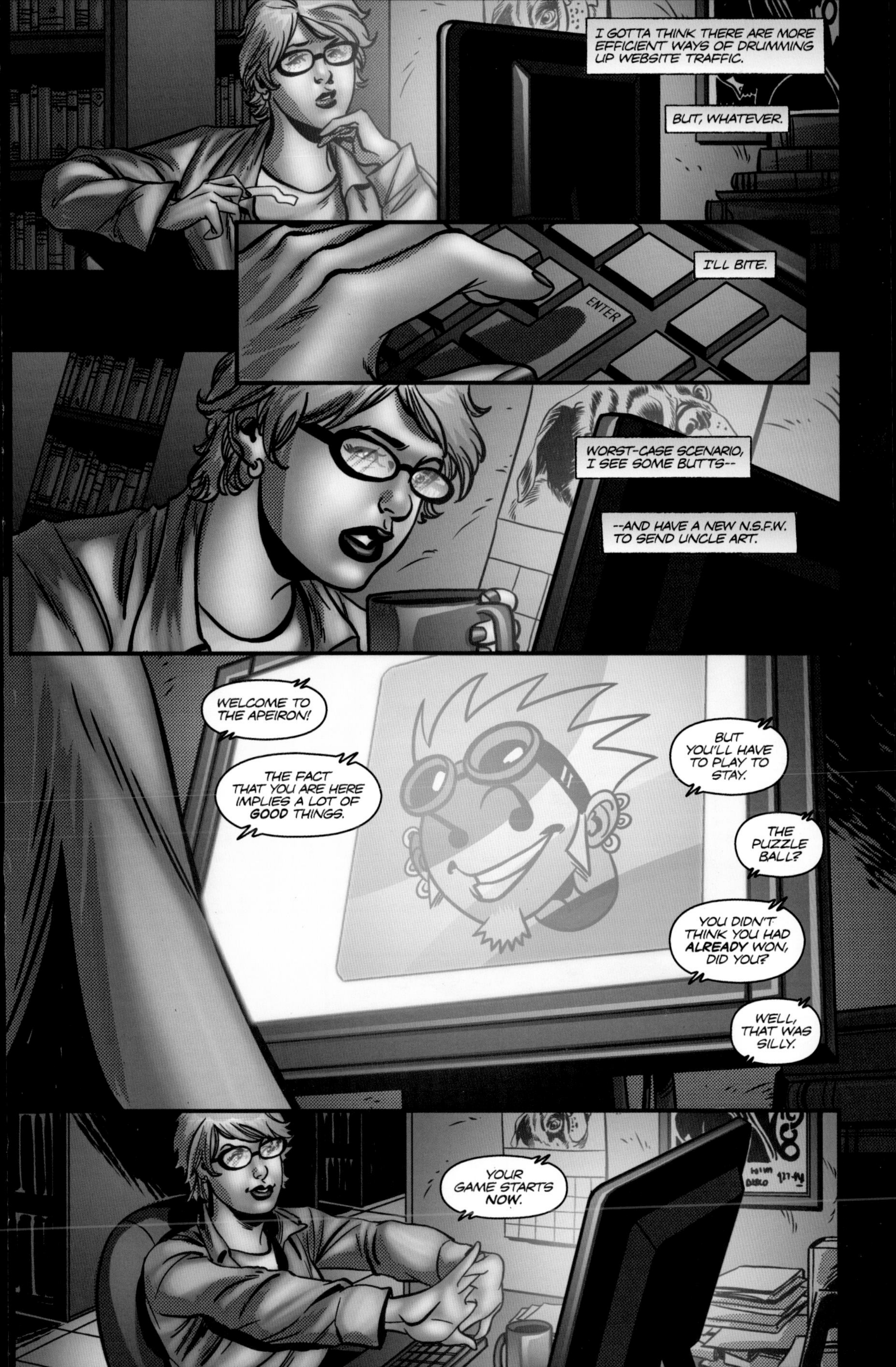
I GOTTA THINK THERE ARE MORE EFFICIENT WAYS OF DRUMMING UP WEBSITE TRAFFIC.
BUT, WHATEVER.
I'LL BITE.
ENTER
WORST-CASE SCENARIO, I SEE SOME BUTTS--
--AND HAVE A NEW N.S.F.W. TO SEND UNCLE ART.
WELCOME TO THE APEIRON!
THE FACT THAT YOU ARE HERE IMPLIES A LOT OF GOOD THINGS.
BUT YOU'LL HAVE TO PLAY TO STAY.
THE PUZZLE BALL?
YOU DIDN'T THINK YOU HAD ALREADY WON, DID YOU?
WELL, THAT WAS SILLY.
YOUR GAME STARTS NOW.

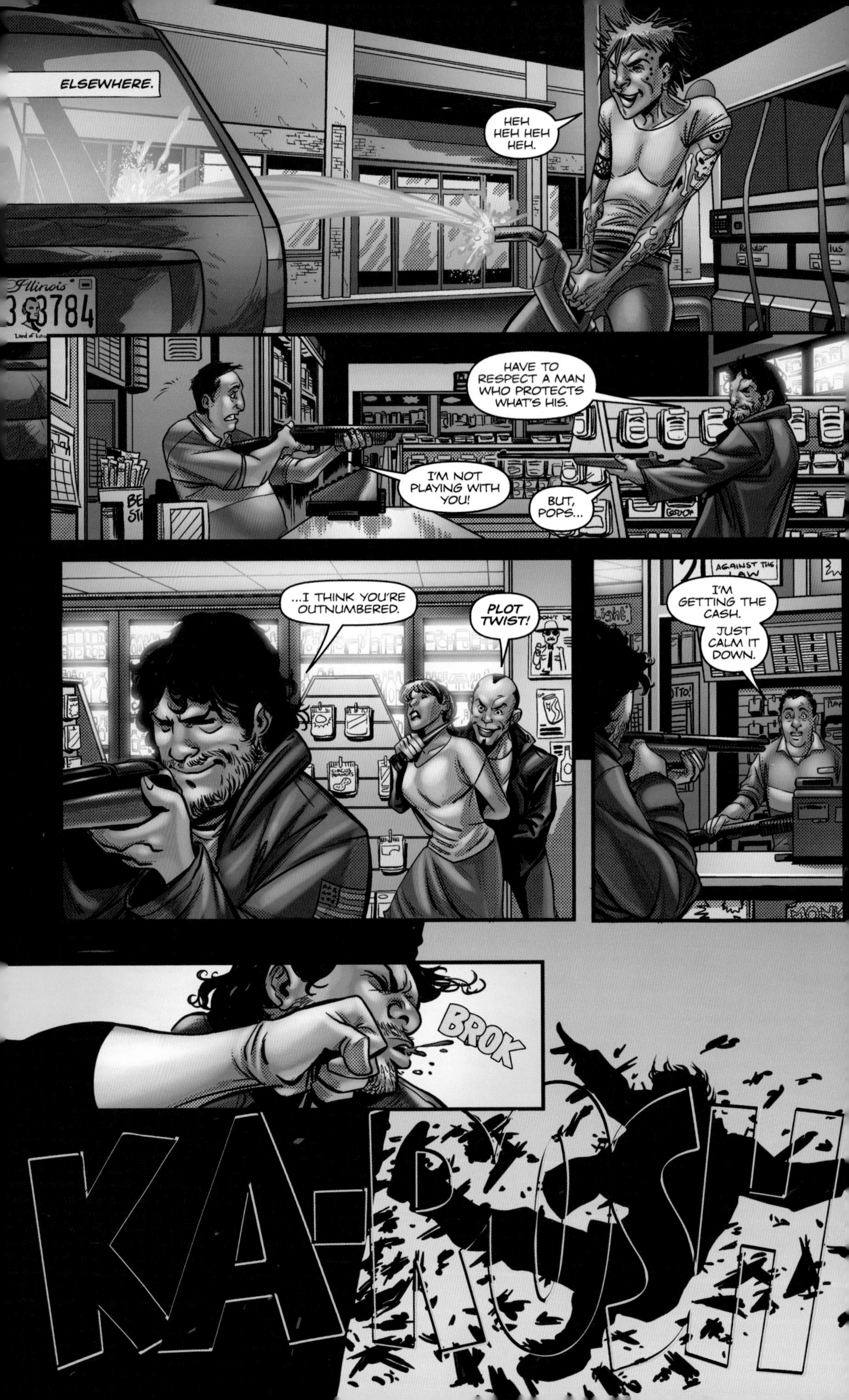
ELSEWHERE.
HEH HEH HEH HEH.
Illinois
3784
Regular
HAVE TO RESPECT A MAN WHO PROTECTS WHAT'S HIS.
I'M NOT PLAYING WITH YOU!
BUT, POPS...
...I THINK YOU'RE OUTNUMBERED.
PLOT TWIST!
AGAINST THE LAW
I'M GETTING THE CASH.
JUST CALM IT DOWN.
BROK
KA-PUSH

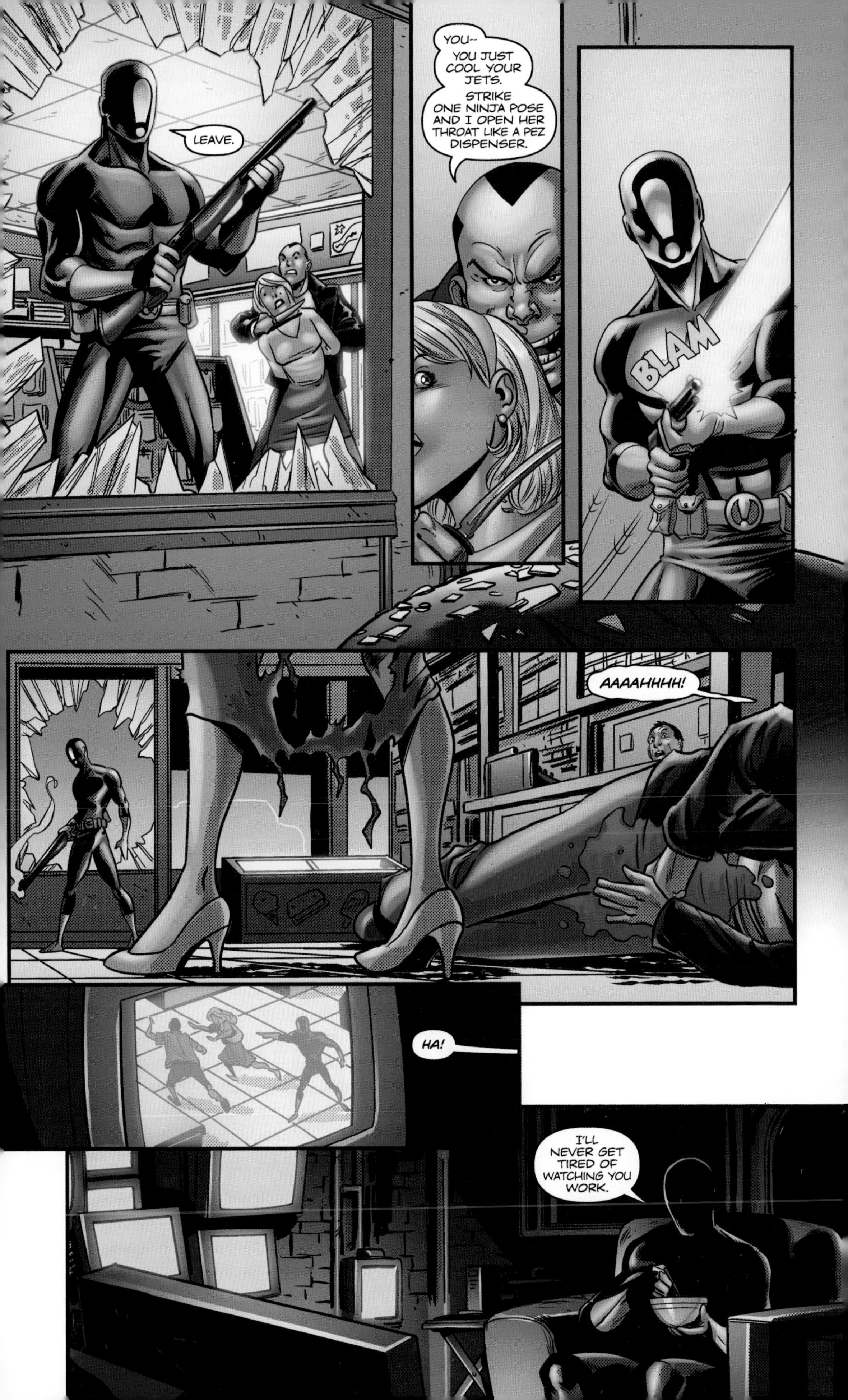
LEAVE.
YOU--
YOU JUST COOL YOUR JETS.
STRIKE ONE NINJA POSE AND I OPEN HER THROAT LIKE A PEZ DISPENSER.
BLAM
AAAAHHHH!
HA!
I'LL NEVER GET TIRED OF WATCHING YOU WORK.

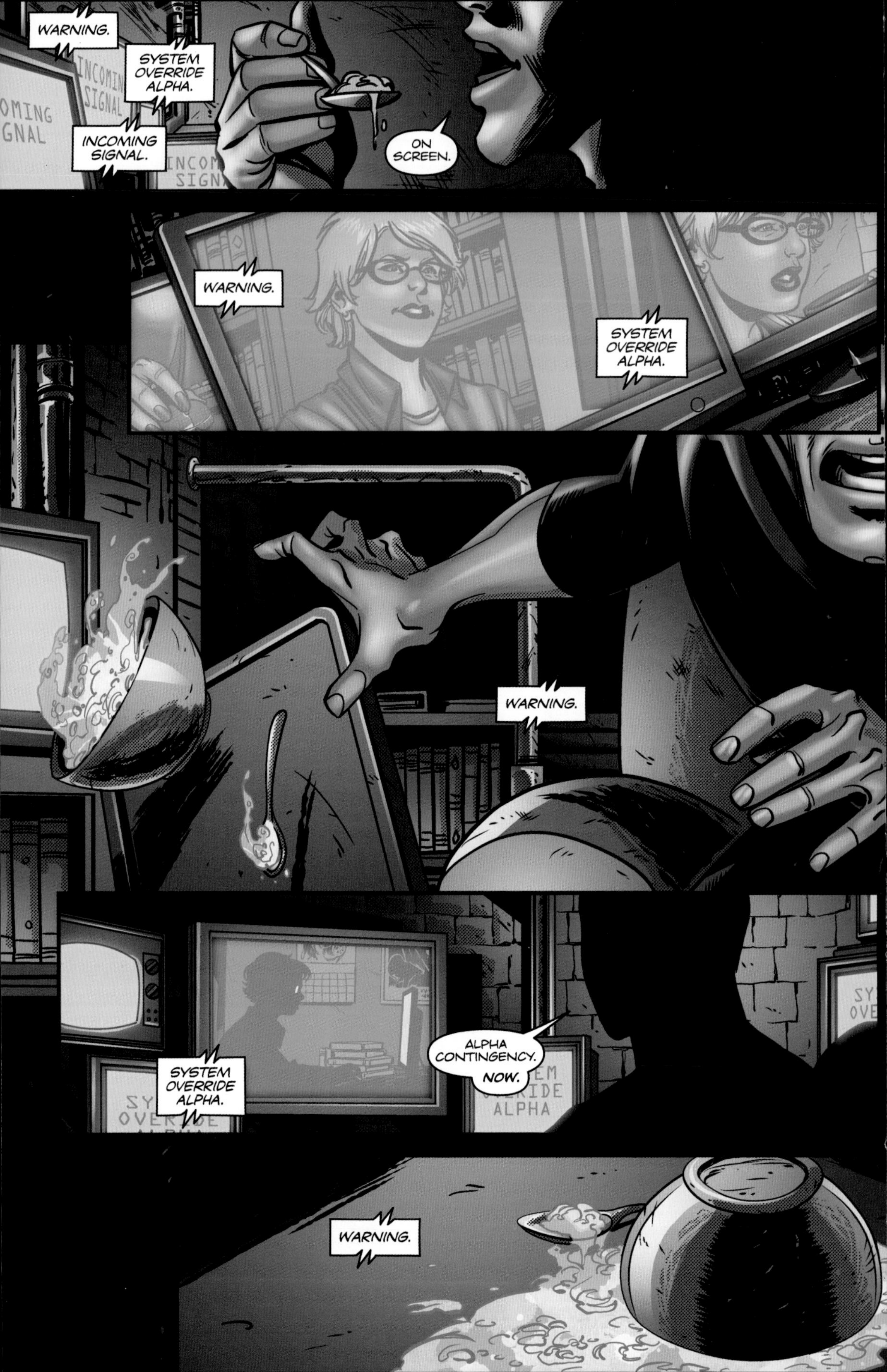
WARNING.
SYSTEM OVERRIDE ALPHA.
INCOMING SIGNAL.
INCOMING SIGNAL.
ON SCREEN.
WARNING.
SYSTEM OVERRIDE ALPHA.
WARNING.
SYSTEM OVERRIDE ALPHA.
ALPHA CONTINGENCY. NOW.
SYSTEM OVERRIDE ALPHA
WARNING.

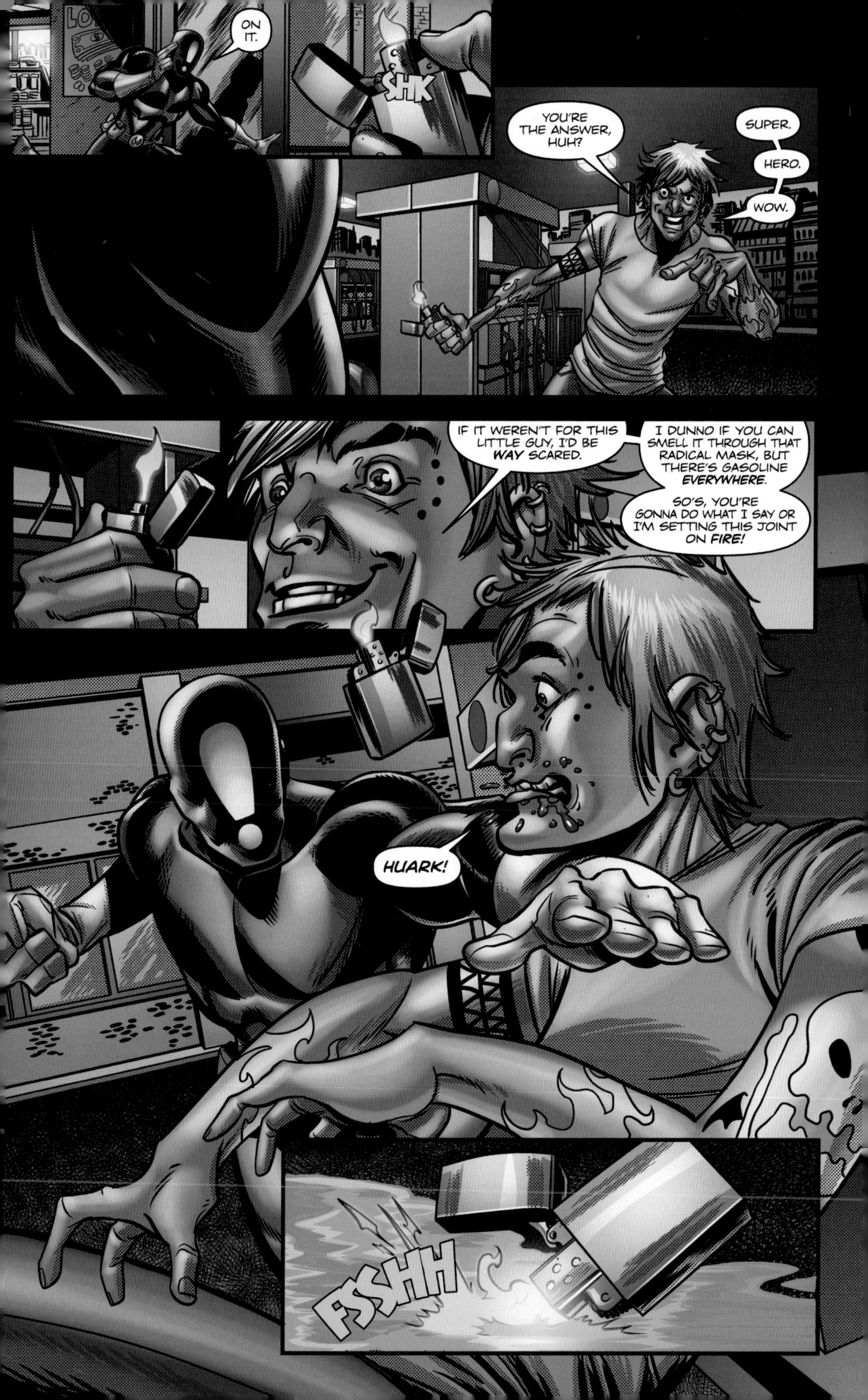
ON IT.
SHK
YOU'RE THE ANSWER, HUH?
SUPER.
HERO.
WOW.
IF IT WEREN'T FOR THIS LITTLE GUY, I'D BE *WAY* SCARED.
I DUNNO IF YOU CAN SMELL IT THROUGH THAT RADICAL MASK, BUT THERE'S GASOLINE *EVERYWHERE*.
SO'S, YOU'RE GONNA DO WHAT I SAY OR I'M SETTING THIS JOINT ON *FIRE!*
HUARK!
FSSHH

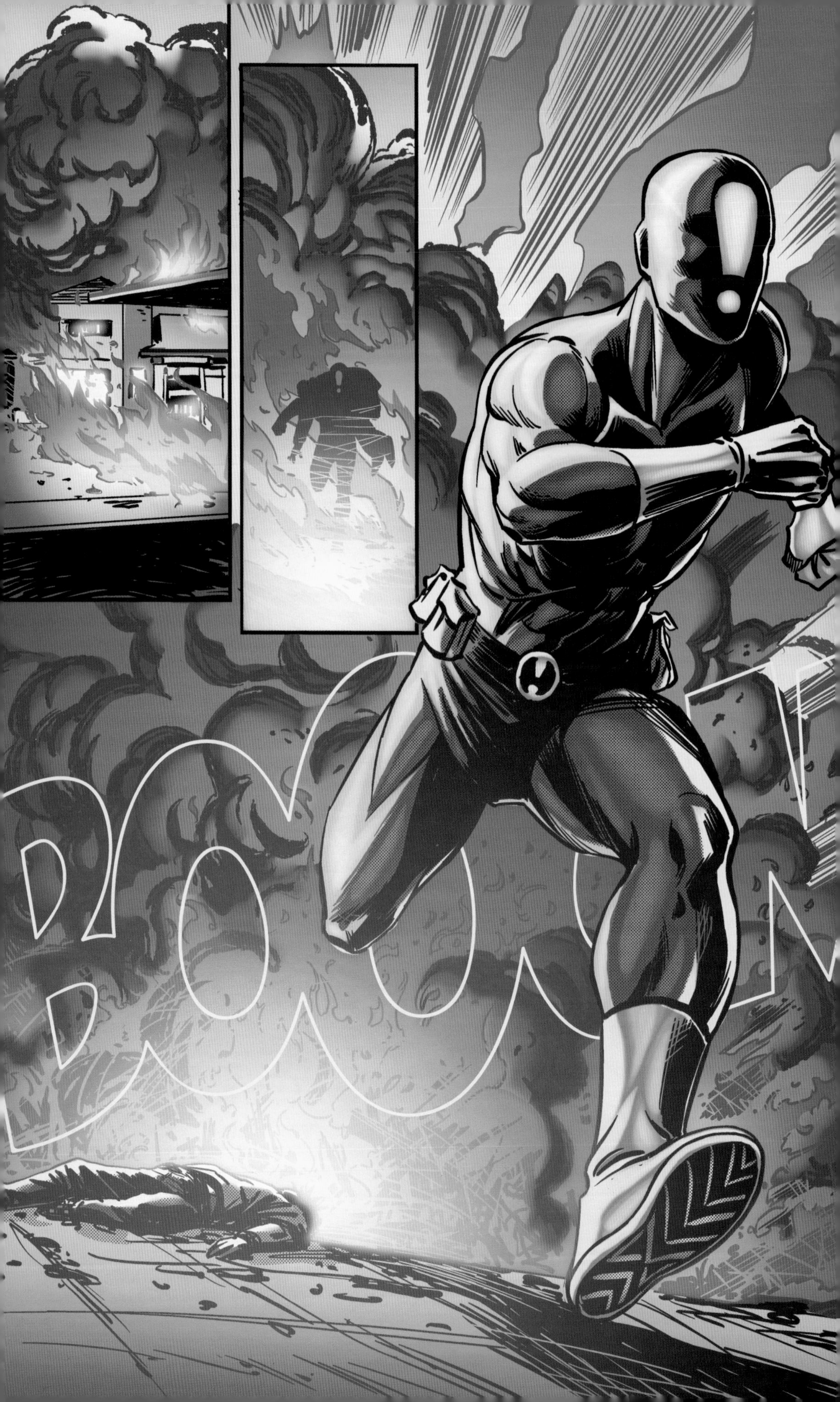
BOOOM

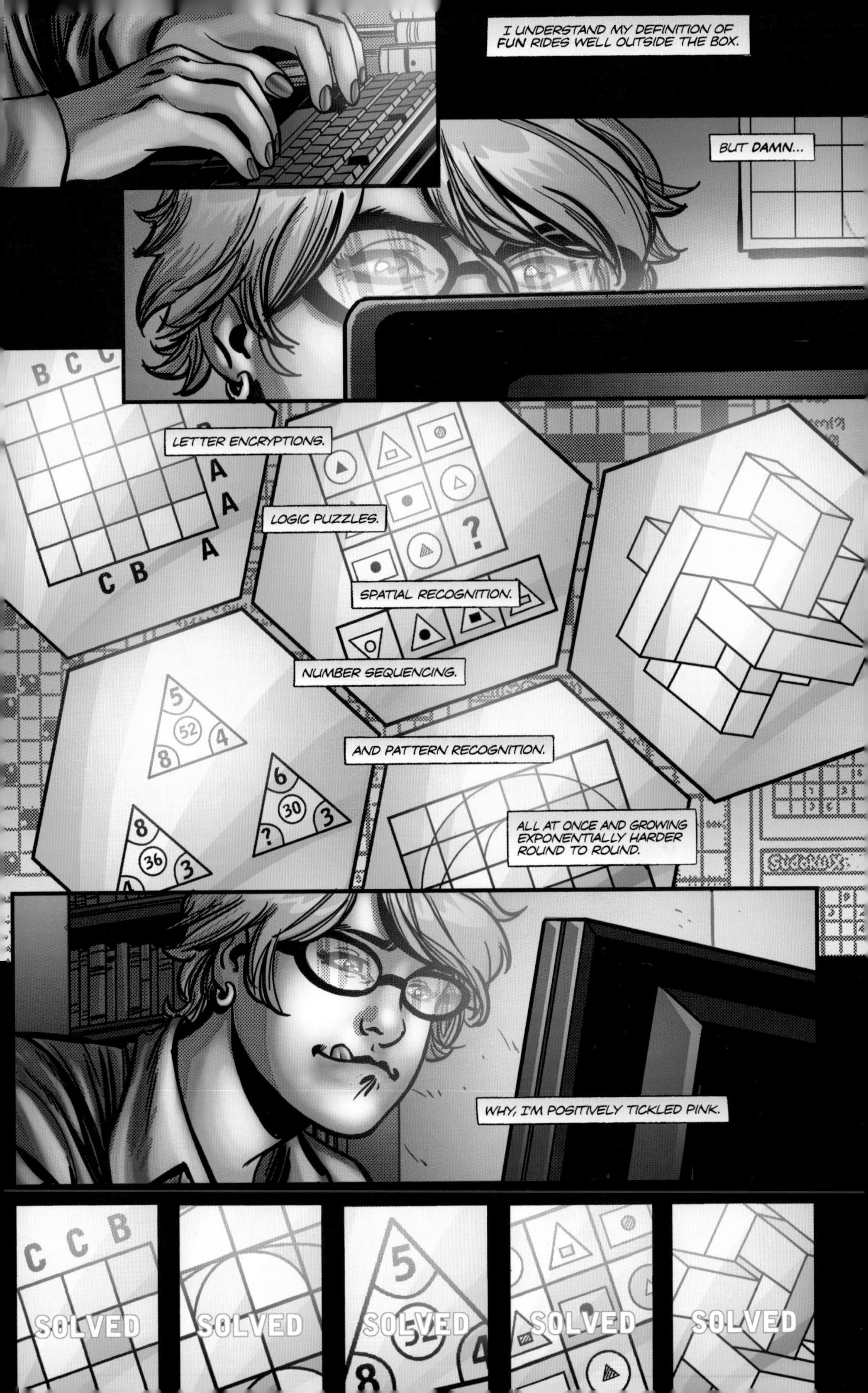
I UNDERSTAND MY DEFINITION OF FUN RIDES WELL OUTSIDE THE BOX.
BUT DAMN...
LETTER ENCRYPTIONS.
LOGIC PUZZLES.
SPATIAL RECOGNITION.
NUMBER SEQUENCING.
AND PATTERN RECOGNITION.
ALL AT ONCE AND GROWING EXPONENTIALLY HARDER ROUND TO ROUND.
WHY, I'M POSITIVELY TICKLED PINK.
SOLVED
SOLVED
SOLVED
SOLVED
SOLVED

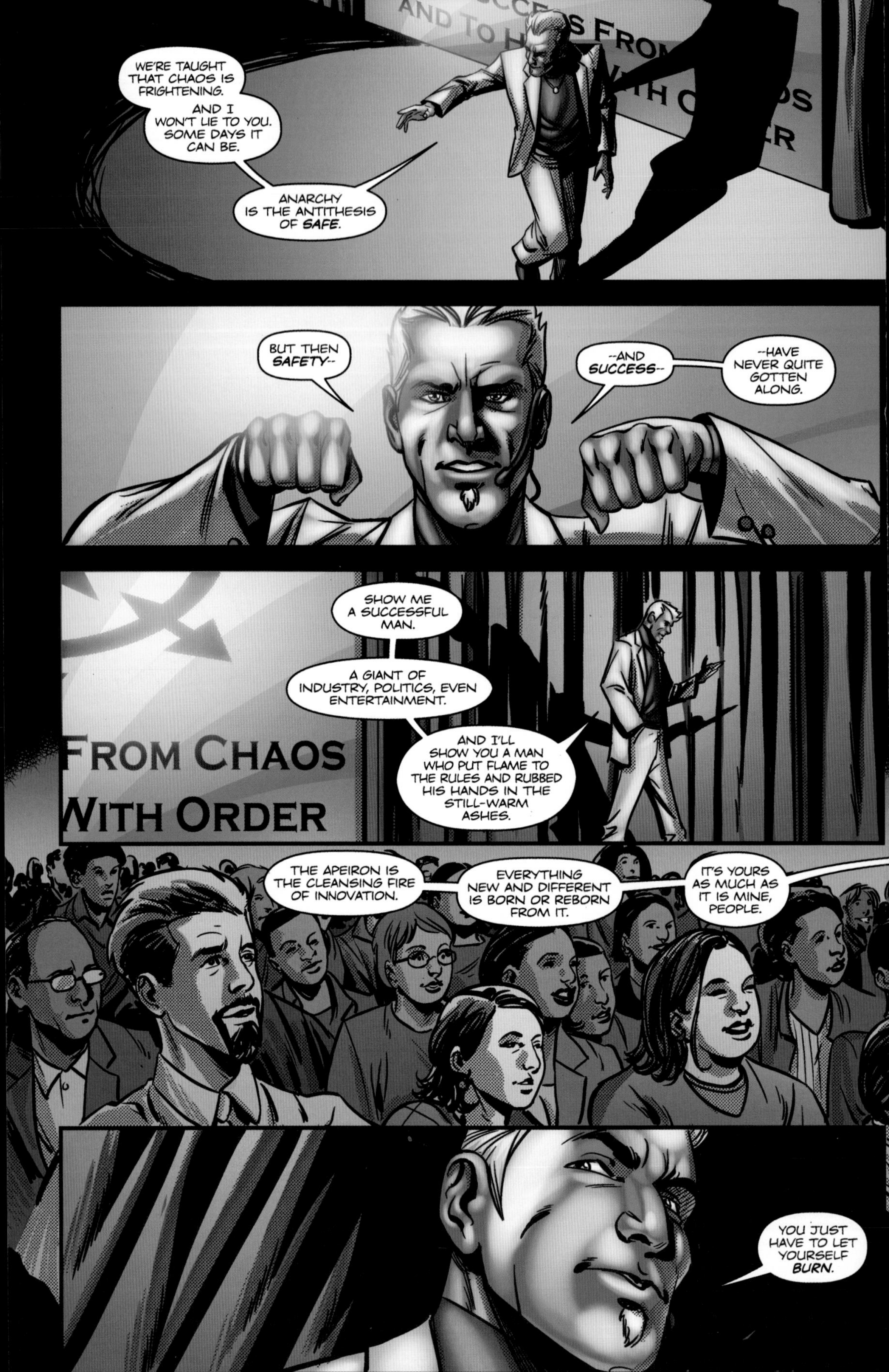
WE'RE TAUGHT THAT CHAOS IS FRIGHTENING.
AND I WON'T LIE TO YOU. SOME DAYS IT CAN BE.
ANARCHY IS THE ANTITHESIS OF SAFE.
BUT THEN SAFETY--
--AND SUCCESS--
--HAVE NEVER QUITE GOTTEN ALONG.
FROM CHAOS
WITH ORDER
SHOW ME A SUCCESSFUL MAN.
A GIANT OF INDUSTRY, POLITICS, EVEN ENTERTAINMENT.
AND I'LL SHOW YOU A MAN WHO PUT FLAME TO THE RULES AND RUBBED HIS HANDS IN THE STILL-WARM ASHES.
THE APEIRON IS THE CLEANSING FIRE OF INNOVATION.
EVERYTHING NEW AND DIFFERENT IS BORN OR REBORN FROM IT.
IT'S YOURS AS MUCH AS IT IS MINE, PEOPLE.
YOU JUST HAVE TO LET YOURSELF BURN.

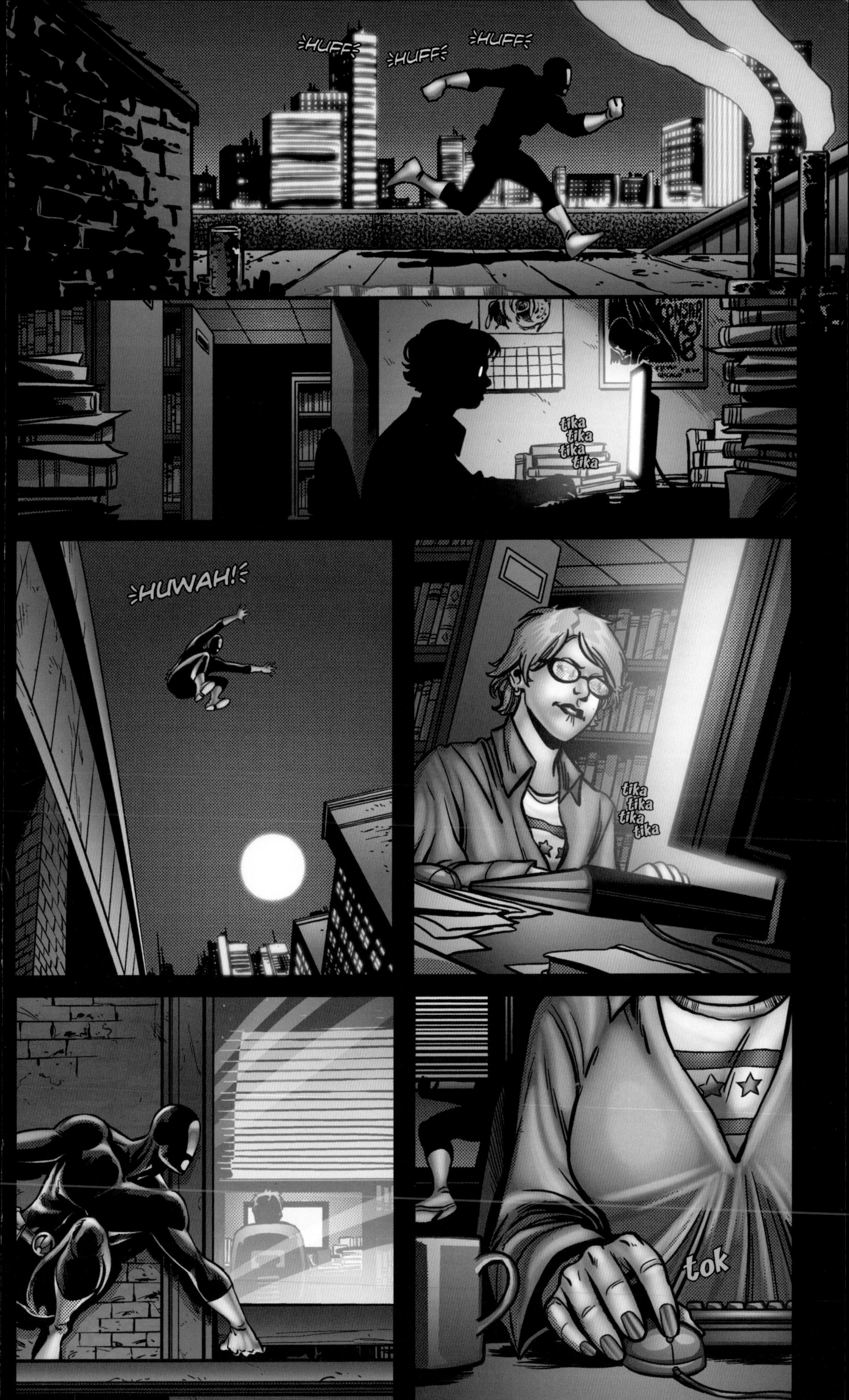
HUFF
HUFF
HUFF
tika tika tika tika
HUWAH!
tika tika tika tika
tok

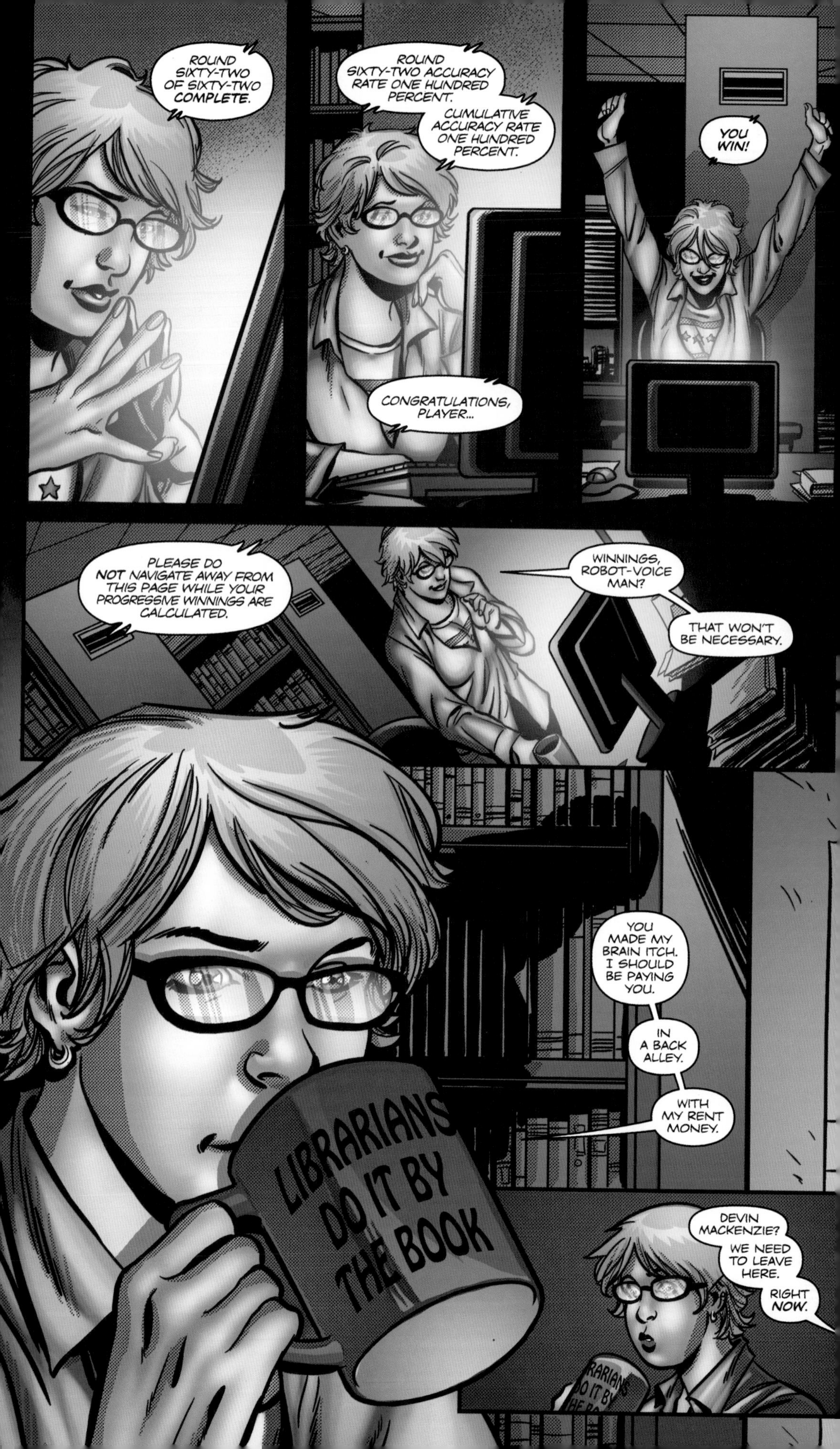
ROUND SIXTY-TWO OF SIXTY-TWO COMPLETE.
ROUND SIXTY-TWO ACCURACY RATE ONE HUNDRED PERCENT.
CUMULATIVE ACCURACY RATE ONE HUNDRED PERCENT.
CONGRATULATIONS, PLAYER...
YOU WIN!
PLEASE DO NOT NAVIGATE AWAY FROM THIS PAGE WHILE YOUR PROGRESSIVE WINNINGS ARE CALCULATED.
WINNINGS, ROBOT-VOICE MAN?
THAT WON'T BE NECESSARY.
YOU MADE MY BRAIN ITCH. I SHOULD BE PAYING YOU.
IN A BACK ALLEY.
WITH MY RENT MONEY.
LIBRARIANS DO IT BY THE BOOK
DEVIN MACKENZIE?
WE NEED TO LEAVE HERE.
RIGHT NOW.

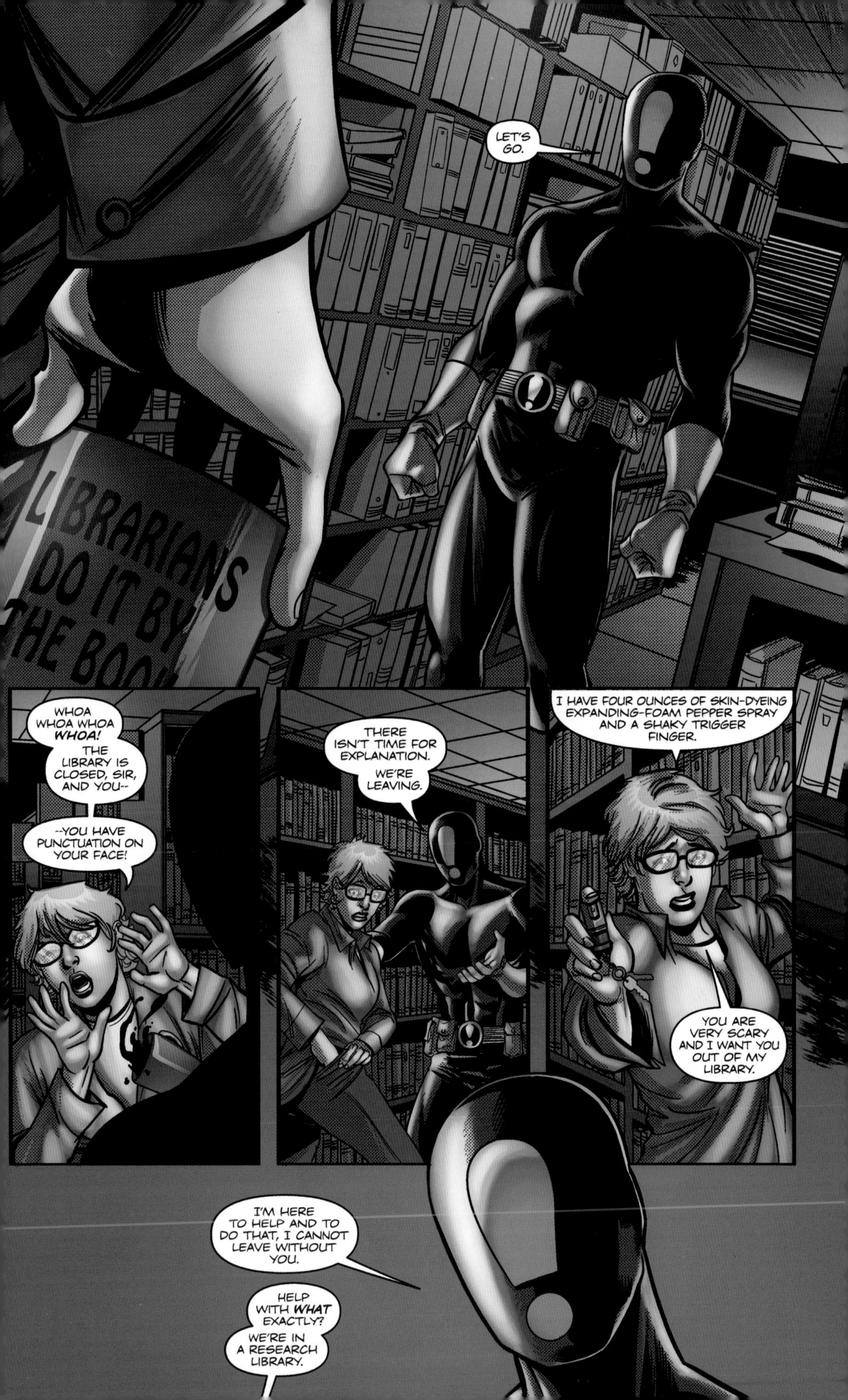
LIBRARIANS DO IT BY THE BOOK
LET'S GO.
WHOA WHOA WHOA WHOA! THE LIBRARY IS CLOSED, SIR, AND YOU--
--YOU HAVE PUNCTUATION ON YOUR FACE!
THERE ISN'T TIME FOR EXPLANATION.
WE'RE LEAVING.
I HAVE FOUR OUNCES OF SKIN-DYEING EXPANDING-FOAM PEPPER SPRAY AND A SHAKY TRIGGER FINGER.
YOU ARE VERY SCARY AND I WANT YOU OUT OF MY LIBRARY.
I'M HERE TO HELP AND TO DO THAT, I CANNOT LEAVE WITHOUT YOU.
HELP WITH WHAT EXACTLY?
WE'RE IN A RESEARCH LIBRARY.

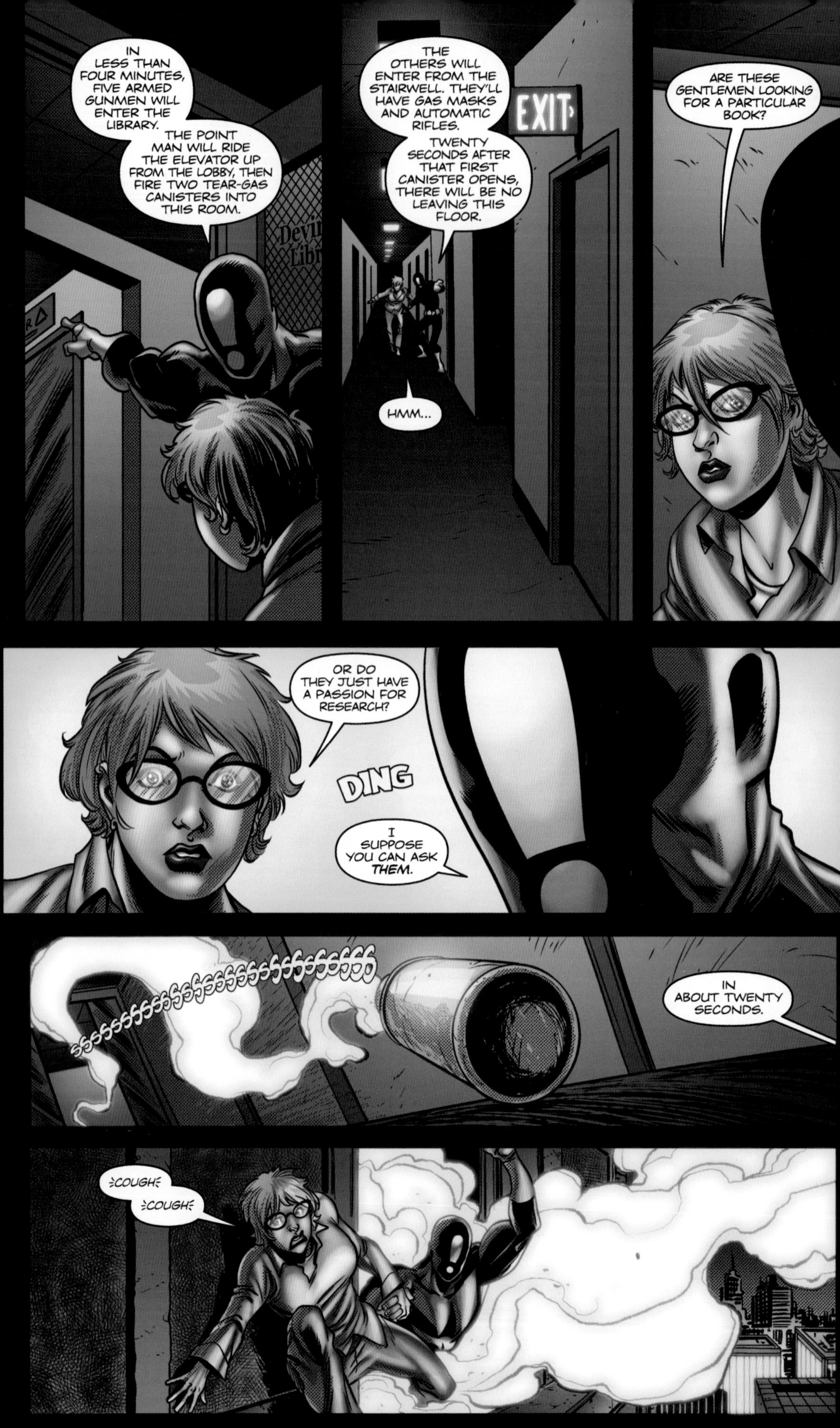

IN LESS THAN FOUR MINUTES, FIVE ARMED GUNMEN WILL ENTER THE LIBRARY.
THE POINT MAN WILL RIDE THE ELEVATOR UP FROM THE LOBBY, THEN FIRE TWO TEAR-GAS CANISTERS INTO THIS ROOM.
THE OTHERS WILL ENTER FROM THE STAIRWELL. THEY'LL HAVE GAS MASKS AND AUTOMATIC RIFLES.
EXIT
TWENTY SECONDS AFTER THAT FIRST CANISTER OPENS, THERE WILL BE NO LEAVING THIS FLOOR.
HMM...
ARE THESE GENTLEMEN LOOKING FOR A PARTICULAR BOOK?
OR DO THEY JUST HAVE A PASSION FOR RESEARCH?
DING
I SUPPOSE YOU CAN ASK *THEM*.
SSSSSSSSSSSSSSSSSSSSSSSSSSSSSSSSS
IN ABOUT TWENTY SECONDS.
COUGH
COUGH

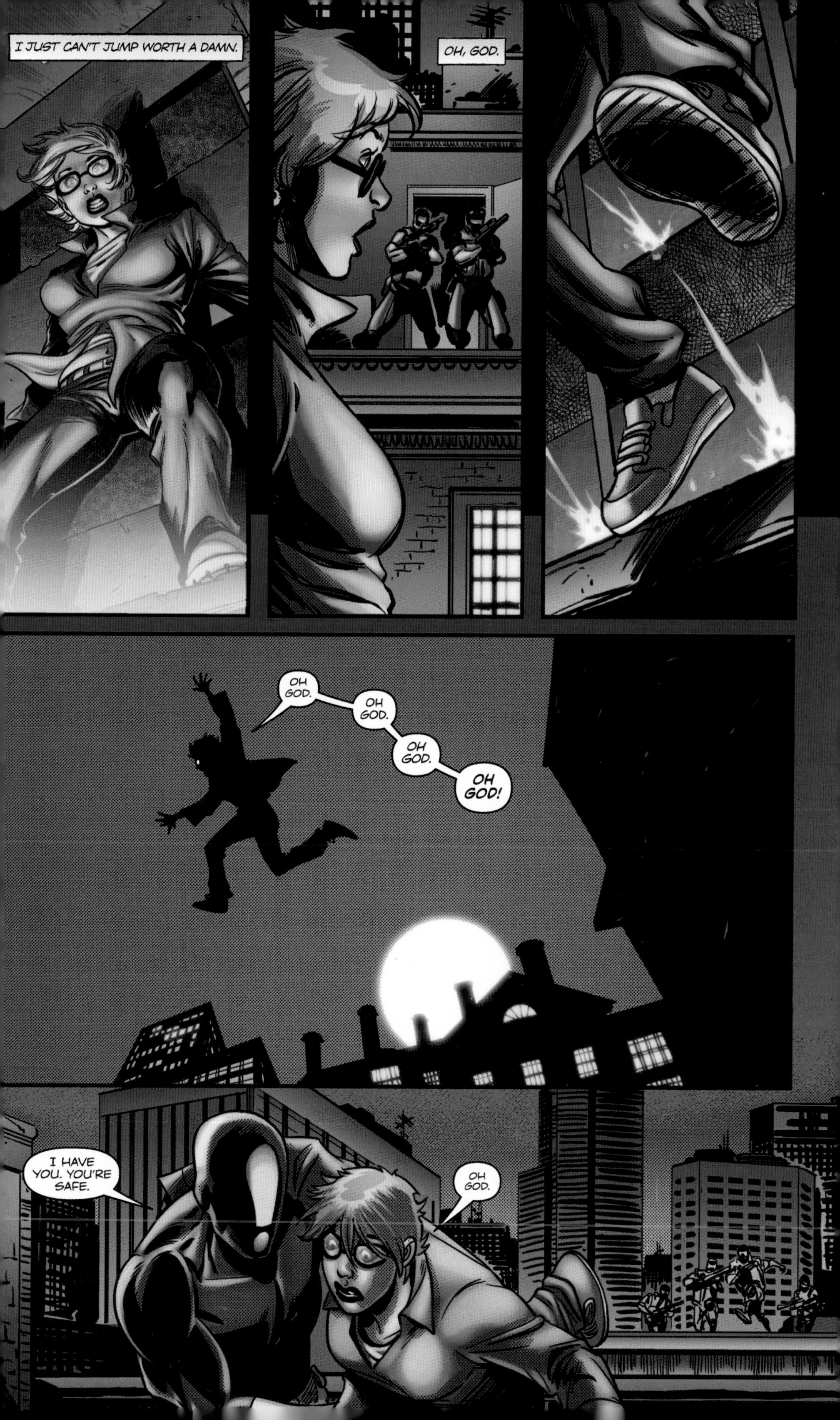
I JUST CAN'T JUMP WORTH A DAMN.
OH, GOD.
OH GOD.
OH GOD.
OH GOD.
OH GOD!
I HAVE YOU. YOU'RE SAFE.
OH GOD.

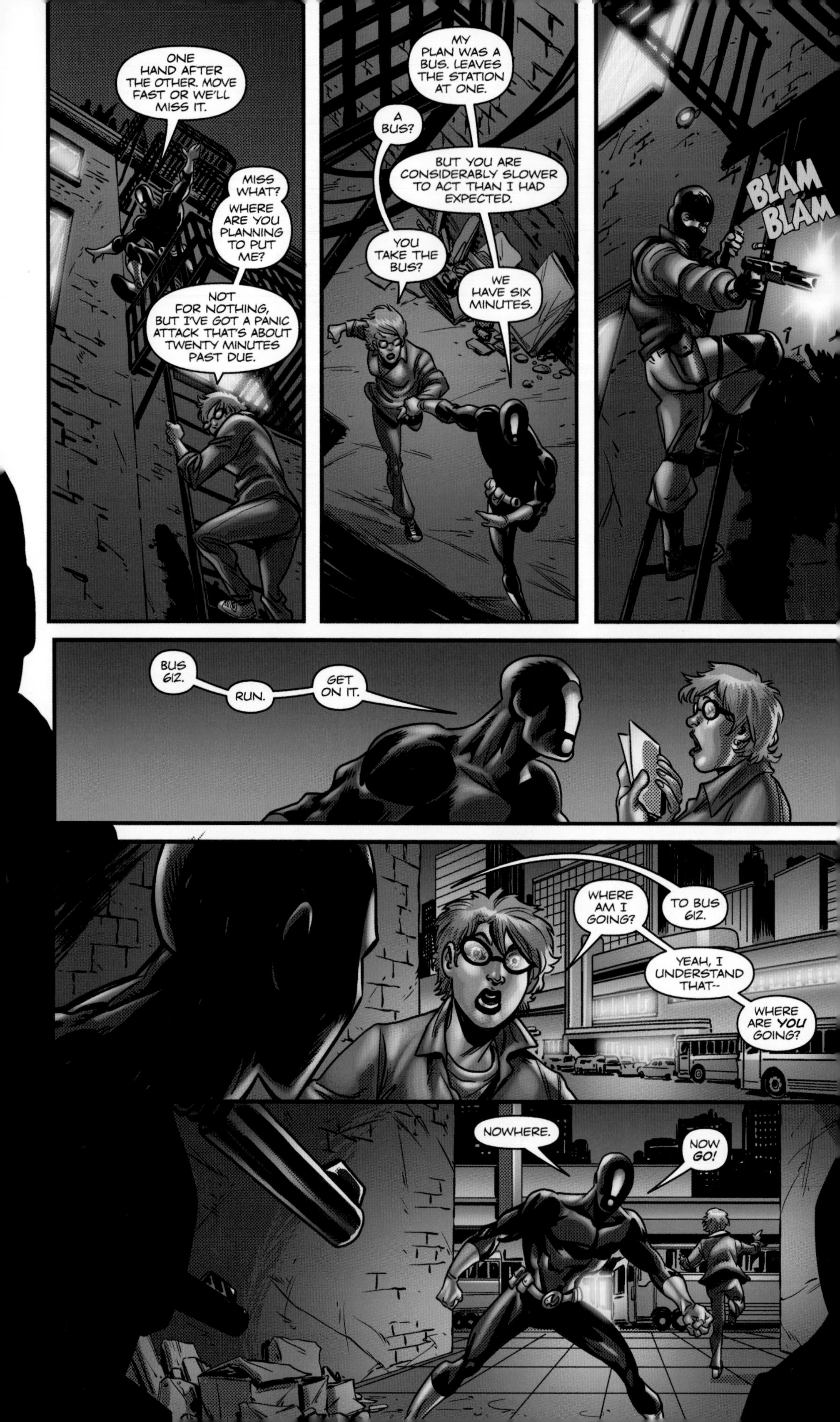
ONE HAND AFTER THE OTHER. MOVE FAST OR WE'LL MISS IT.
MISS WHAT? WHERE ARE YOU PLANNING TO PUT ME?
NOT FOR NOTHING, BUT I'VE GOT A PANIC ATTACK THAT'S ABOUT TWENTY MINUTES PAST DUE.
MY PLAN WAS A BUS. LEAVES THE STATION AT ONE.
A BUS?
BUT YOU ARE CONSIDERABLY SLOWER TO ACT THAN I HAD EXPECTED.
YOU TAKE THE BUS?
WE HAVE SIX MINUTES.
BLAM BLAM
BUS 612.
RUN.
GET ON IT.
WHERE AM I GOING?
TO BUS 612.
YEAH, I UNDERSTAND THAT--
WHERE ARE *YOU* GOING?
NOWHERE.
NOW *GO!*

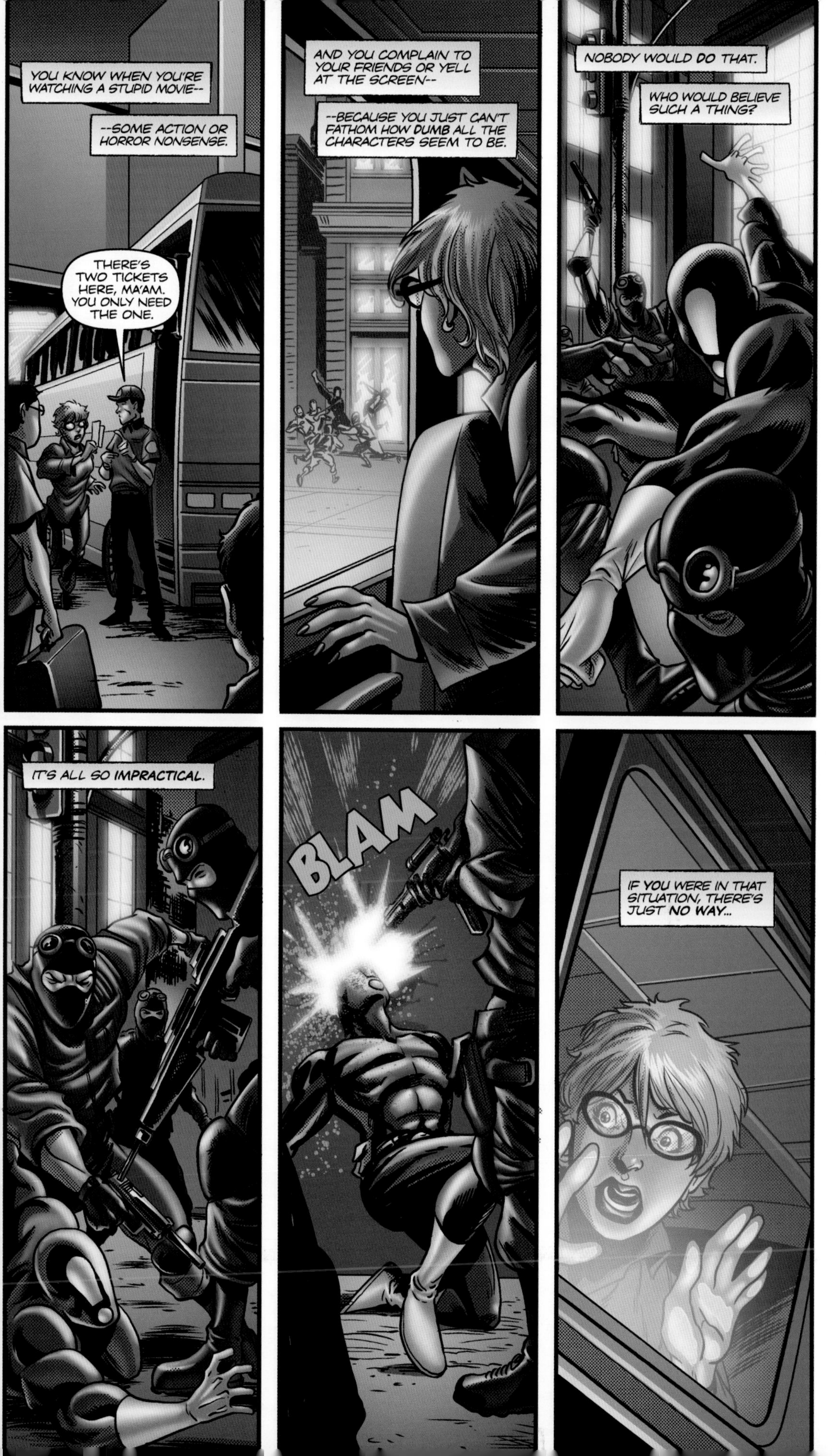
YOU KNOW WHEN YOU'RE WATCHING A STUPID MOVIE--
--SOME ACTION OR HORROR NONSENSE.
THERE'S TWO TICKETS HERE, MA'AM. YOU ONLY NEED THE ONE.
AND YOU COMPLAIN TO YOUR FRIENDS OR YELL AT THE SCREEN--
--BECAUSE YOU JUST CAN'T FATHOM HOW DUMB ALL THE CHARACTERS SEEM TO BE.
NOBODY WOULD DO THAT.
WHO WOULD BELIEVE SUCH A THING?
IT'S ALL SO IMPRACTICAL.
BLAM
IF YOU WERE IN THAT SITUATION, THERE'S JUST NO WAY...

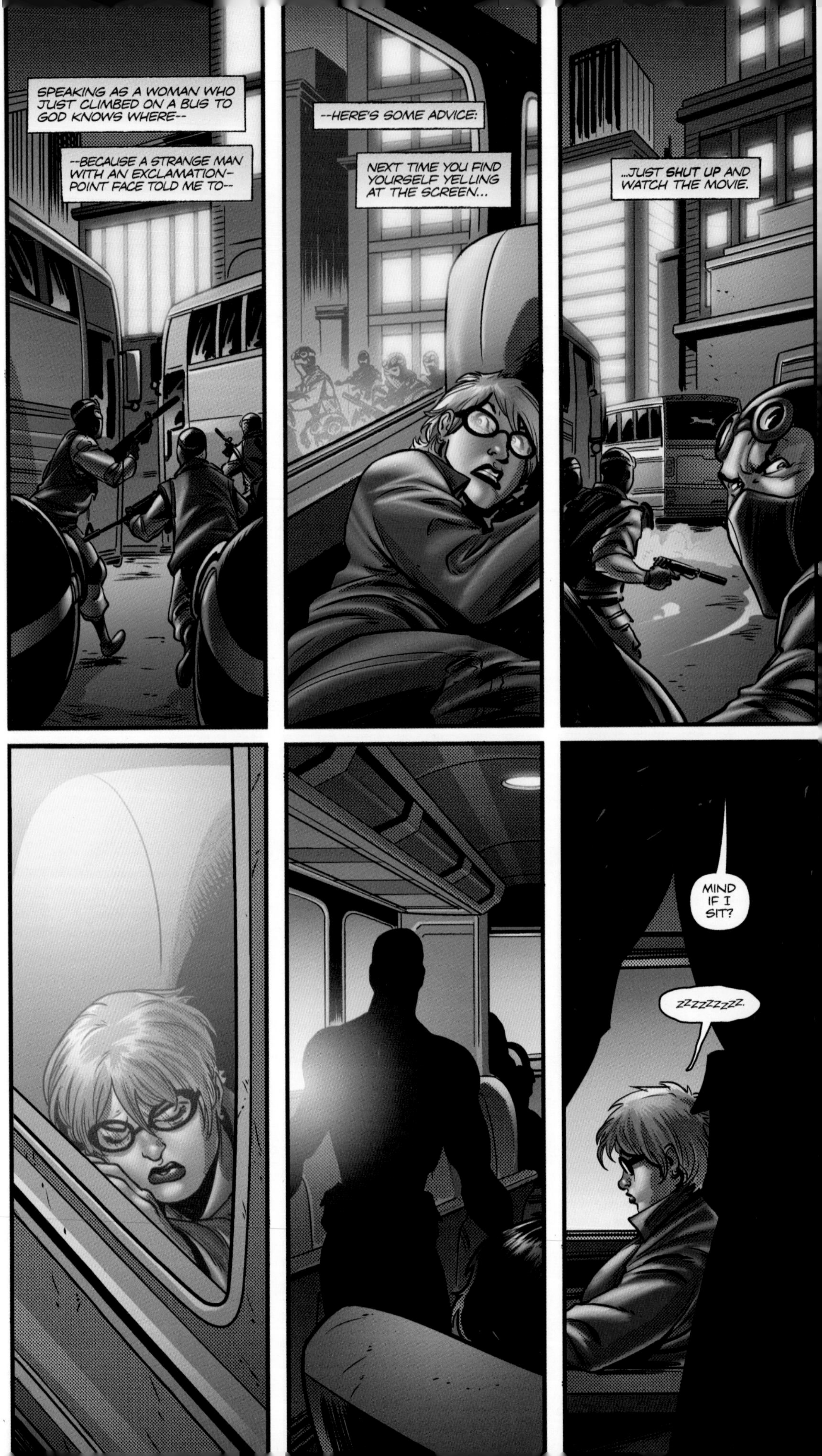
SPEAKING AS A WOMAN WHO JUST CLIMBED ON A BUS TO GOD KNOWS WHERE--
--BECAUSE A STRANGE MAN WITH AN EXCLAMATION-POINT FACE TOLD ME TO--
--HERE'S SOME ADVICE:
NEXT TIME YOU FIND YOURSELF YELLING AT THE SCREEN...
...JUST SHUT UP AND WATCH THE MOVIE.
MIND IF I SIT?
ZZZZZZZZZ.

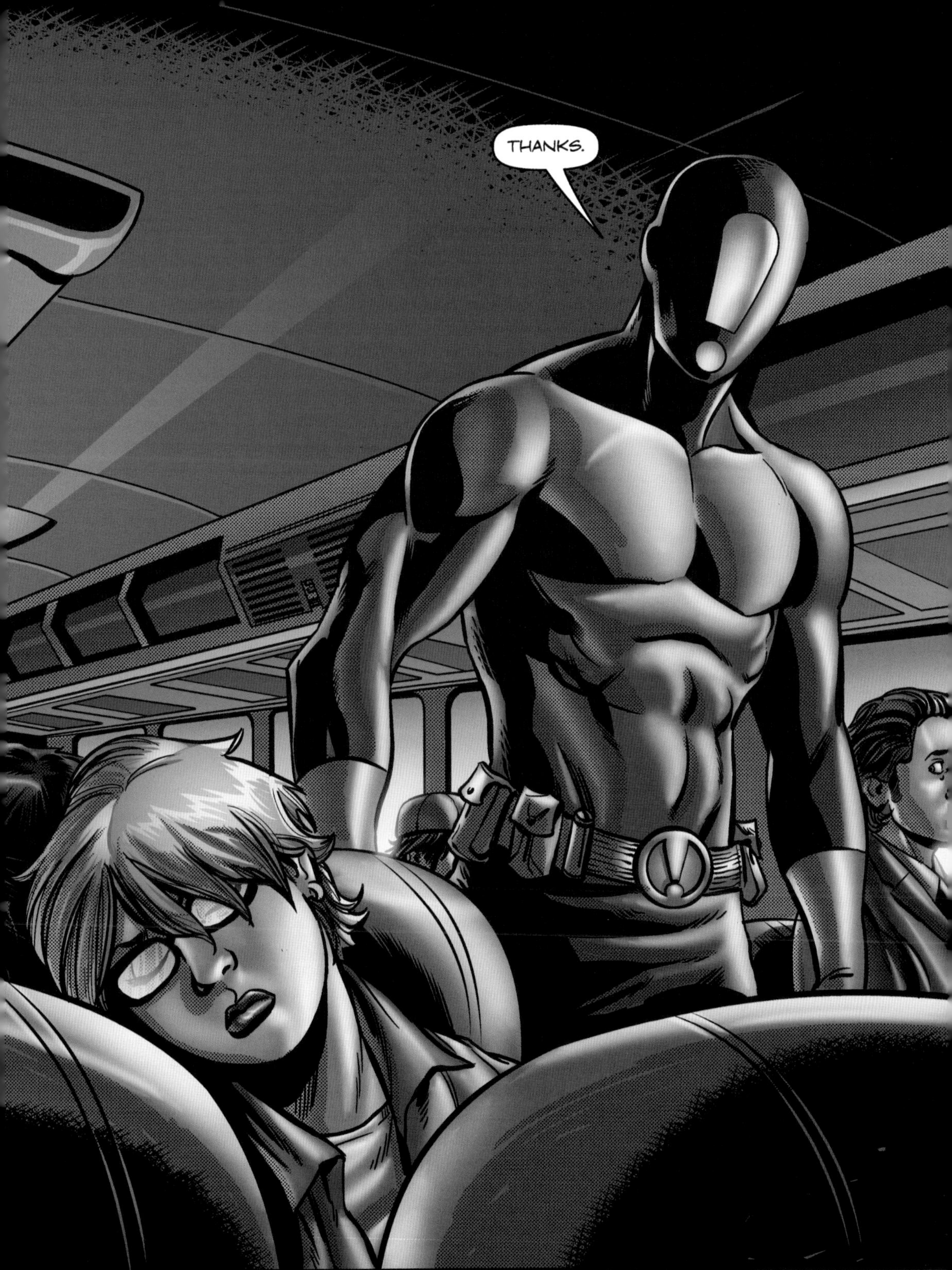
THANKS.

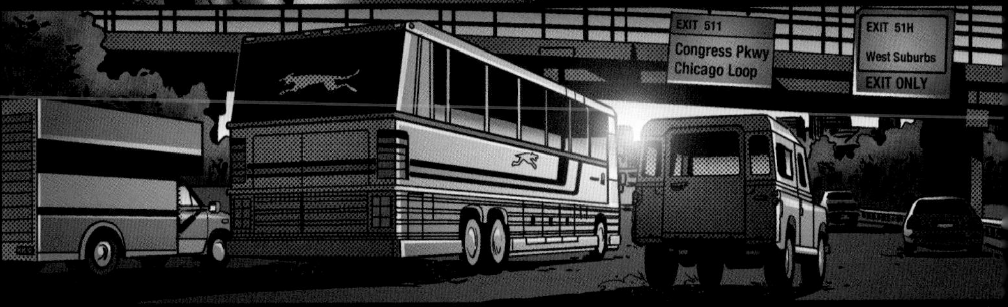
EXIT 511
Congress Pkwy
Chicago Loop
EXIT 51H
West Suburbs
EXIT ONLY

CHAPTER 2

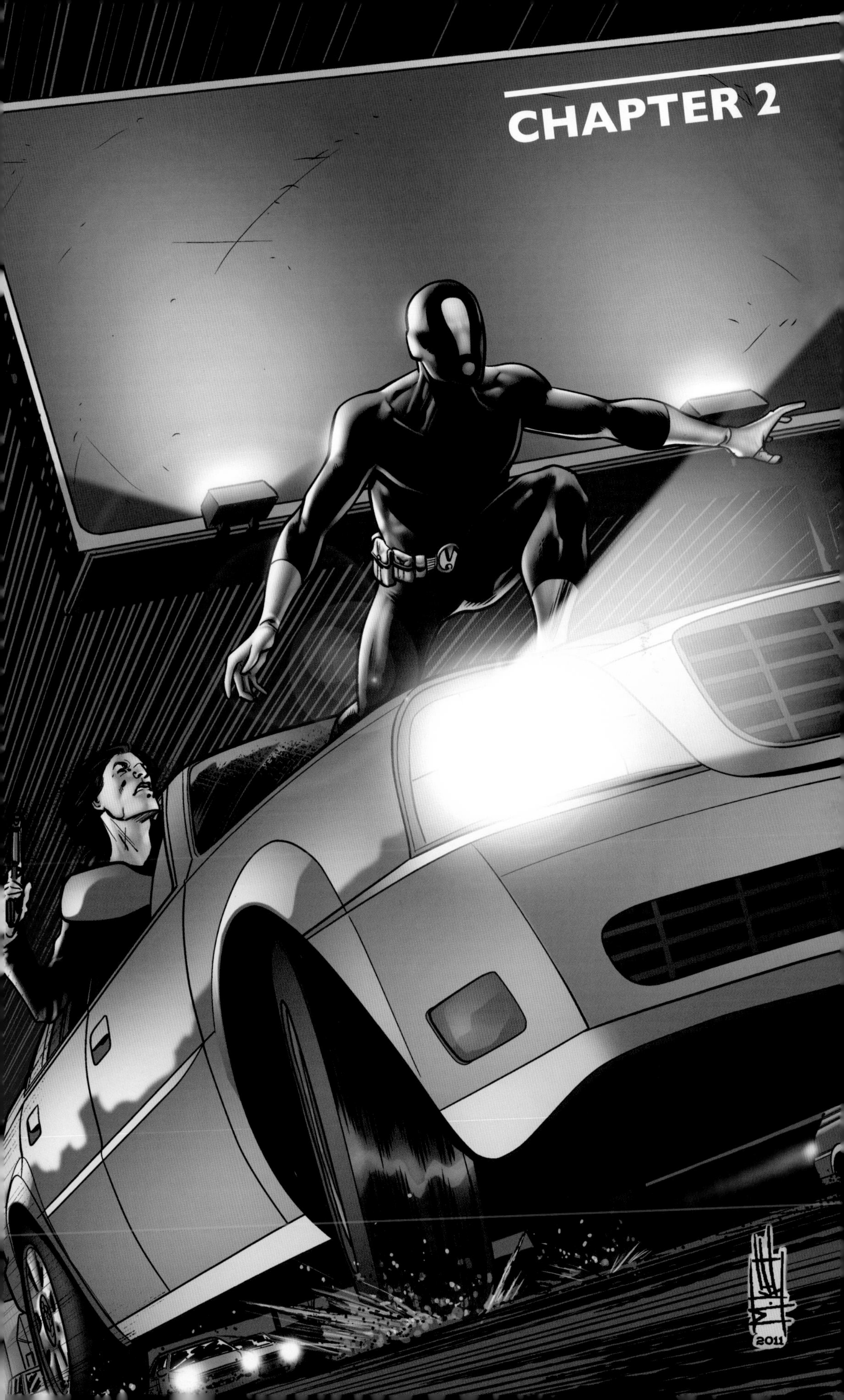
2011

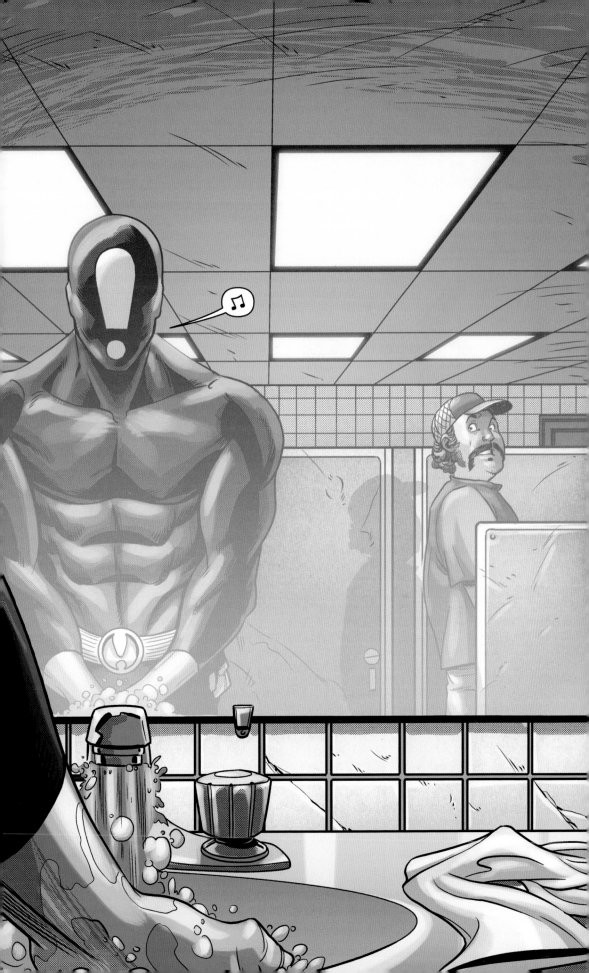

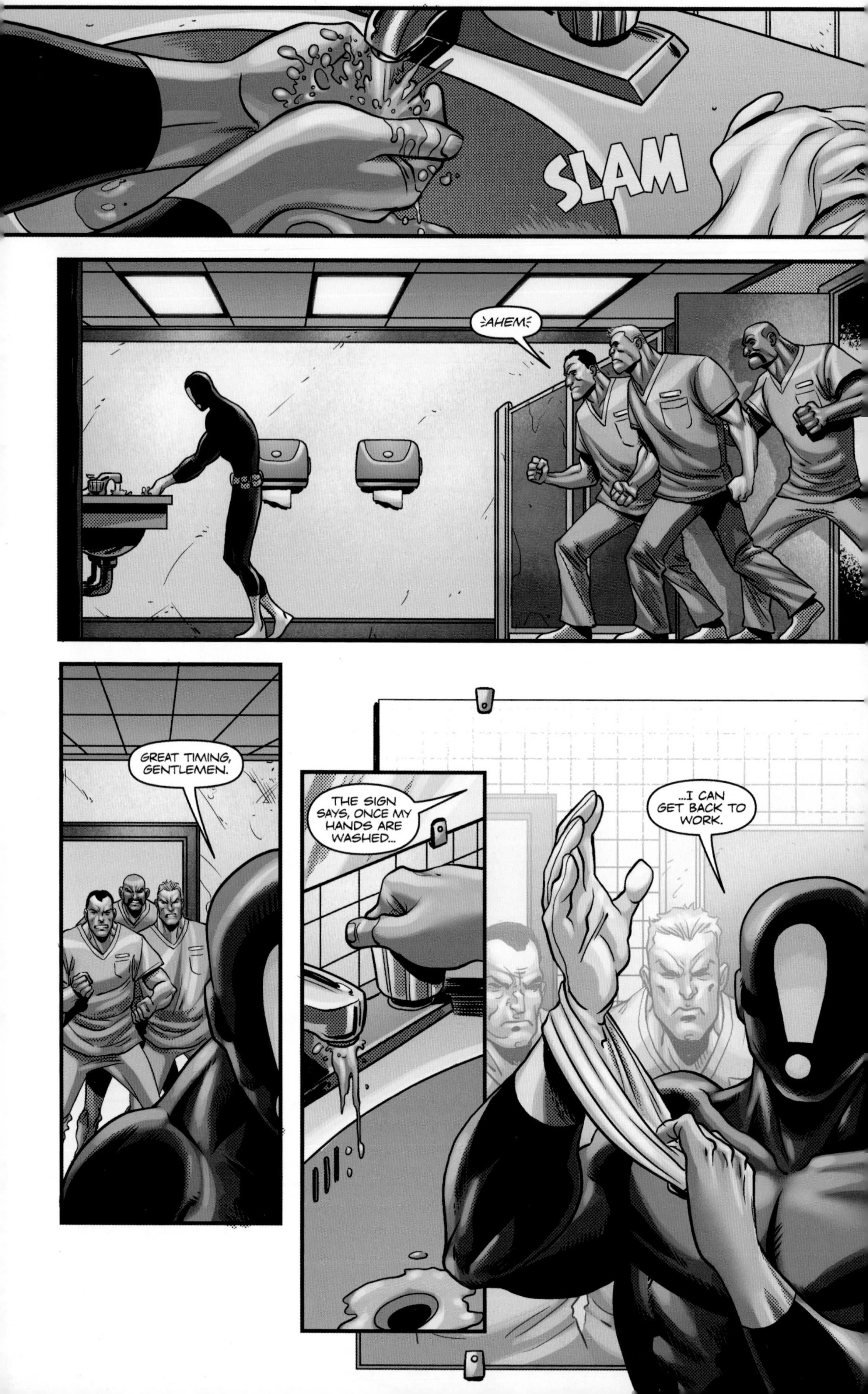
SLAM
AHEM
GREAT TIMING, GENTLEMEN.
THE SIGN SAYS, ONCE MY HANDS ARE WASHED...
...I CAN GET BACK TO WORK.

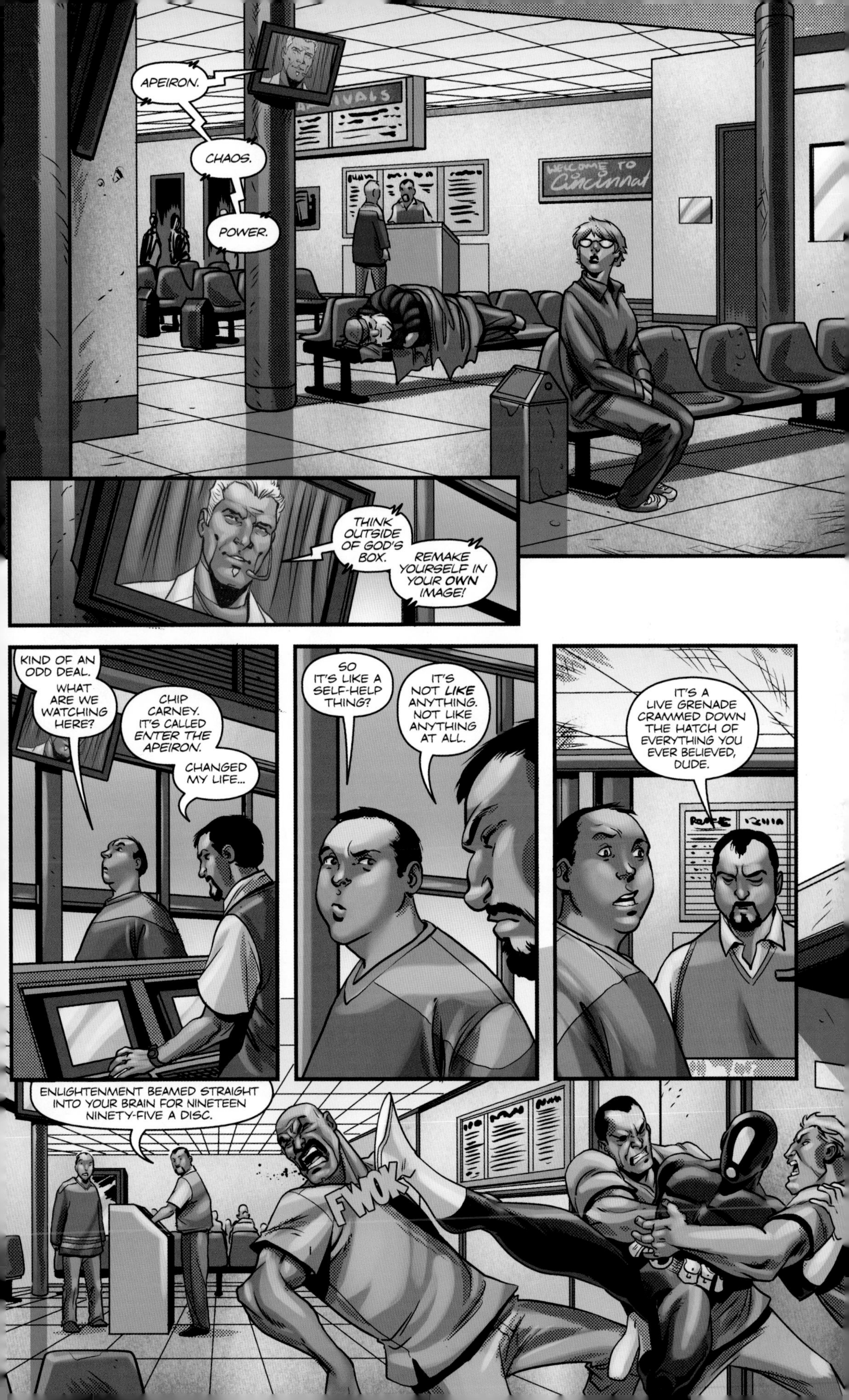
APEIRON.
CHAOS.
POWER.
ARRIVALS
WELCOME TO Cincinnati
THINK OUTSIDE OF GOD'S BOX.
REMAKE YOURSELF IN YOUR OWN IMAGE!
KIND OF AN ODD DEAL. WHAT ARE WE WATCHING HERE?
CHIP CARNEY. IT'S CALLED ENTER THE APEIRON.
CHANGED MY LIFE...
SO IT'S LIKE A SELF-HELP THING?
IT'S NOT LIKE ANYTHING. NOT LIKE ANYTHING AT ALL.
IT'S A LIVE GRENADE CRAMMED DOWN THE HATCH OF EVERYTHING YOU EVER BELIEVED, DUDE.
ENLIGHTENMENT BEAMED STRAIGHT INTO YOUR BRAIN FOR NINETEEN NINETY-FIVE A DISC.
FWOK

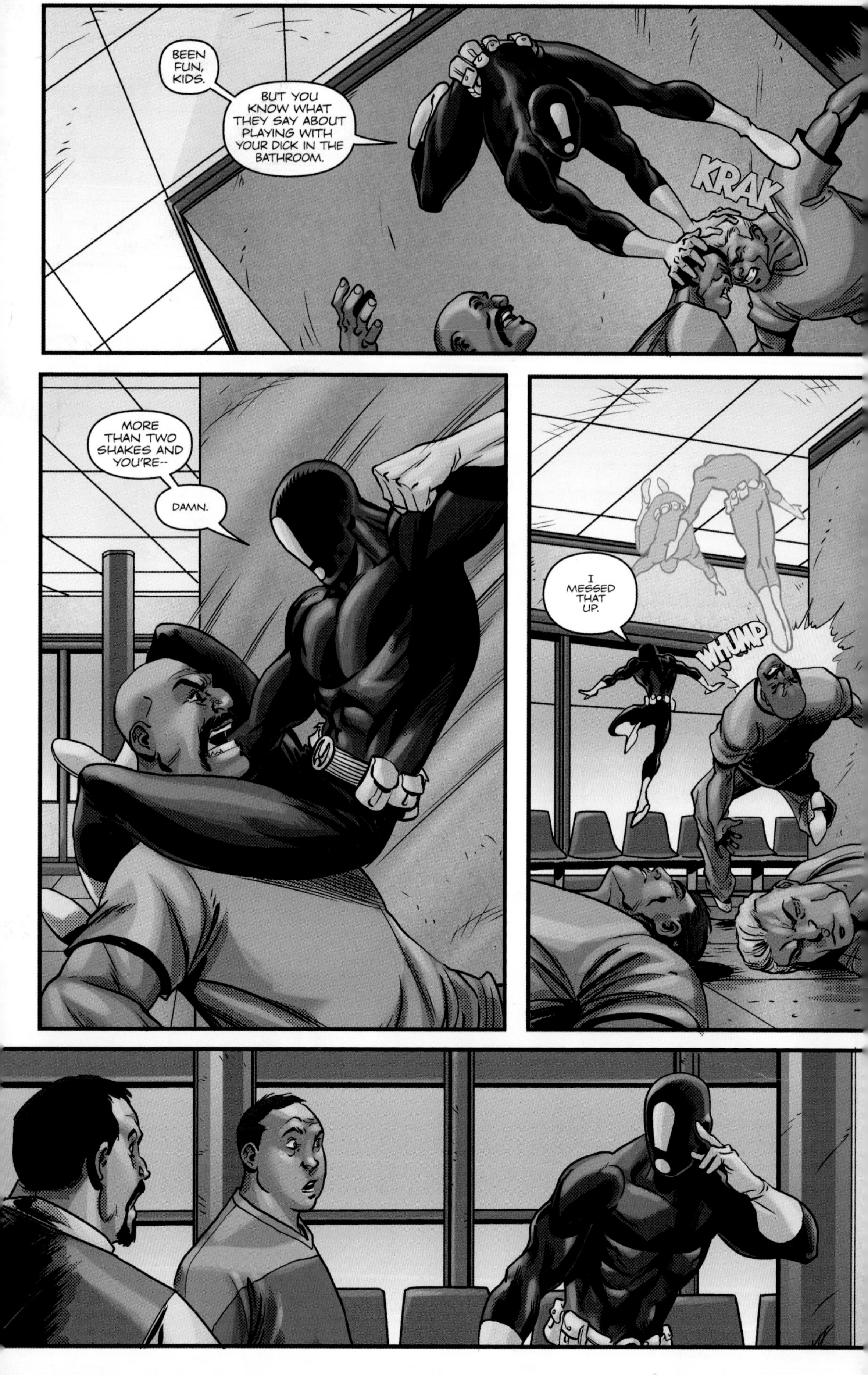

BEEN FUN, KIDS.
BUT YOU KNOW WHAT THEY SAY ABOUT PLAYING WITH YOUR DICK IN THE BATHROOM.
KRAK
MORE THAN TWO SHAKES AND YOU'RE--
DAMN.
I MESSED THAT UP.
WHUMP

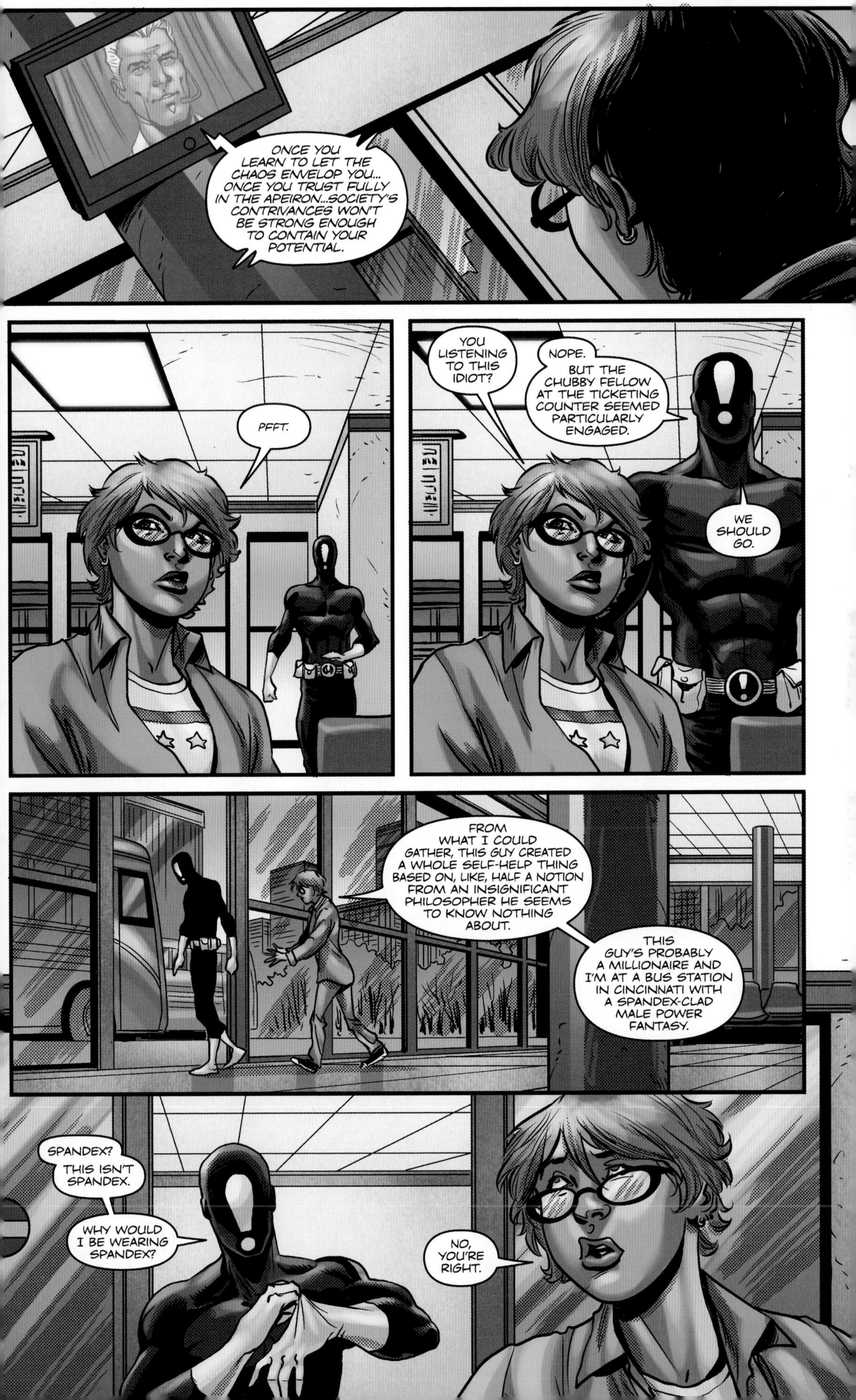

ONCE YOU LEARN TO LET THE CHAOS ENVELOP YOU... ONCE YOU TRUST FULLY IN THE APEIRON...SOCIETY'S CONTRIVANCES WON'T BE STRONG ENOUGH TO CONTAIN YOUR POTENTIAL.
PFFT.
YOU LISTENING TO THIS IDIOT?
NOPE.
BUT THE CHUBBY FELLOW AT THE TICKETING COUNTER SEEMED PARTICULARLY ENGAGED.
WE SHOULD GO.
FROM WHAT I COULD GATHER, THIS GUY CREATED A WHOLE SELF-HELP THING BASED ON, LIKE, HALF A NOTION FROM AN INSIGNIFICANT PHILOSOPHER HE SEEMS TO KNOW NOTHING ABOUT.
THIS GUY'S PROBABLY A MILLIONAIRE AND I'M AT A BUS STATION IN CINCINNATI WITH A SPANDEX-CLAD MALE POWER FANTASY.
SPANDEX?
THIS ISN'T SPANDEX.
WHY WOULD I BE WEARING SPANDEX?
NO, YOU'RE RIGHT.

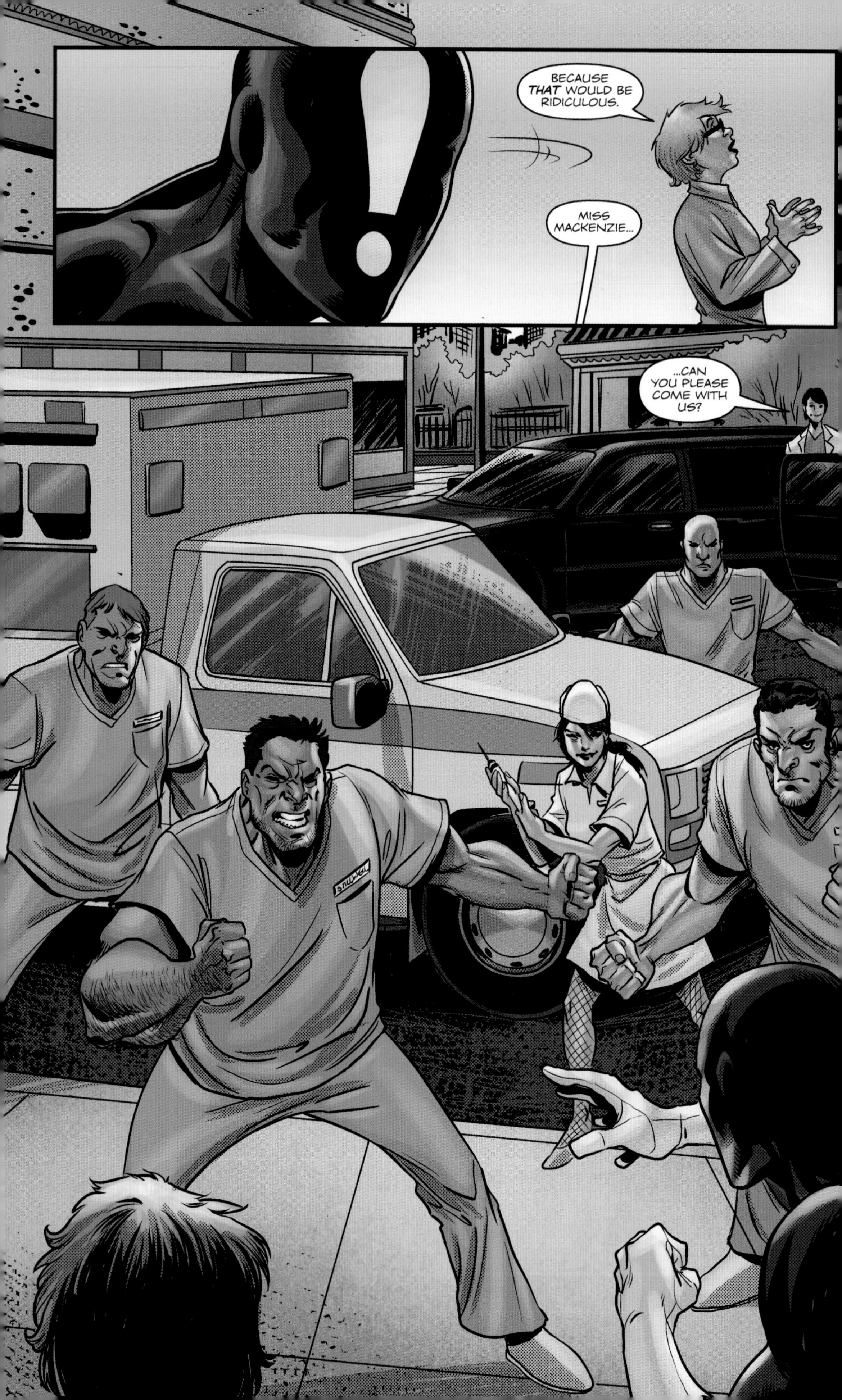

BECAUSE THAT WOULD BE RIDICULOUS.
MISS MACKENZIE...
...CAN YOU PLEASE COME WITH US?

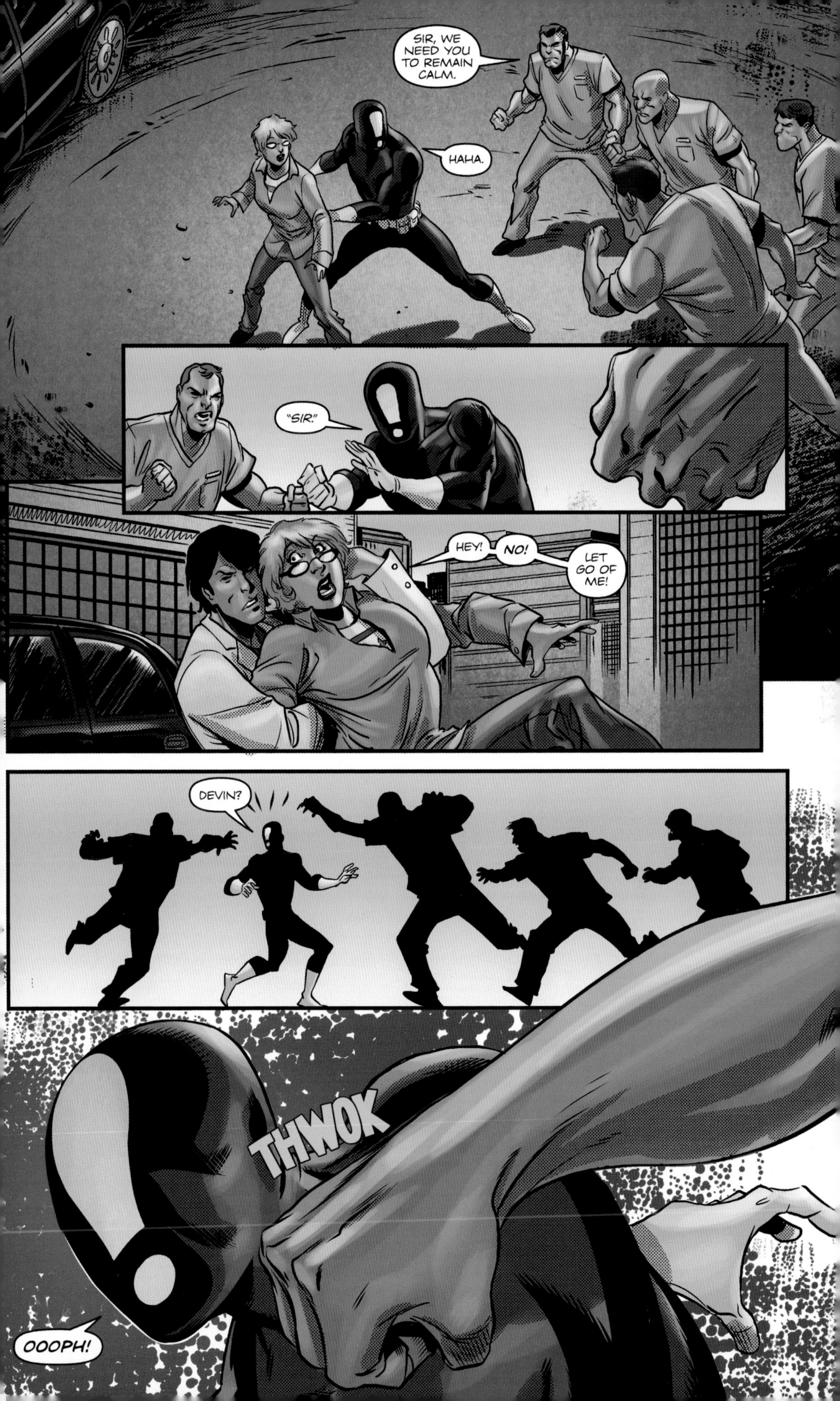

SIR, WE NEED YOU TO REMAIN CALM.
HAHA.
"SIR."
HEY!
NO!
LET GO OF ME!
DEVIN?
THWOK
OOOPH!

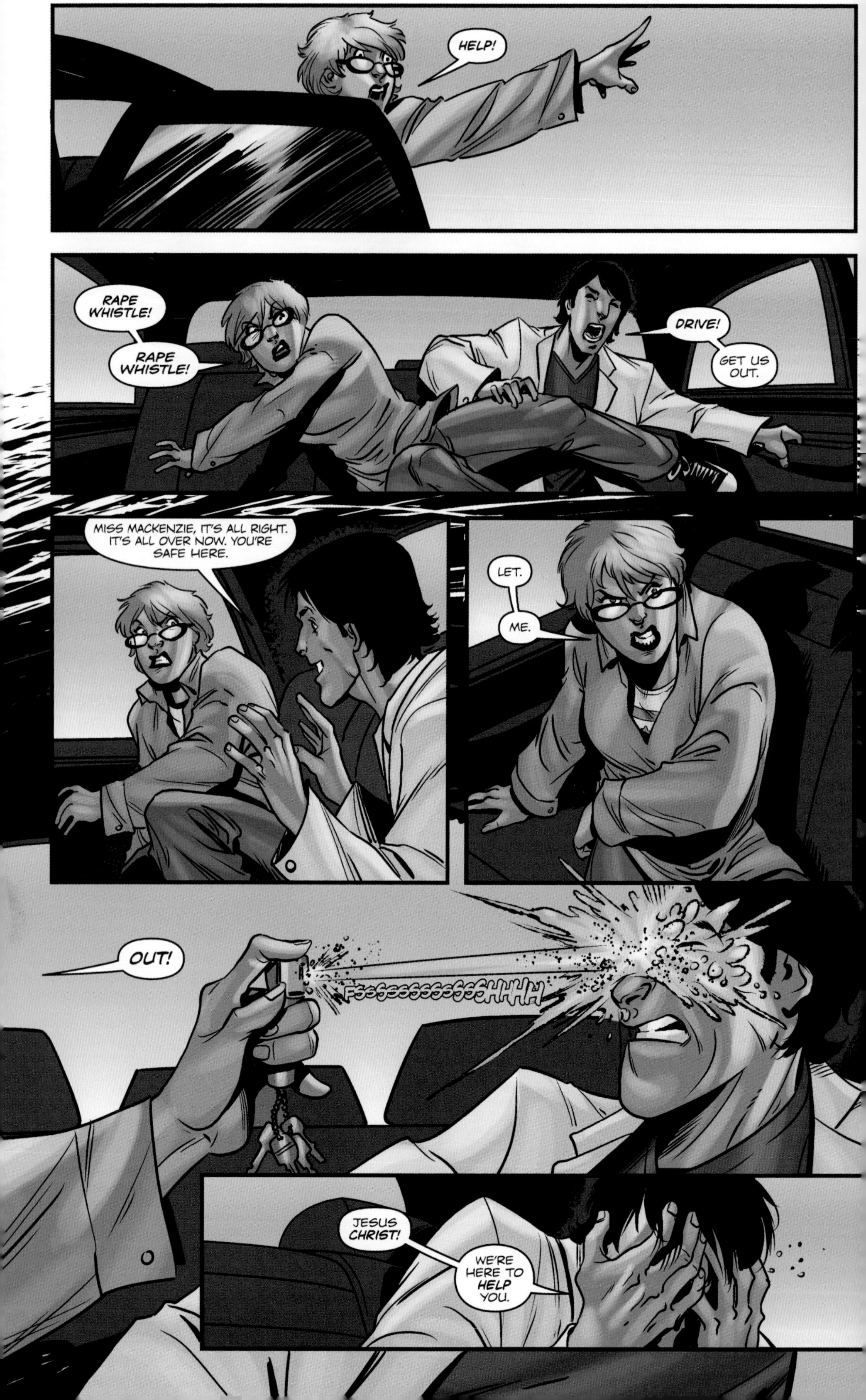

HELP!
RAPE WHISTLE!
RAPE WHISTLE!
DRIVE!
GET US OUT.
MISS MACKENZIE, IT'S ALL RIGHT. IT'S ALL OVER NOW. YOU'RE SAFE HERE.
LET.
ME.
OUT!
FSSSSSSSSSSSSHHHH
JESUS CHRIST!
WE'RE HERE TO HELP YOU.

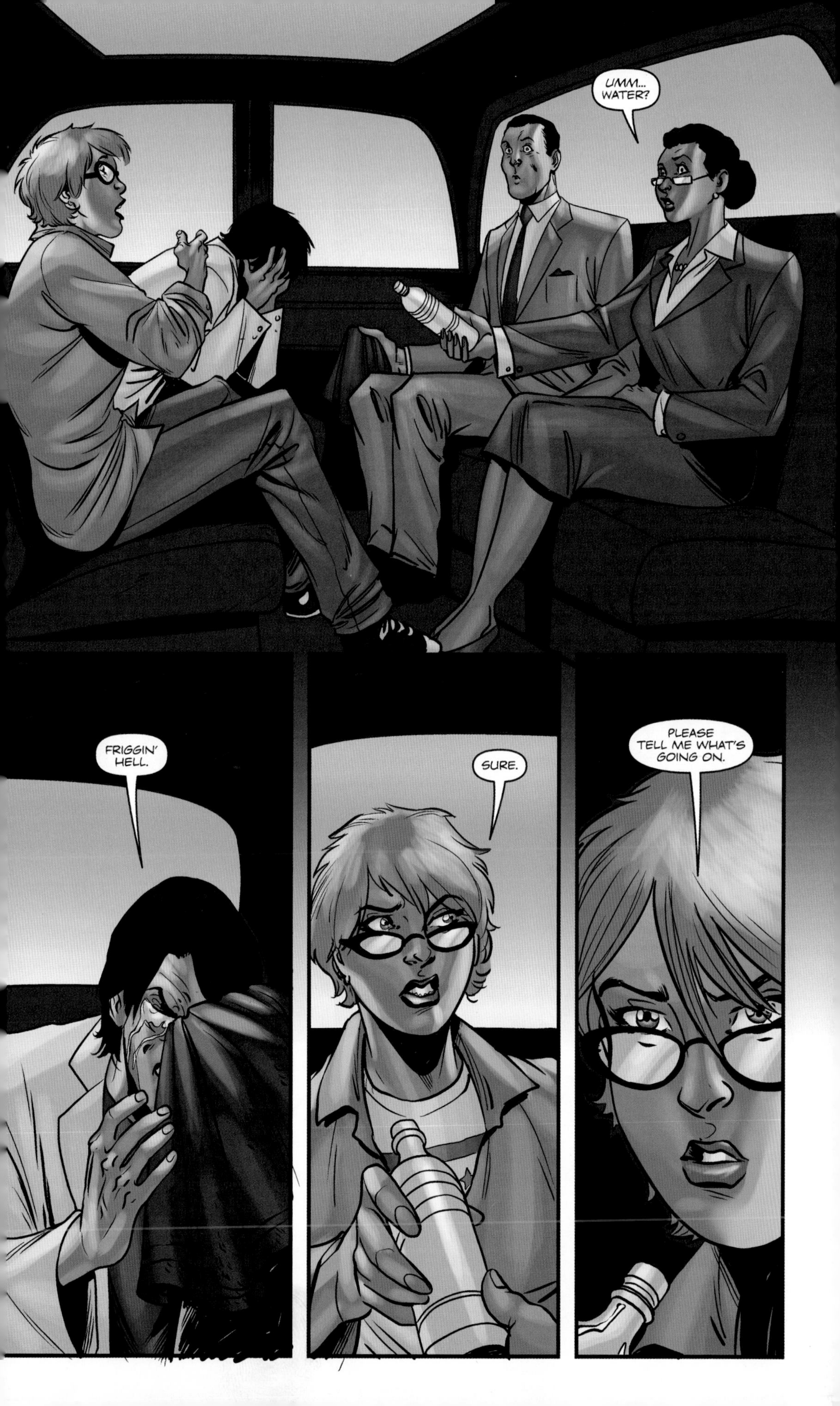
UMM... WATER?
FRIGGIN' HELL.
SURE.
PLEASE TELL ME WHAT'S GOING ON.

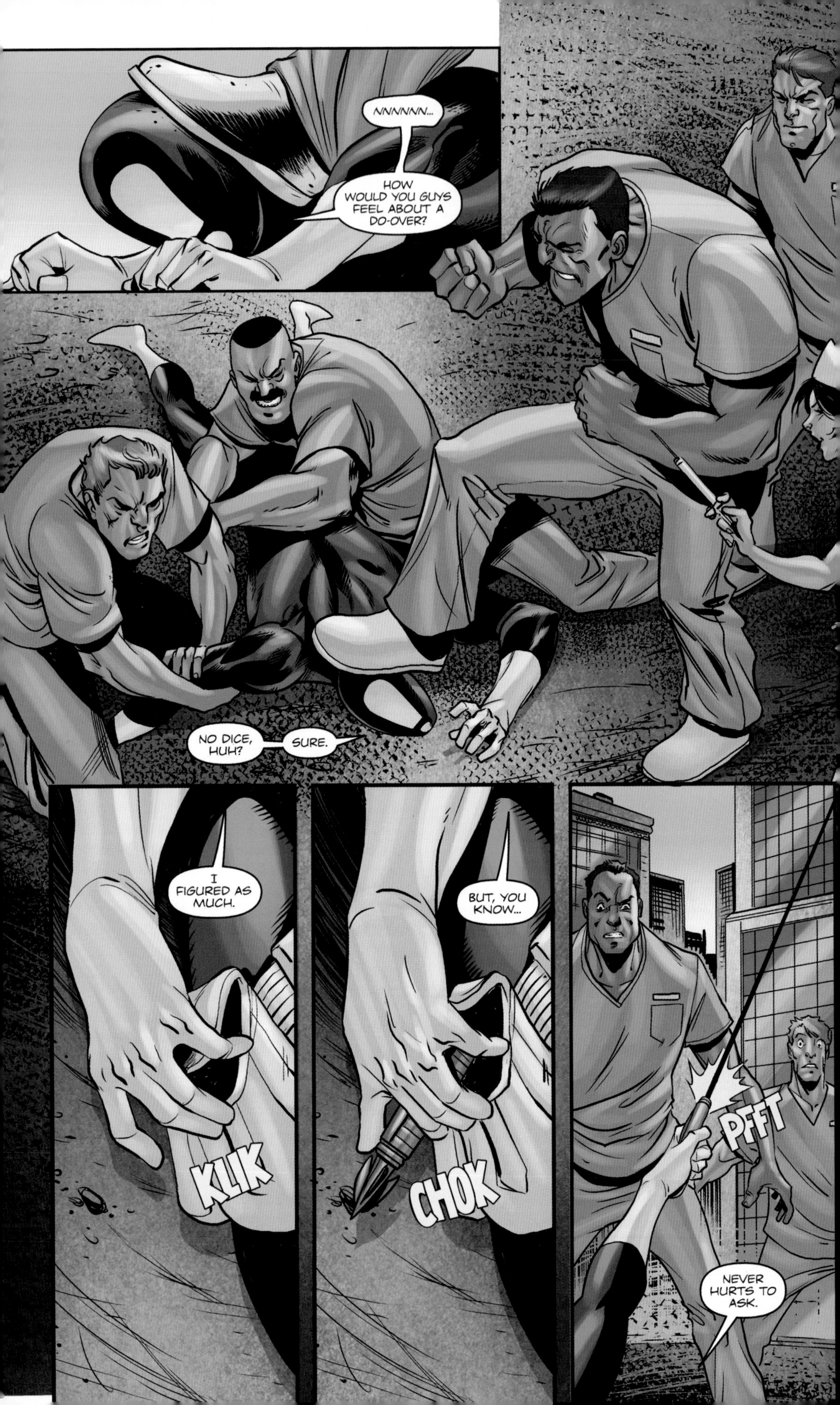

NNNNNN...
HOW WOULD YOU GUYS FEEL ABOUT A DO-OVER?
NO DICE, HUH?
SURE.
I FIGURED AS MUCH.
KLIK
BUT, YOU KNOW...
CHOK
PFFT
NEVER HURTS TO ASK.

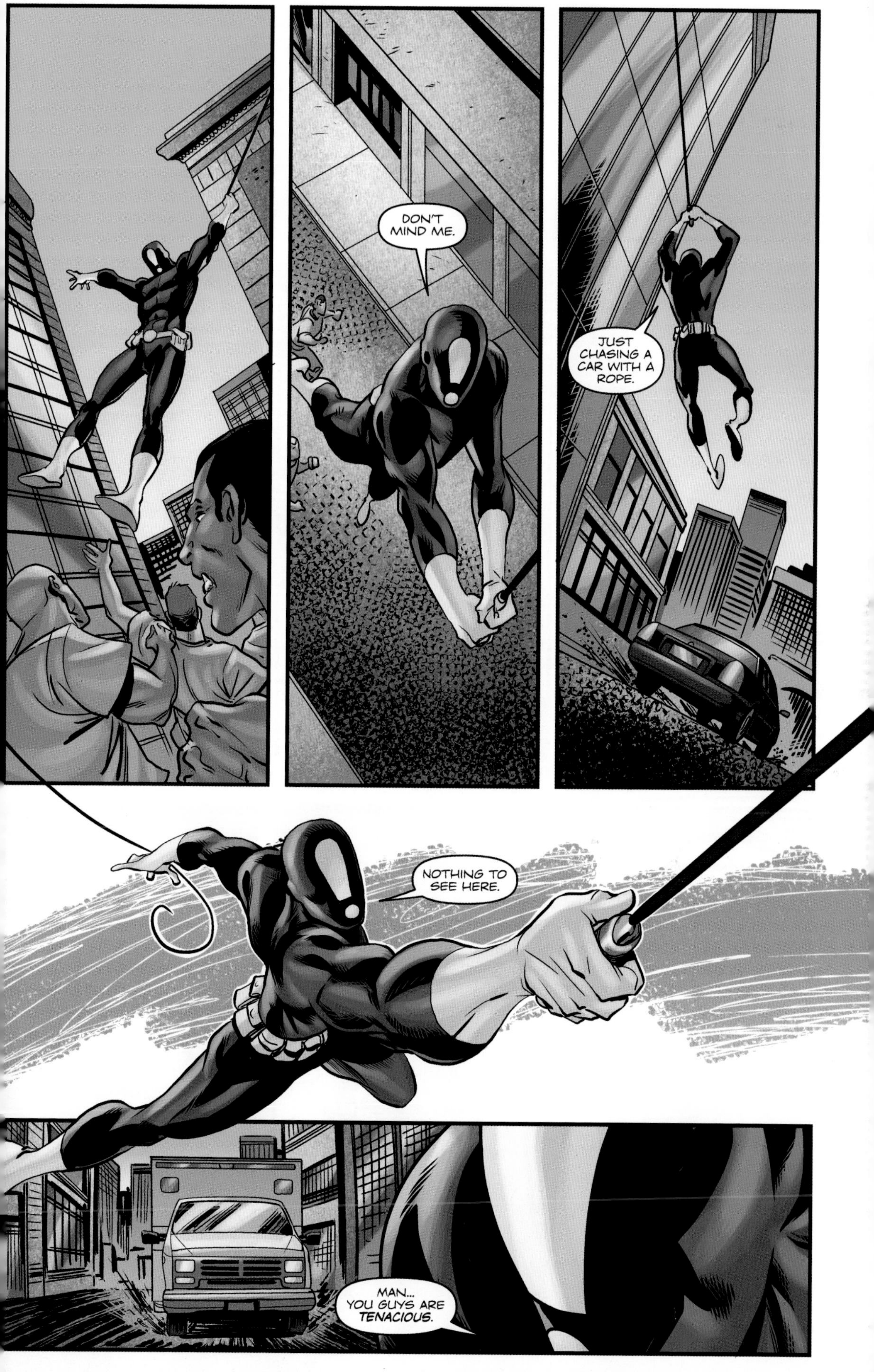
DON'T MIND ME.
JUST CHASING A CAR WITH A ROPE.
NOTHING TO SEE HERE.
MAN... YOU GUYS ARE TENACIOUS.

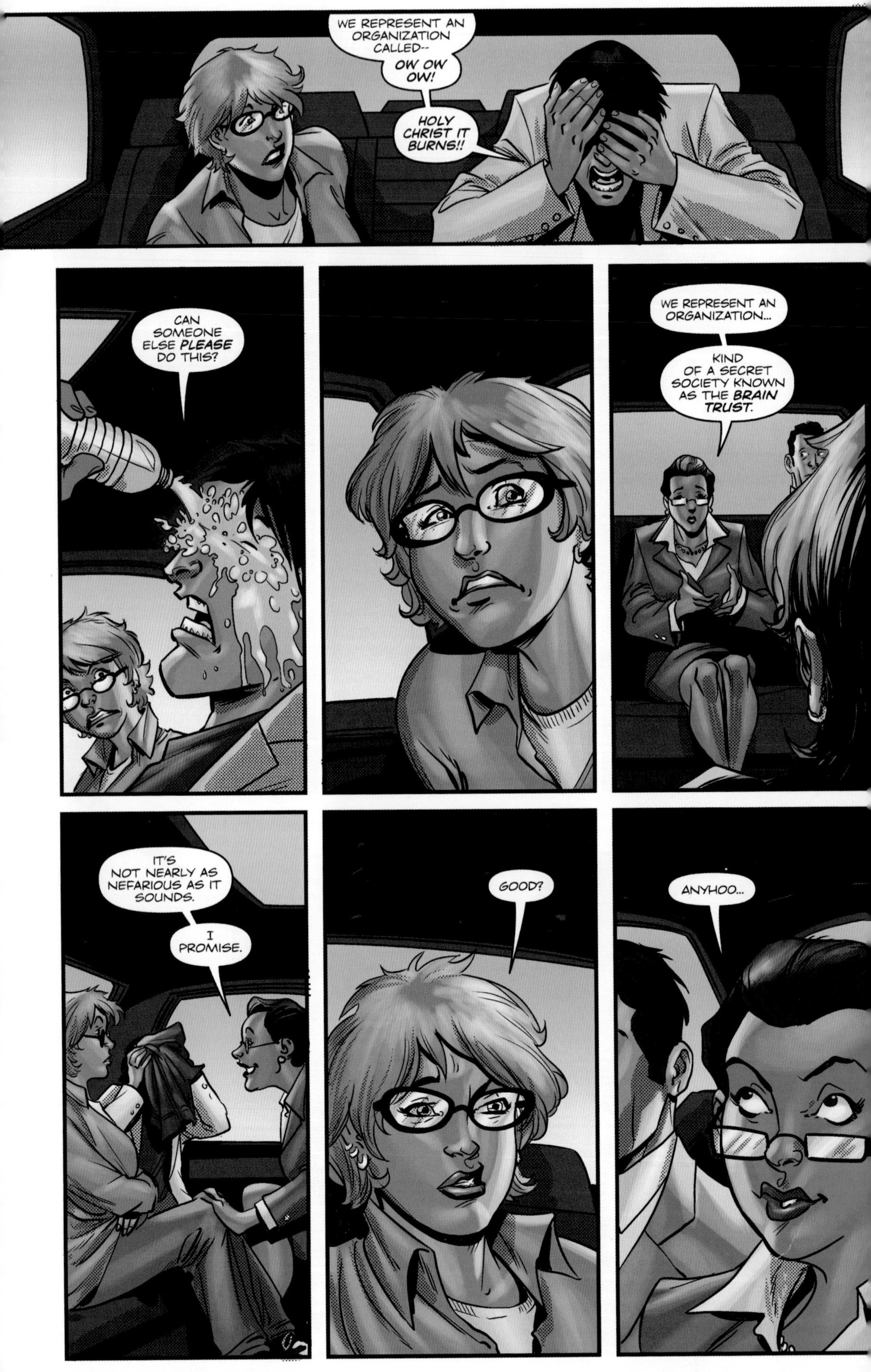
WE REPRESENT AN ORGANIZATION CALLED--
OW OW OW!
HOLY CHRIST IT BURNS!!
CAN SOMEONE ELSE PLEASE DO THIS?
WE REPRESENT AN ORGANIZATION...
KIND OF A SECRET SOCIETY KNOWN AS THE BRAIN TRUST.
IT'S NOT NEARLY AS NEFARIOUS AS IT SOUNDS.
I PROMISE.
GOOD?
ANYHOO...

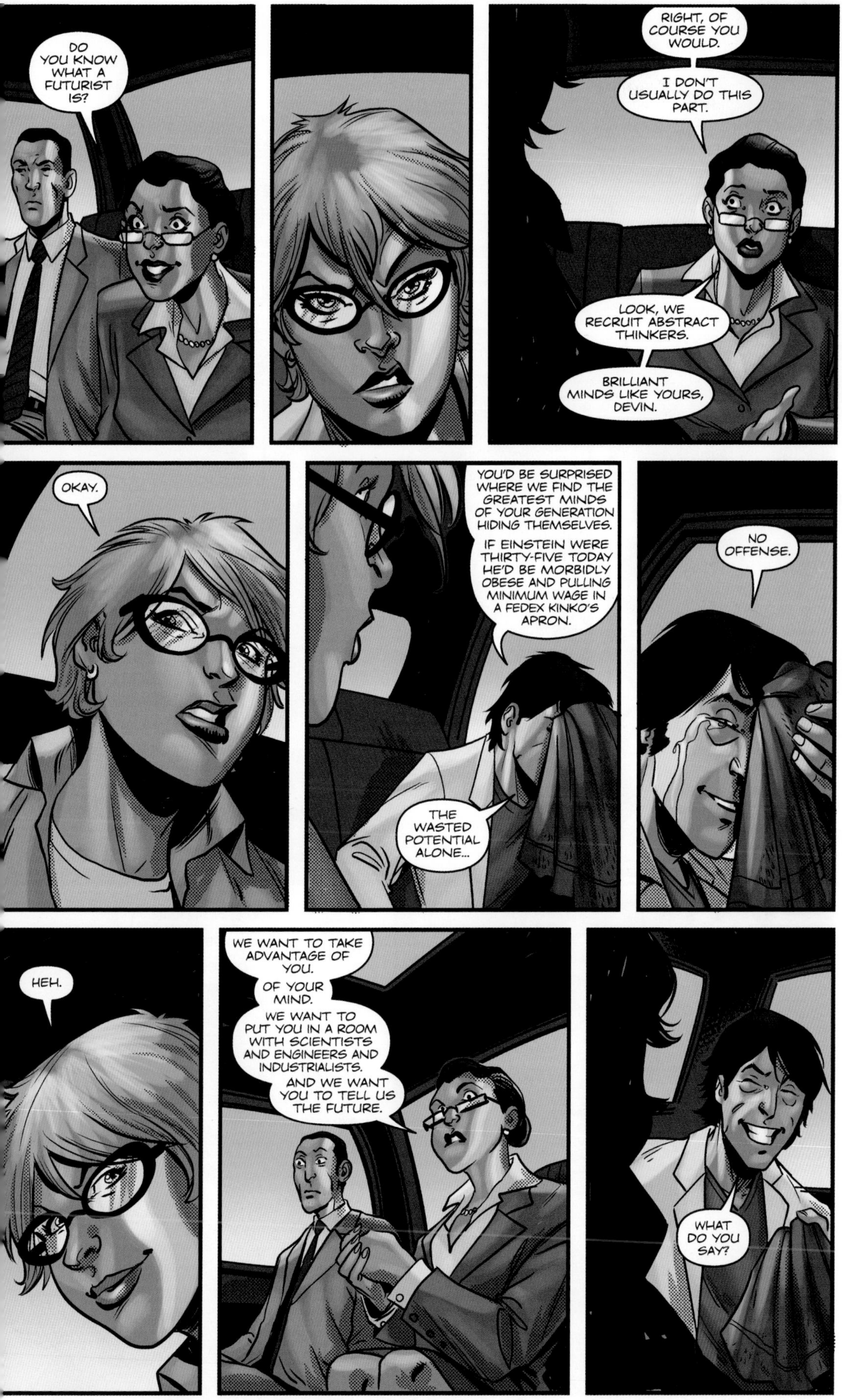
DO YOU KNOW WHAT A FUTURIST IS?
RIGHT, OF COURSE YOU WOULD.
I DON'T USUALLY DO THIS PART.
LOOK, WE RECRUIT ABSTRACT THINKERS.
BRILLIANT MINDS LIKE YOURS, DEVIN.
OKAY.
YOU'D BE SURPRISED WHERE WE FIND THE GREATEST MINDS OF YOUR GENERATION HIDING THEMSELVES.
IF EINSTEIN WERE THIRTY-FIVE TODAY HE'D BE MORBIDLY OBESE AND PULLING MINIMUM WAGE IN A FEDEX KINKO'S APRON.
THE WASTED POTENTIAL ALONE...
NO OFFENSE.
HEH.
WE WANT TO TAKE ADVANTAGE OF YOU.
OF YOUR MIND.
WE WANT TO PUT YOU IN A ROOM WITH SCIENTISTS AND ENGINEERS AND INDUSTRIALISTS.
AND WE WANT YOU TO TELL US THE FUTURE.
WHAT DO YOU SAY?

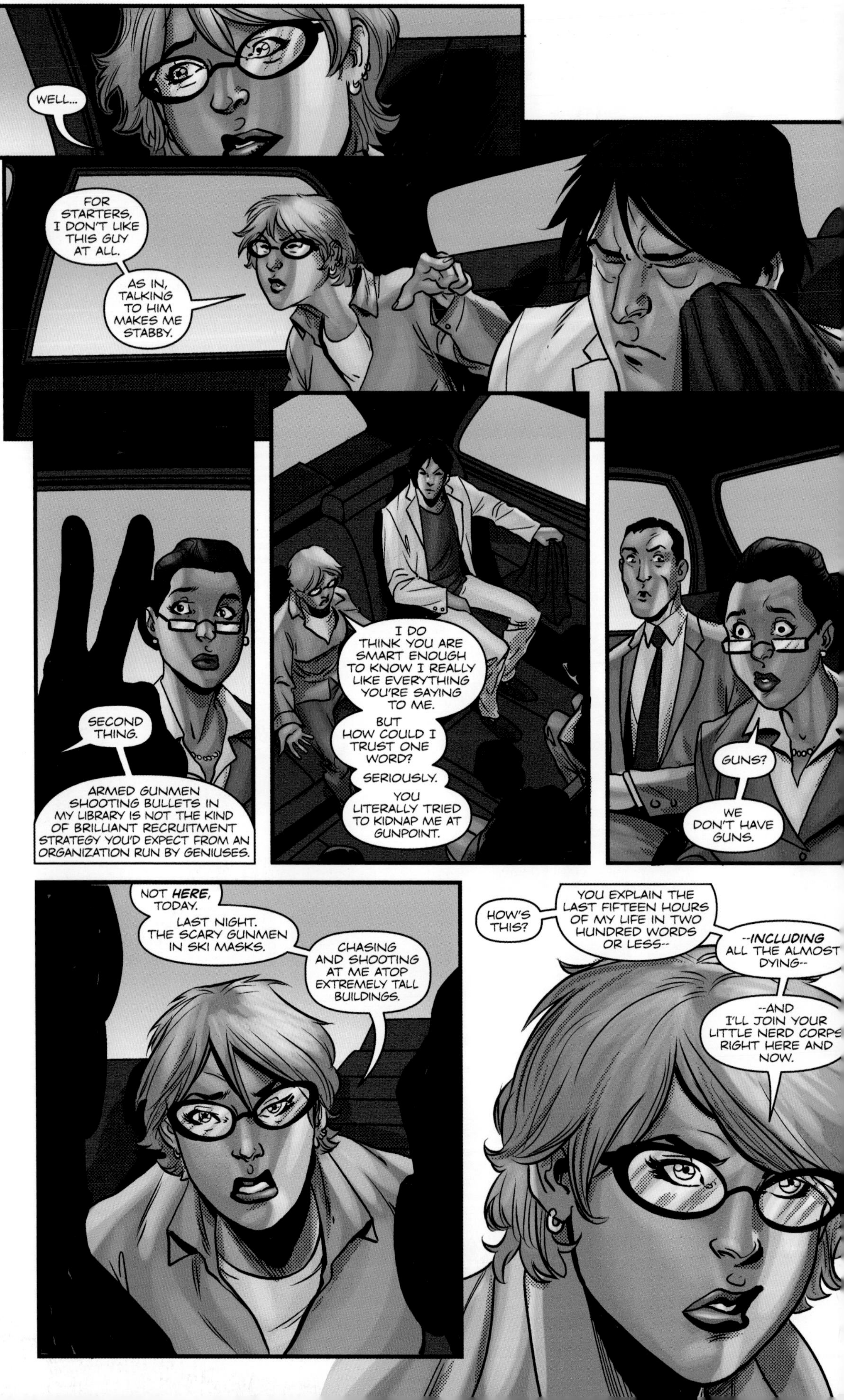
WELL...
FOR STARTERS, I DON'T LIKE THIS GUY AT ALL.
AS IN, TALKING TO HIM MAKES ME STABBY.
SECOND THING.
ARMED GUNMEN SHOOTING BULLETS IN MY LIBRARY IS NOT THE KIND OF BRILLIANT RECRUITMENT STRATEGY YOU'D EXPECT FROM AN ORGANIZATION RUN BY GENIUSES.
I DO THINK YOU ARE SMART ENOUGH TO KNOW I REALLY LIKE EVERYTHING YOU'RE SAYING TO ME.
BUT HOW COULD I TRUST ONE WORD?
SERIOUSLY.
YOU LITERALLY TRIED TO KIDNAP ME AT GUNPOINT.
GUNS?
WE DON'T HAVE GUNS.
NOT *HERE*, TODAY.
LAST NIGHT. THE SCARY GUNMEN IN SKI MASKS.
CHASING AND SHOOTING AT ME ATOP EXTREMELY TALL BUILDINGS.
HOW'S THIS?
YOU EXPLAIN THE LAST FIFTEEN HOURS OF MY LIFE IN TWO HUNDRED WORDS OR LESS--
--*INCLUDING* ALL THE ALMOST DYING--
--AND I'LL JOIN YOUR LITTLE NERD CORPS RIGHT HERE AND NOW.

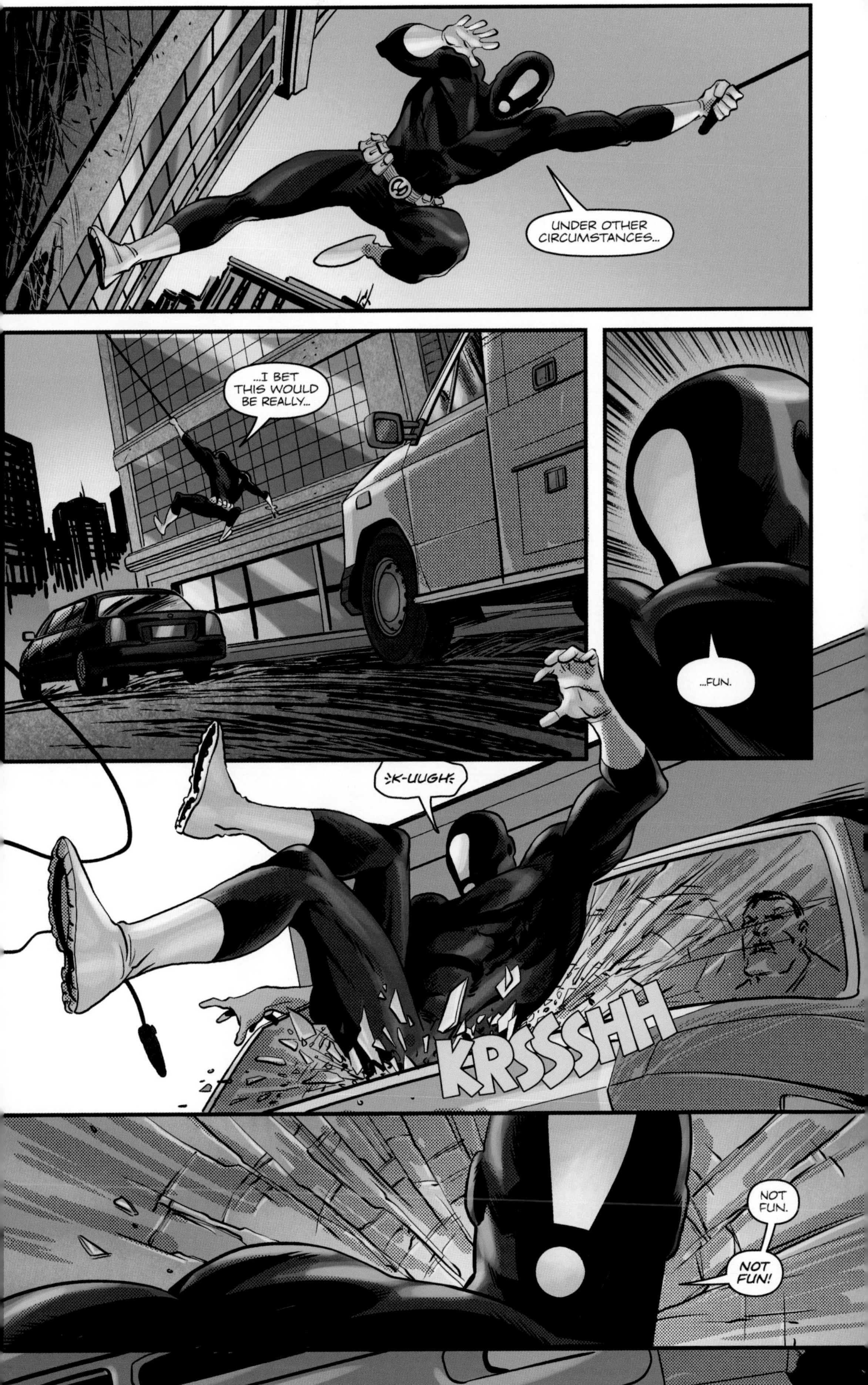
UNDER OTHER CIRCUMSTANCES...
...I BET THIS WOULD BE REALLY...
...FUN.
K-UUGH
KRSSSHH
NOT FUN.
NOT FUN!

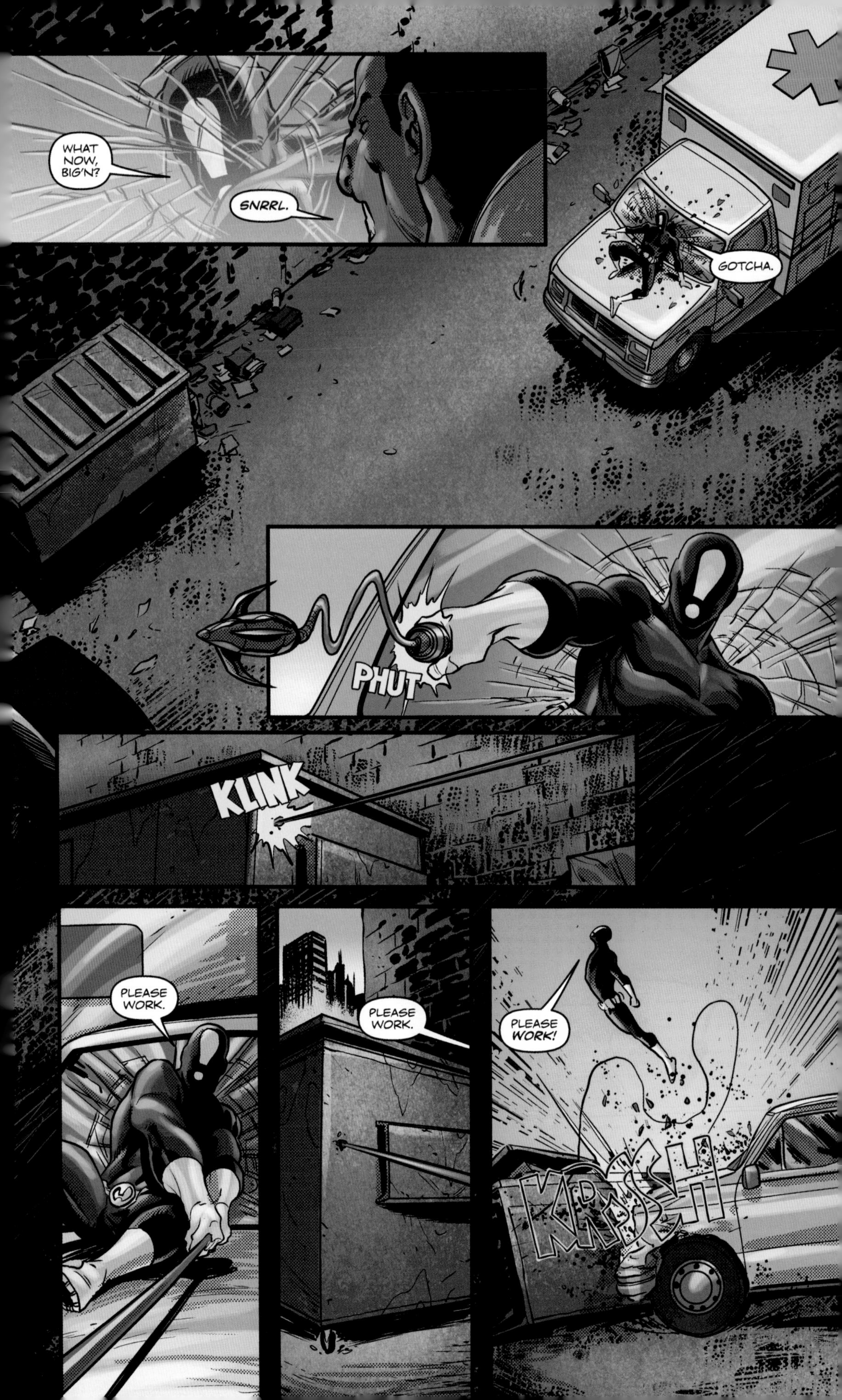
WHAT NOW, BIG'N?
SNRRL.
GOTCHA.
PHUT
KLINK
PLEASE WORK.
PLEASE WORK.
PLEASE WORK!
KRASH

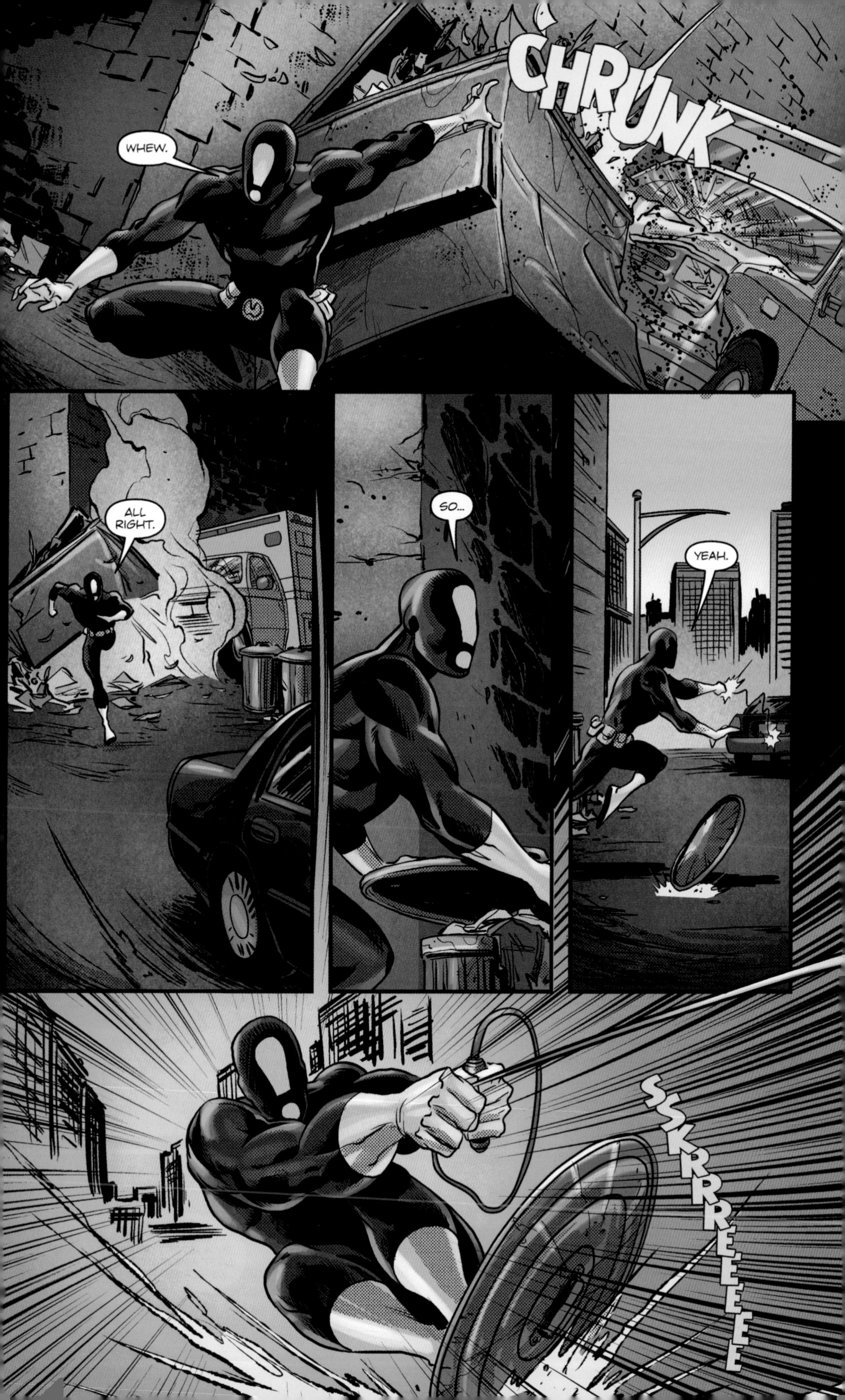
WHEW.
CHRUNK
ALL RIGHT.
SO...
YEAH.
SSKRREEEEE

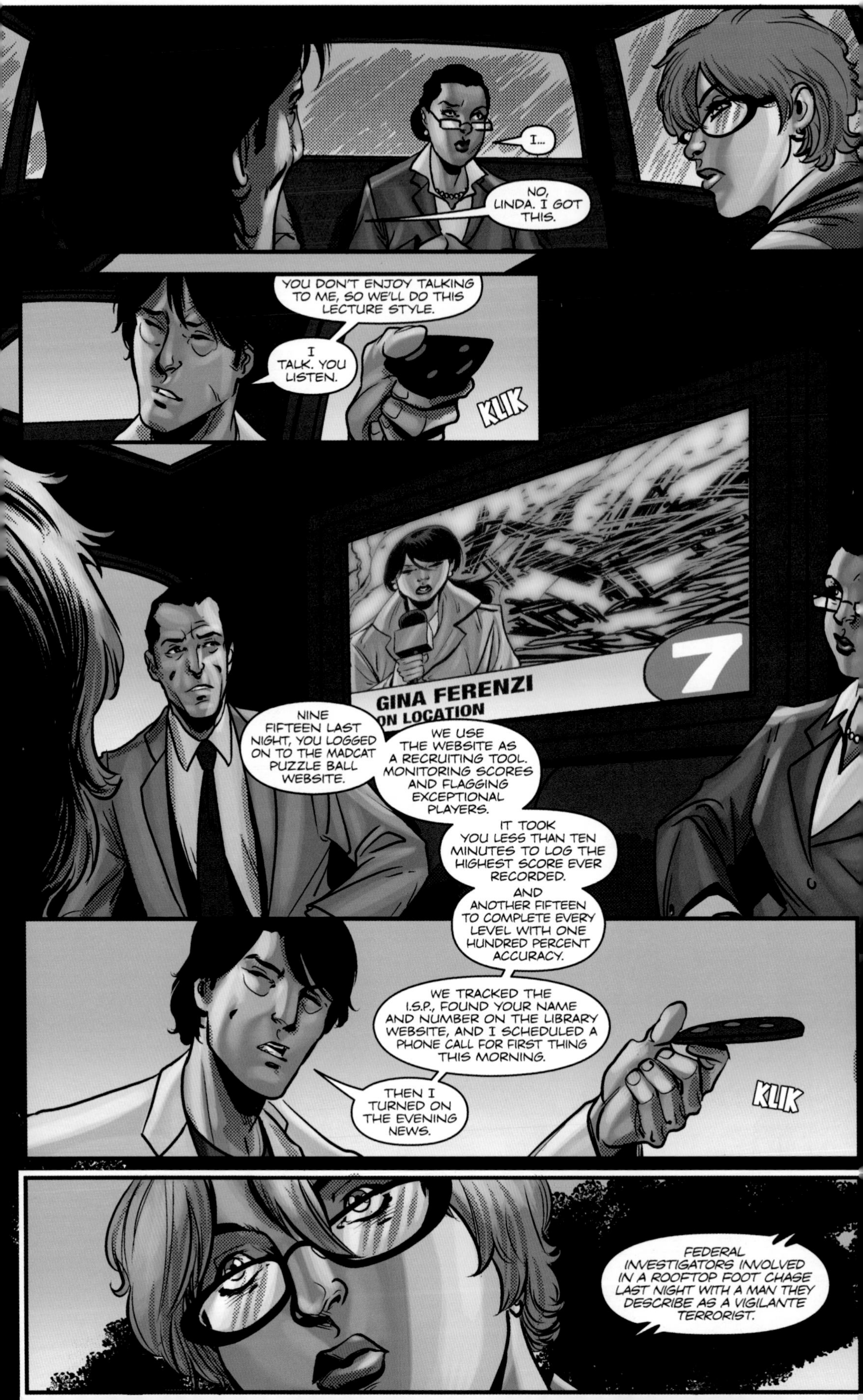
I...
NO, LINDA. I GOT THIS.
YOU DON'T ENJOY TALKING TO ME, SO WE'LL DO THIS LECTURE STYLE.
I TALK. YOU LISTEN.
KLIK
GINA FERENZI
ON LOCATION
7
NINE FIFTEEN LAST NIGHT, YOU LOGGED ON TO THE MADCAT PUZZLE BALL WEBSITE.
WE USE THE WEBSITE AS A RECRUITING TOOL. MONITORING SCORES AND FLAGGING EXCEPTIONAL PLAYERS.
IT TOOK YOU LESS THAN TEN MINUTES TO LOG THE HIGHEST SCORE EVER RECORDED.
AND ANOTHER FIFTEEN TO COMPLETE EVERY LEVEL WITH ONE HUNDRED PERCENT ACCURACY.
WE TRACKED THE I.S.P., FOUND YOUR NAME AND NUMBER ON THE LIBRARY WEBSITE, AND I SCHEDULED A PHONE CALL FOR FIRST THING THIS MORNING.
THEN I TURNED ON THE EVENING NEWS.
KLIK
FEDERAL INVESTIGATORS INVOLVED IN A ROOFTOP FOOT CHASE LAST NIGHT WITH A MAN THEY DESCRIBE AS A VIGILANTE TERRORIST.

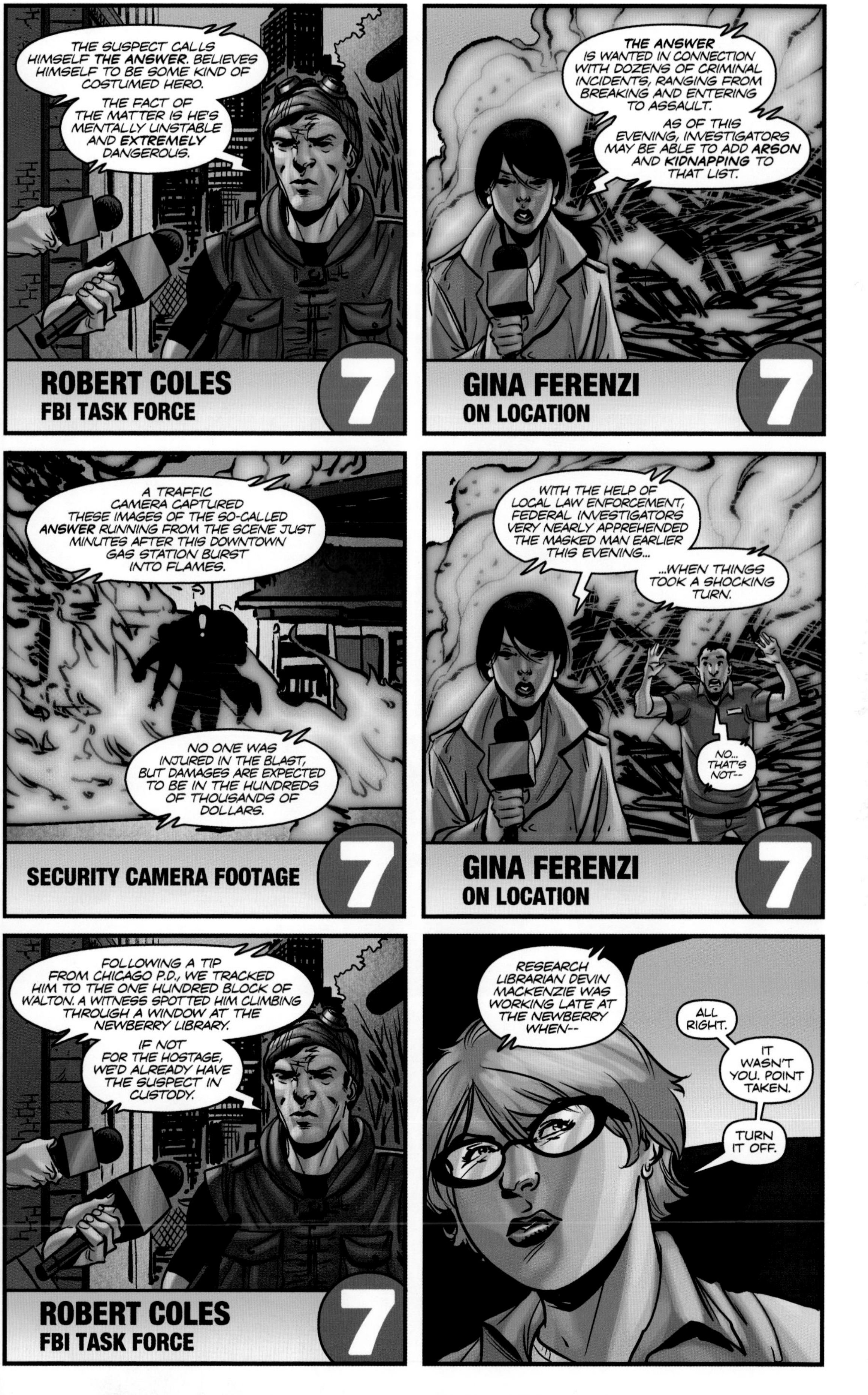
THE SUSPECT CALLS HIMSELF THE ANSWER. BELIEVES HIMSELF TO BE SOME KIND OF COSTUMED HERO.
THE FACT OF THE MATTER IS HE'S MENTALLY UNSTABLE AND EXTREMELY DANGEROUS.
ROBERT COLES
FBI TASK FORCE
7
THE ANSWER IS WANTED IN CONNECTION WITH DOZENS OF CRIMINAL INCIDENTS, RANGING FROM BREAKING AND ENTERING TO ASSAULT.
AS OF THIS EVENING, INVESTIGATORS MAY BE ABLE TO ADD ARSON AND KIDNAPPING TO THAT LIST.
GINA FERENZI
ON LOCATION
7
A TRAFFIC CAMERA CAPTURED THESE IMAGES OF THE SO-CALLED ANSWER RUNNING FROM THE SCENE JUST MINUTES AFTER THIS DOWNTOWN GAS STATION BURST INTO FLAMES.
NO ONE WAS INJURED IN THE BLAST, BUT DAMAGES ARE EXPECTED TO BE IN THE HUNDREDS OF THOUSANDS OF DOLLARS.
SECURITY CAMERA FOOTAGE
7
WITH THE HELP OF LOCAL LAW ENFORCEMENT, FEDERAL INVESTIGATORS VERY NEARLY APPREHENDED THE MASKED MAN EARLIER THIS EVENING...
...WHEN THINGS TOOK A SHOCKING TURN.
NO... THAT'S NOT--
GINA FERENZI
ON LOCATION
7
FOLLOWING A TIP FROM CHICAGO P.D., WE TRACKED HIM TO THE ONE HUNDRED BLOCK OF WALTON. A WITNESS SPOTTED HIM CLIMBING THROUGH A WINDOW AT THE NEWBERRY LIBRARY.
IF NOT FOR THE HOSTAGE, WE'D ALREADY HAVE THE SUSPECT IN CUSTODY.
ROBERT COLES
FBI TASK FORCE
7
RESEARCH LIBRARIAN DEVIN MACKENZIE WAS WORKING LATE AT THE NEWBERRY WHEN--
ALL RIGHT.
IT WASN'T YOU. POINT TAKEN.
TURN IT OFF.

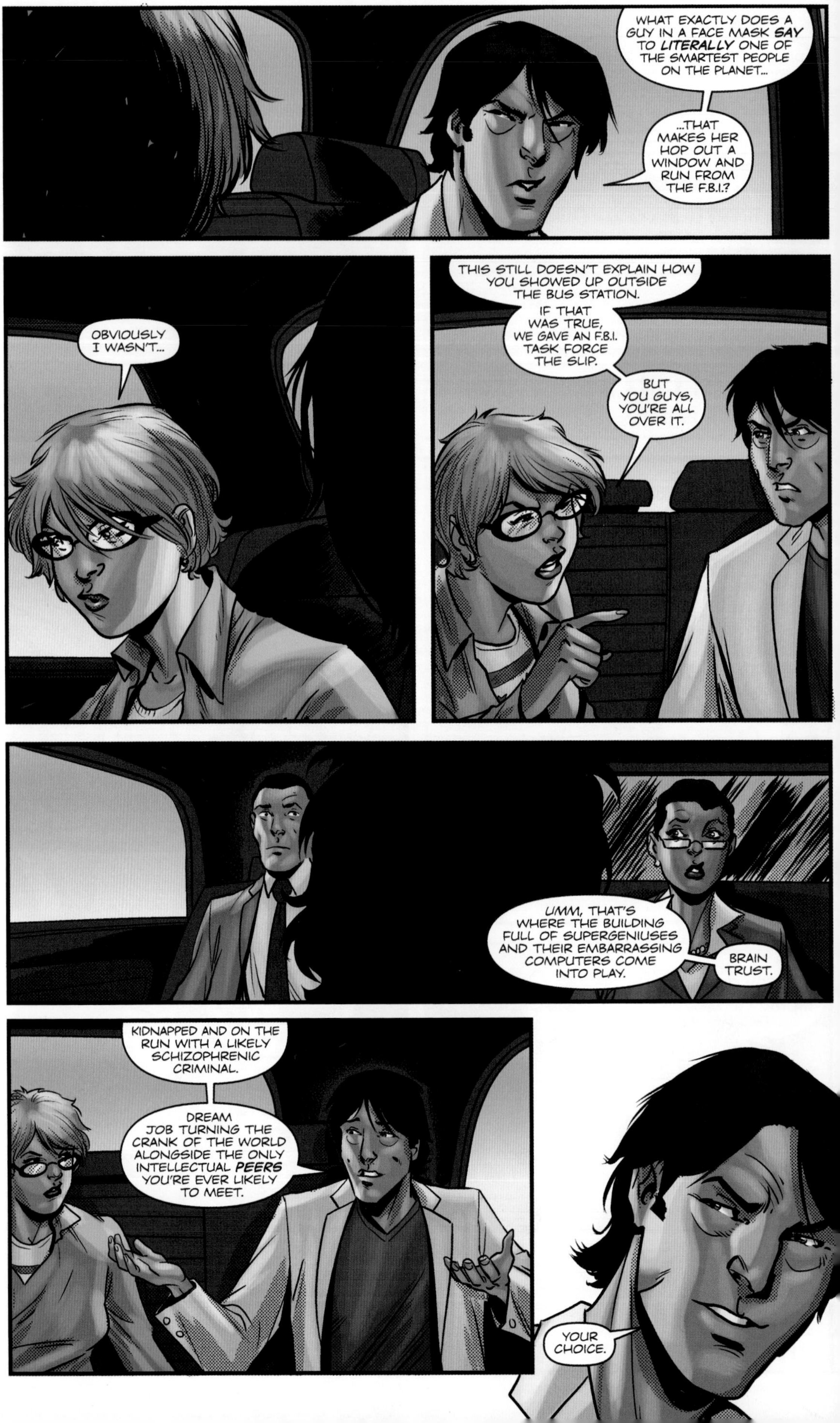
WHAT EXACTLY DOES A GUY IN A FACE MASK *SAY* TO *LITERALLY* ONE OF THE SMARTEST PEOPLE ON THE PLANET...
...THAT MAKES HER HOP OUT A WINDOW AND RUN FROM THE F.B.I.?
OBVIOUSLY I WASN'T...
THIS STILL DOESN'T EXPLAIN HOW YOU SHOWED UP OUTSIDE THE BUS STATION.
IF THAT WAS TRUE, WE GAVE AN F.B.I. TASK FORCE THE SLIP.
BUT YOU GUYS, YOU'RE ALL OVER IT.
UMM, THAT'S WHERE THE BUILDING FULL OF SUPERGENIUSES AND THEIR EMBARRASSING COMPUTERS COME INTO PLAY.
BRAIN TRUST.
KIDNAPPED AND ON THE RUN WITH A LIKELY SCHIZOPHRENIC CRIMINAL.
DREAM JOB TURNING THE CRANK OF THE WORLD ALONGSIDE THE ONLY INTELLECTUAL *PEERS* YOU'RE EVER LIKELY TO MEET.
YOUR CHOICE.

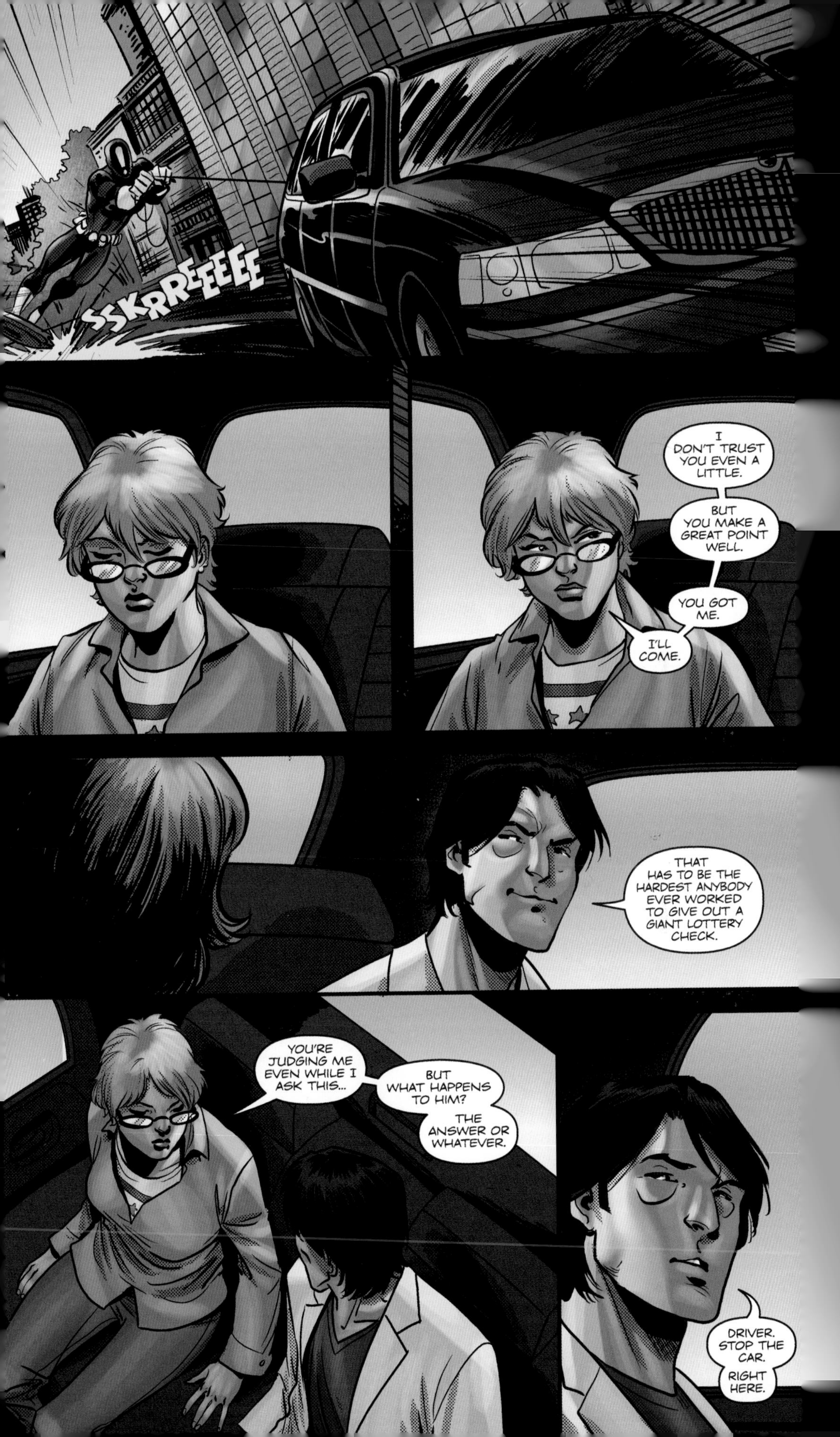
SSKRREEEEE
I DON'T TRUST YOU EVEN A LITTLE.
BUT YOU MAKE A GREAT POINT WELL.
YOU GOT ME.
I'LL COME.
THAT HAS TO BE THE HARDEST ANYBODY EVER WORKED TO GIVE OUT A GIANT LOTTERY CHECK.
YOU'RE JUDGING ME EVEN WHILE I ASK THIS...
BUT WHAT HAPPENS TO HIM?
THE ANSWER OR WHATEVER.
DRIVER. STOP THE CAR.
RIGHT HERE.

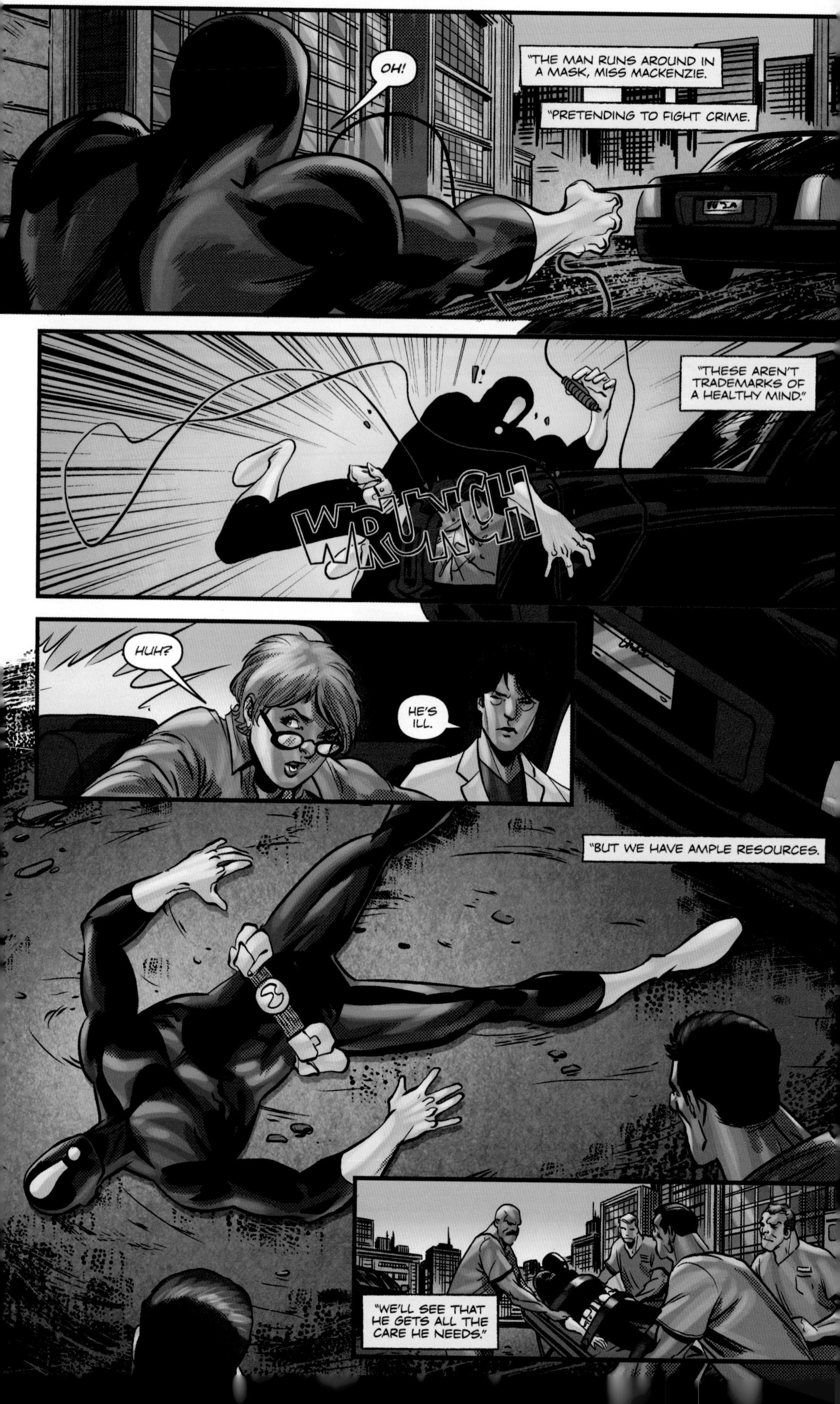
OH!
"THE MAN RUNS AROUND IN A MASK, MISS MACKENZIE.
"PRETENDING TO FIGHT CRIME.
"THESE AREN'T TRADEMARKS OF A HEALTHY MIND."
WRUNCH
HUH?
HE'S ILL.
"BUT WE HAVE AMPLE RESOURCES.
"WE'LL SEE THAT HE GETS ALL THE CARE HE NEEDS."

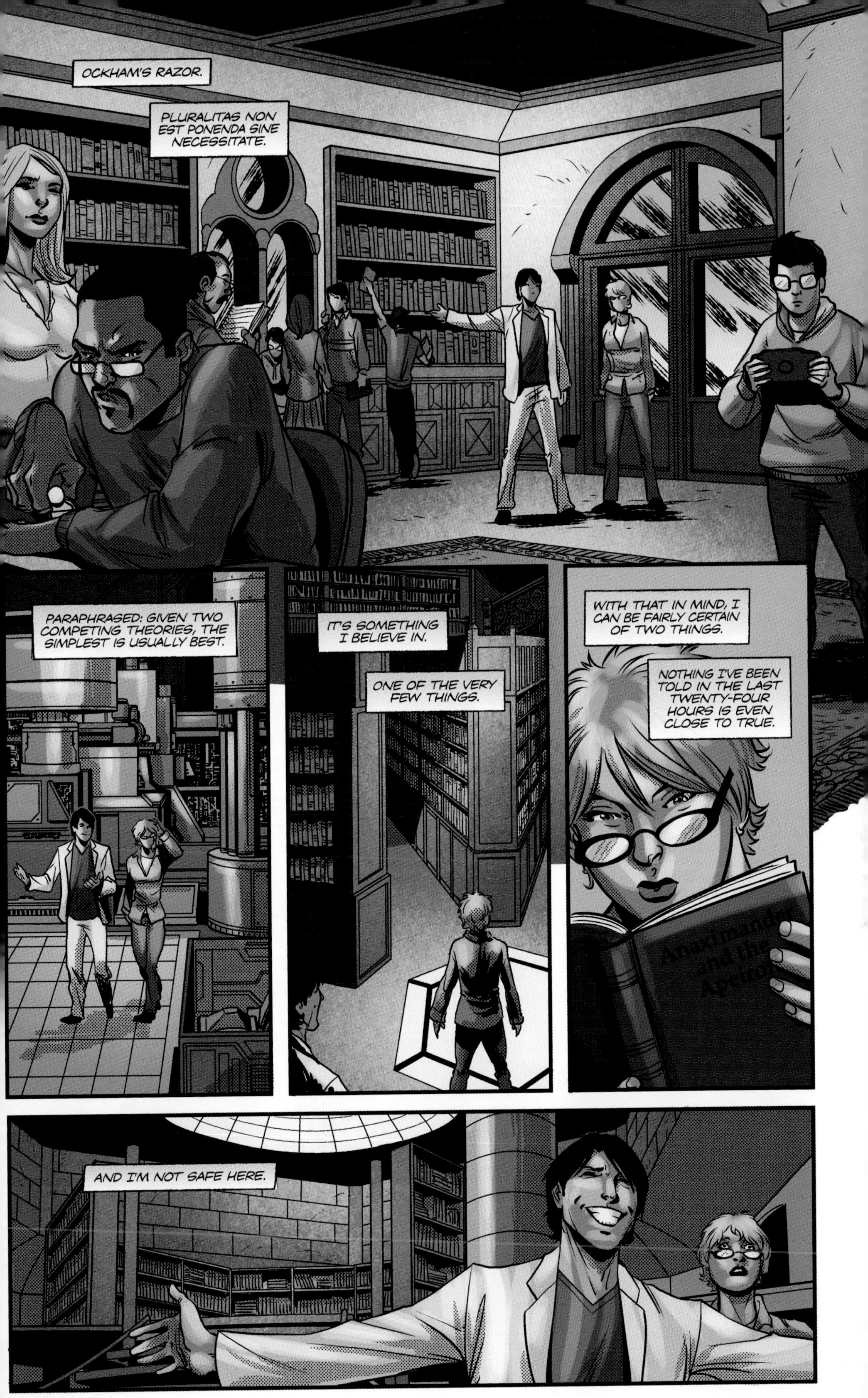
OCKHAM'S RAZOR.
PLURALITAS NON EST PONENDA SINE NECESSITATE.
PARAPHRASED: GIVEN TWO COMPETING THEORIES, THE SIMPLEST IS USUALLY BEST.
IT'S SOMETHING I BELIEVE IN.
ONE OF THE VERY FEW THINGS.
WITH THAT IN MIND, I CAN BE FAIRLY CERTAIN OF TWO THINGS.
NOTHING I'VE BEEN TOLD IN THE LAST TWENTY-FOUR HOURS IS EVEN CLOSE TO TRUE.
Anaximander and the Apeiron
AND I'M NOT SAFE HERE.

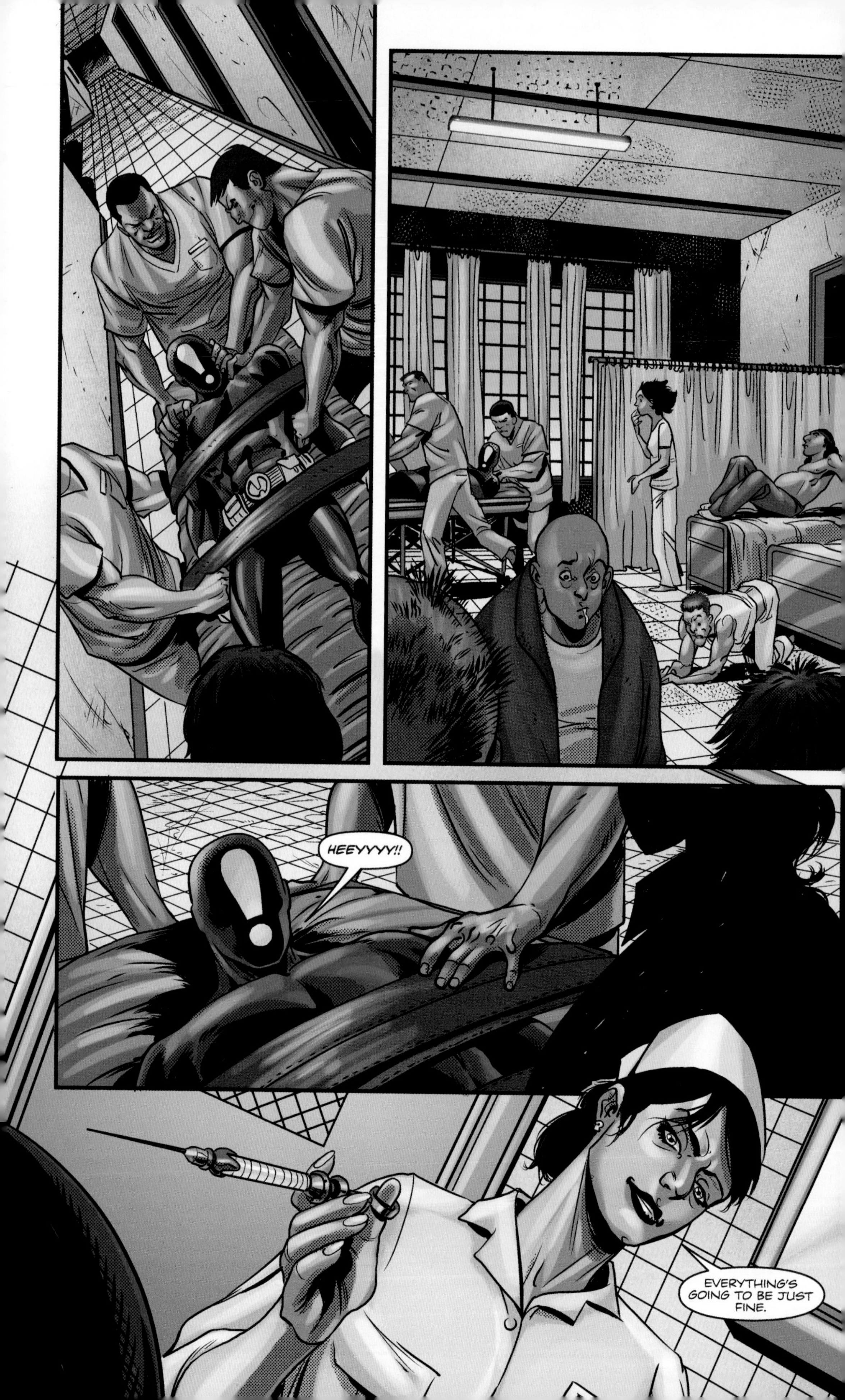
HEEYYYY!!
EVERYTHING'S GOING TO BE JUST FINE.

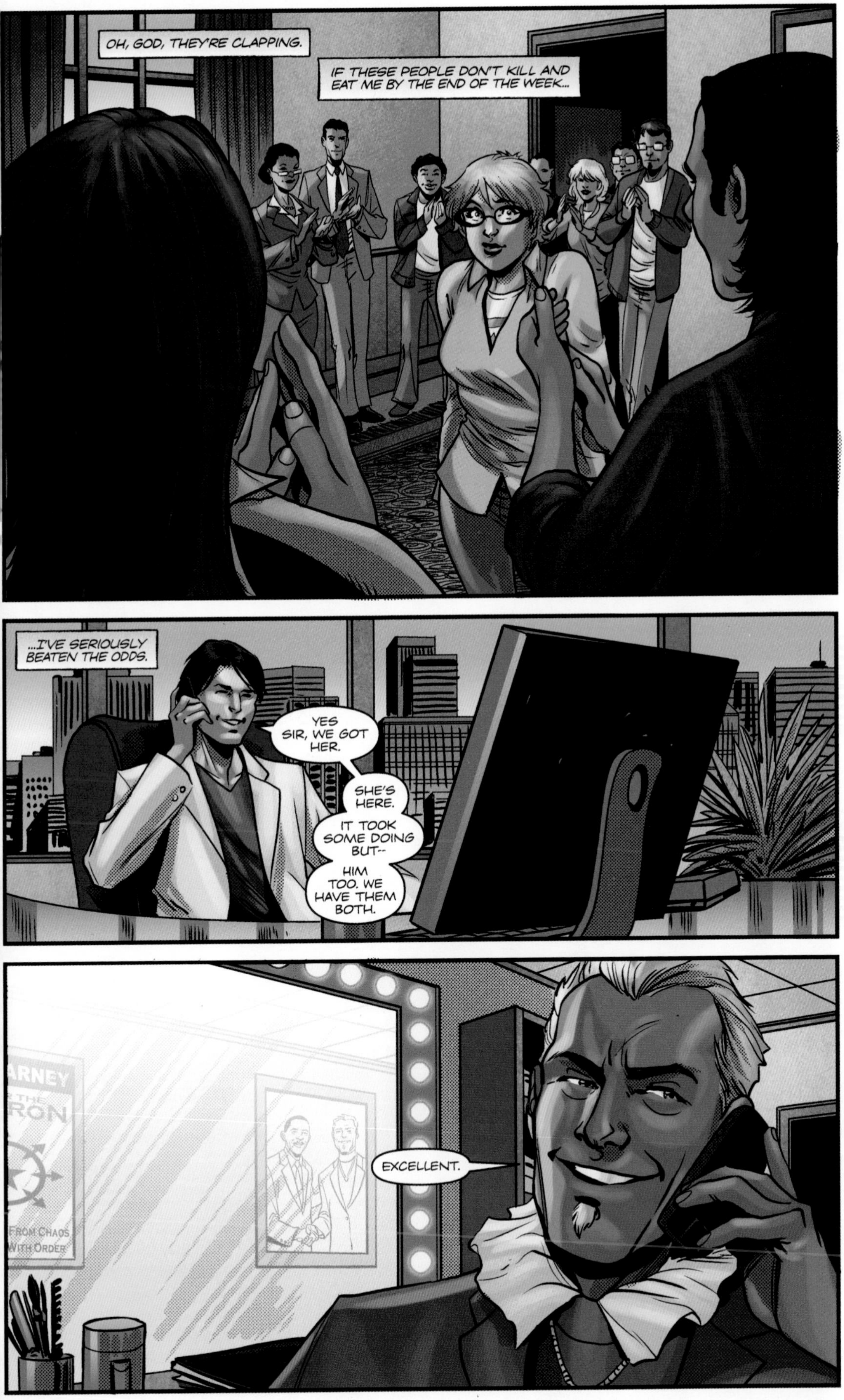
OH, GOD, THEY'RE CLAPPING.
IF THESE PEOPLE DON'T KILL AND EAT ME BY THE END OF THE WEEK...
...I'VE SERIOUSLY BEATEN THE ODDS.
YES SIR, WE GOT HER.
SHE'S HERE.
IT TOOK SOME DOING BUT--
HIM TOO. WE HAVE THEM BOTH.
FROM CHAOS
WITH ORDER
EXCELLENT.

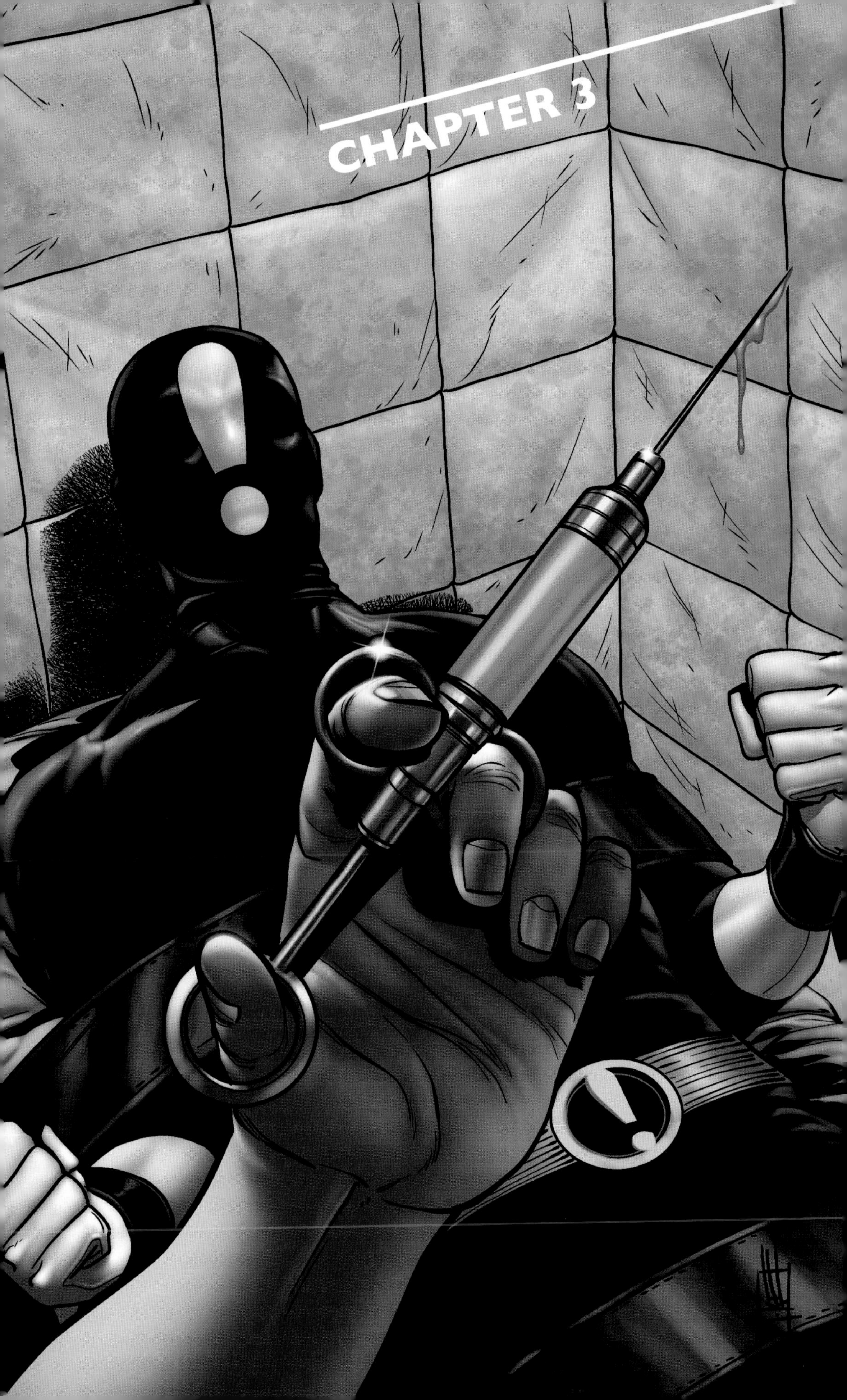
CHAPTER 3

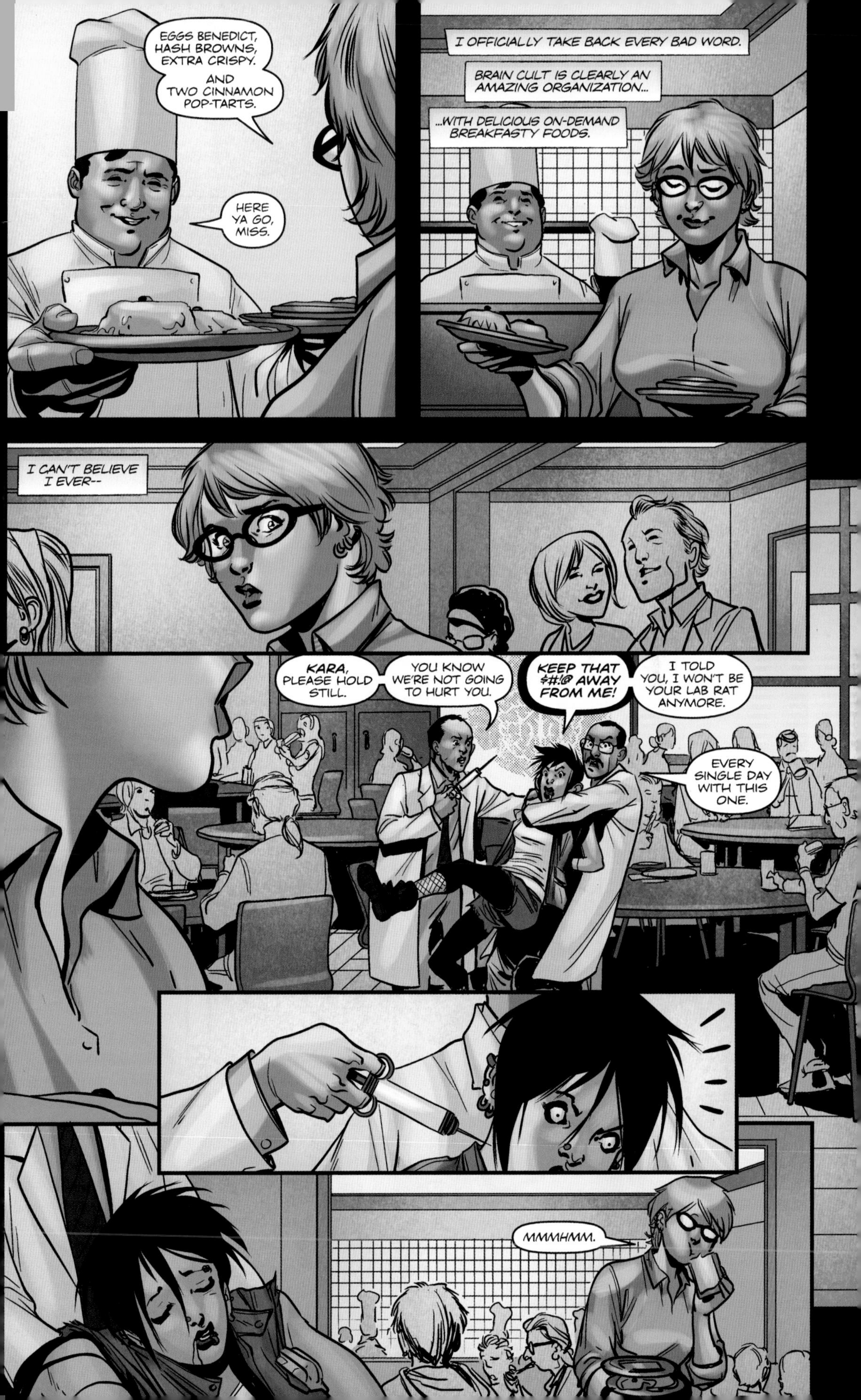
EGGS BENEDICT, HASH BROWNS, EXTRA CRISPY.
AND TWO CINNAMON POP-TARTS.
HERE YA GO, MISS.
I OFFICIALLY TAKE BACK EVERY BAD WORD.
BRAIN CULT IS CLEARLY AN AMAZING ORGANIZATION...
...WITH DELICIOUS ON-DEMAND BREAKFASTY FOODS.
I CAN'T BELIEVE I EVER--
KARA, PLEASE HOLD STILL.
YOU KNOW WE'RE NOT GOING TO HURT YOU.
KEEP THAT $#!@ AWAY FROM ME!
I TOLD YOU, I WON'T BE YOUR LAB RAT ANYMORE.
EVERY SINGLE DAY WITH THIS ONE.
MMMHMM.

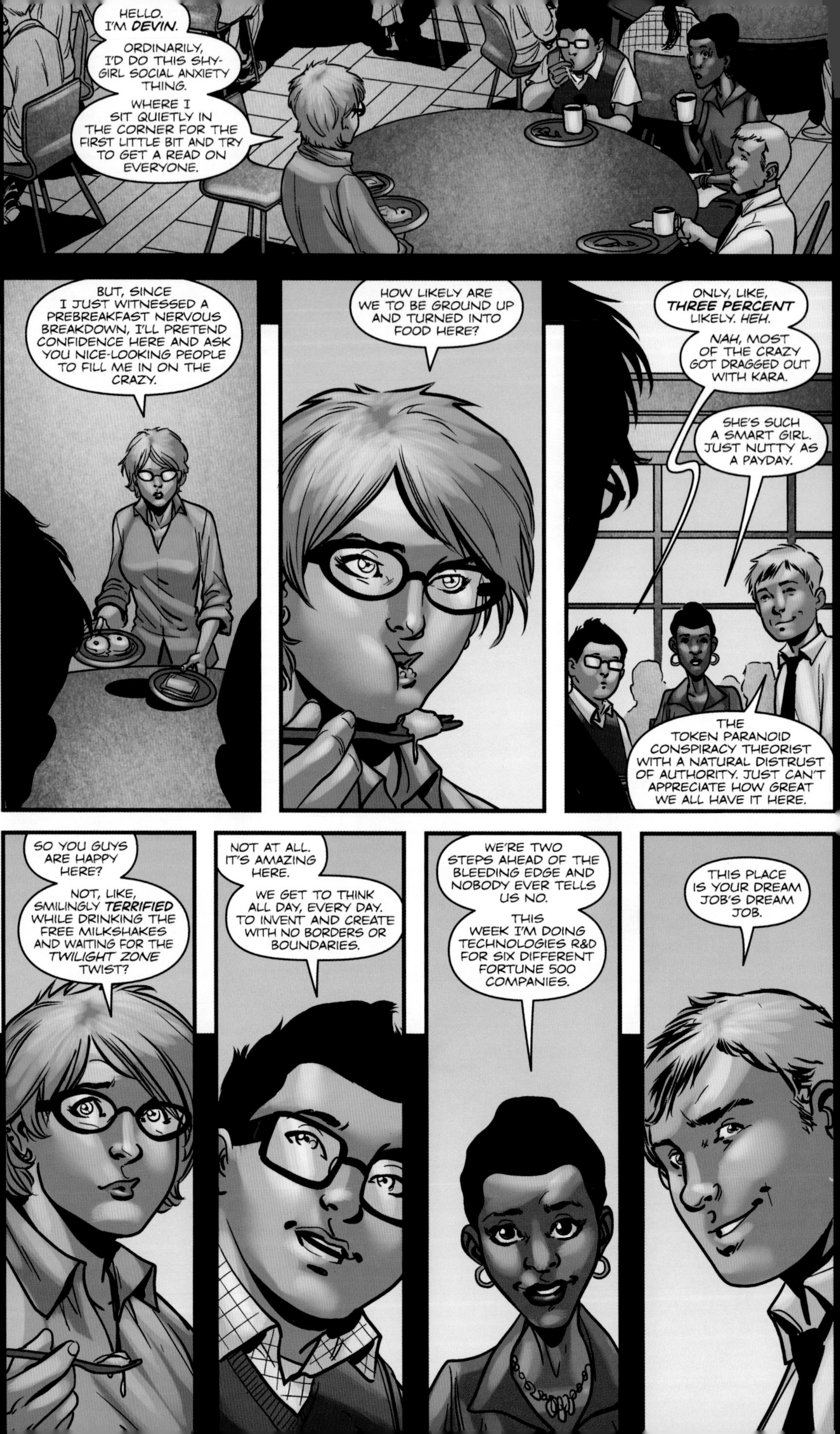

HELLO. I'M *DEVIN*.
ORDINARILY, I'D DO THIS SHY-GIRL SOCIAL ANXIETY THING.
WHERE I SIT QUIETLY IN THE CORNER FOR THE FIRST LITTLE BIT AND TRY TO GET A READ ON EVERYONE.
BUT, SINCE I JUST WITNESSED A PREBREAKFAST NERVOUS BREAKDOWN, I'LL PRETEND CONFIDENCE HERE AND ASK YOU NICE-LOOKING PEOPLE TO FILL ME IN ON THE CRAZY.
HOW LIKELY ARE WE TO BE GROUND UP AND TURNED INTO FOOD HERE?
ONLY, LIKE, ***THREE PERCENT*** LIKELY. HEH.
NAH, MOST OF THE CRAZY GOT DRAGGED OUT WITH KARA.
SHE'S SUCH A SMART GIRL. JUST NUTTY AS A PAYDAY.
THE TOKEN PARANOID CONSPIRACY THEORIST WITH A NATURAL DISTRUST OF AUTHORITY. JUST CAN'T APPRECIATE HOW GREAT WE ALL HAVE IT HERE.
SO YOU GUYS ARE HAPPY HERE?
NOT, LIKE, SMILINGLY *TERRIFIED* WHILE DRINKING THE FREE MILKSHAKES AND WAITING FOR THE *TWILIGHT ZONE* TWIST?
NOT AT ALL. IT'S AMAZING HERE.
WE GET TO THINK ALL DAY, EVERY DAY. TO INVENT AND CREATE WITH NO BORDERS OR BOUNDARIES.
WE'RE TWO STEPS AHEAD OF THE BLEEDING EDGE AND NOBODY EVER TELLS US NO.
THIS WEEK I'M DOING TECHNOLOGIES R&D FOR SIX DIFFERENT FORTUNE 500 COMPANIES.
THIS PLACE IS YOUR DREAM JOB'S DREAM JOB.

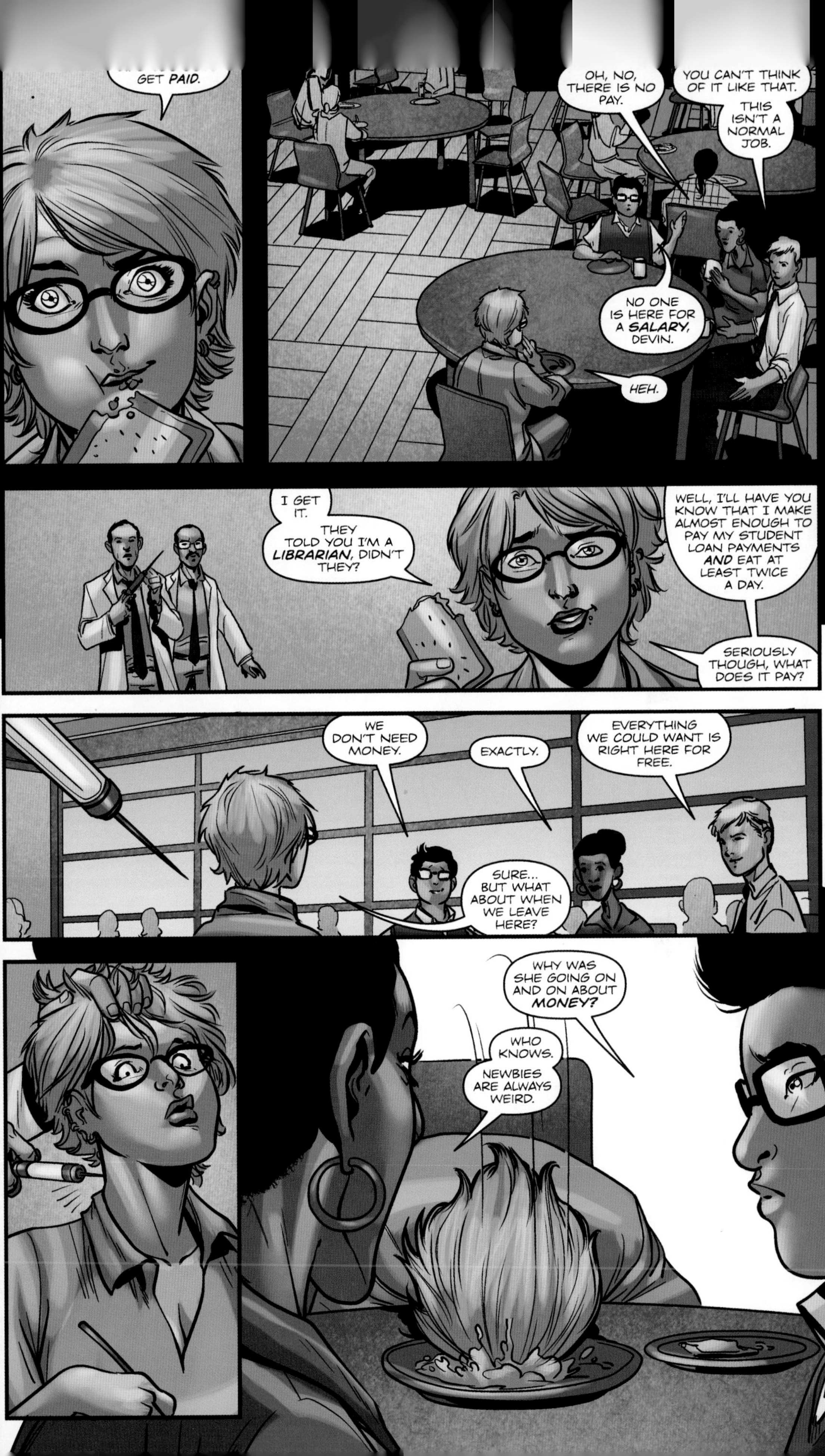
GET PAID.
OH, NO, THERE IS NO PAY.
YOU CAN'T THINK OF IT LIKE THAT.
THIS ISN'T A NORMAL JOB.
NO ONE IS HERE FOR A SALARY, DEVIN.
HEH.
I GET IT.
THEY TOLD YOU I'M A LIBRARIAN, DIDN'T THEY?
WELL, I'LL HAVE YOU KNOW THAT I MAKE ALMOST ENOUGH TO PAY MY STUDENT LOAN PAYMENTS AND EAT AT LEAST TWICE A DAY.
SERIOUSLY THOUGH, WHAT DOES IT PAY?
WE DON'T NEED MONEY.
EXACTLY.
EVERYTHING WE COULD WANT IS RIGHT HERE FOR FREE.
SURE... BUT WHAT ABOUT WHEN WE LEAVE HERE?
WHY WAS SHE GOING ON AND ON ABOUT MONEY?
WHO KNOWS.
NEWBIES ARE ALWAYS WEIRD.

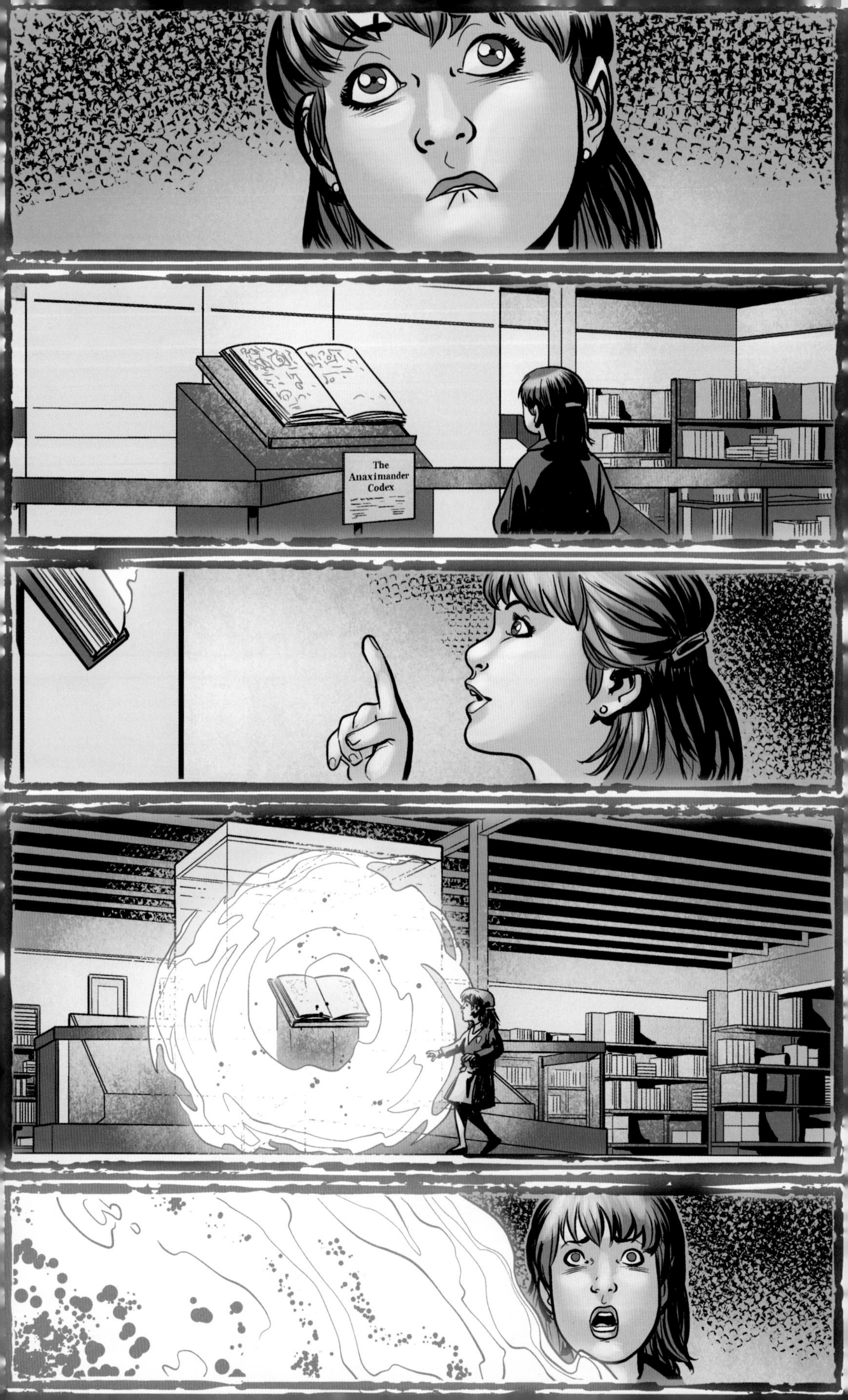
The Anaximander Codex

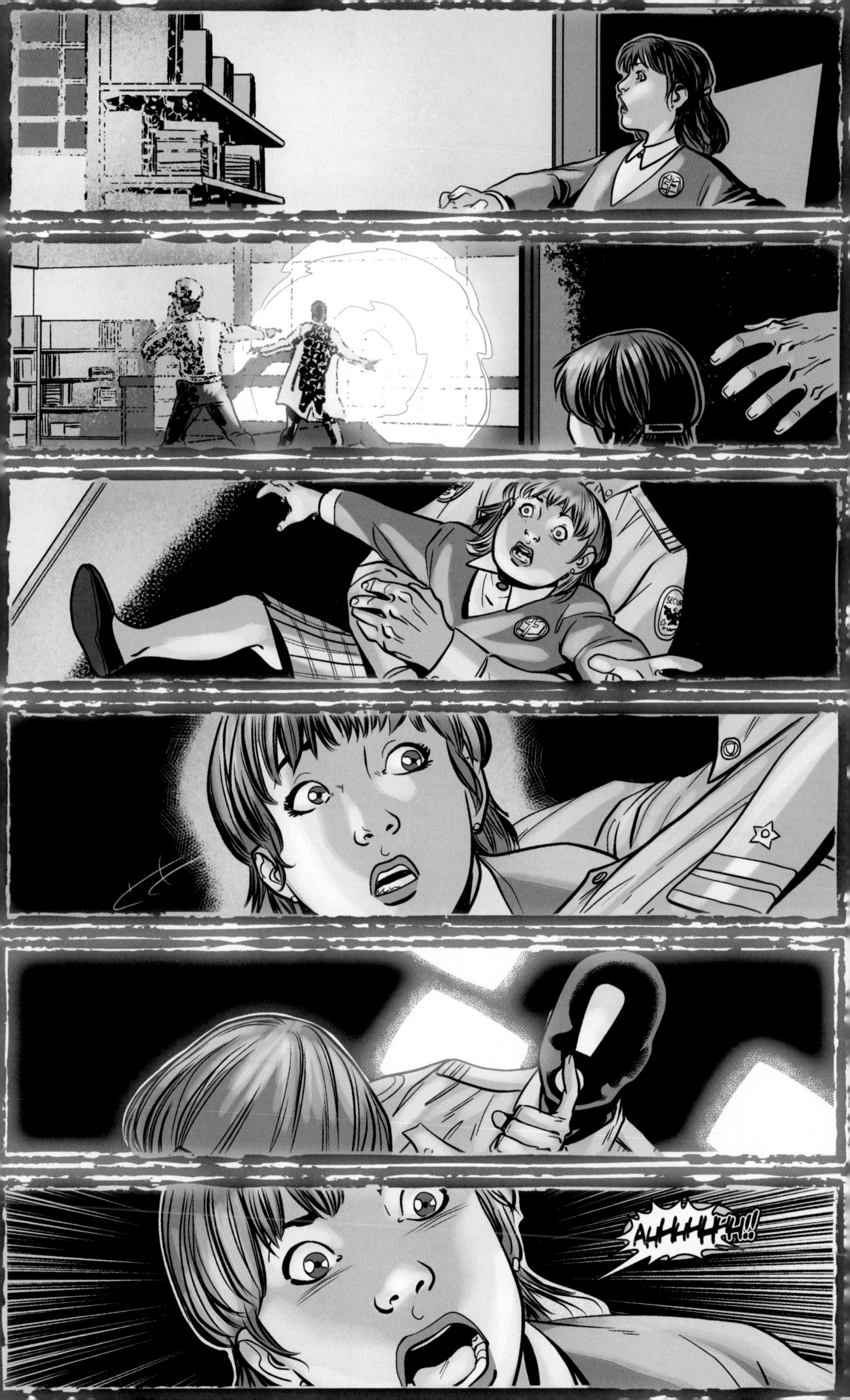
AHHHHHHH!!

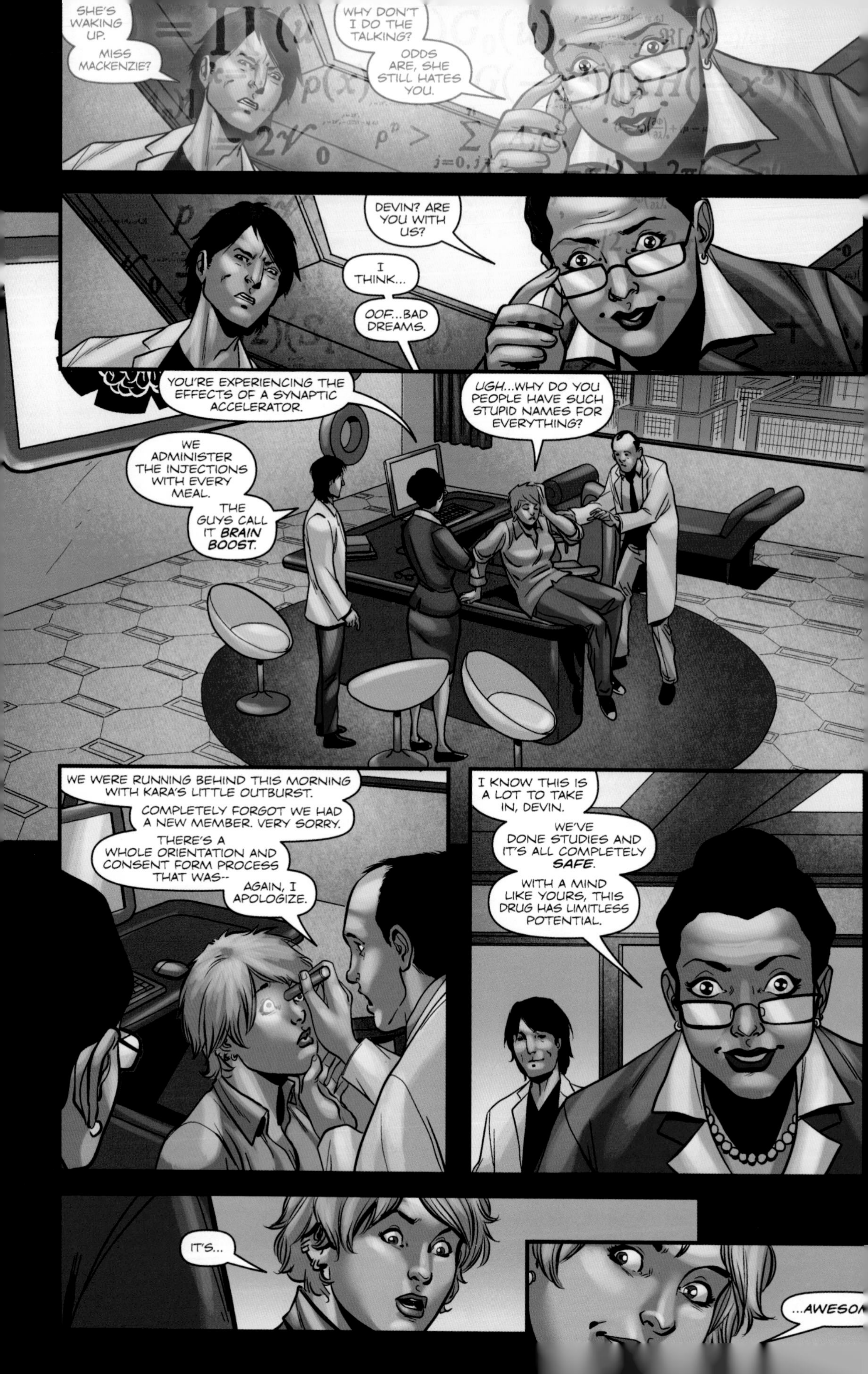
SHE'S WAKING UP.
MISS MACKENZIE?
WHY DON'T I DO THE TALKING?
ODDS ARE, SHE STILL HATES YOU.
DEVIN? ARE YOU WITH US?
I THINK...
OOF...BAD DREAMS.
YOU'RE EXPERIENCING THE EFFECTS OF A SYNAPTIC ACCELERATOR.
UGH...WHY DO YOU PEOPLE HAVE SUCH STUPID NAMES FOR EVERYTHING?
WE ADMINISTER THE INJECTIONS WITH EVERY MEAL.
THE GUYS CALL IT **BRAIN BOOST**.
WE WERE RUNNING BEHIND THIS MORNING WITH KARA'S LITTLE OUTBURST.
COMPLETELY FORGOT WE HAD A NEW MEMBER. VERY SORRY.
THERE'S A WHOLE ORIENTATION AND CONSENT FORM PROCESS THAT WAS--
AGAIN, I APOLOGIZE.
I KNOW THIS IS A LOT TO TAKE IN, DEVIN.
WE'VE DONE STUDIES AND IT'S ALL COMPLETELY ***SAFE***.
WITH A MIND LIKE YOURS, THIS DRUG HAS LIMITLESS POTENTIAL.
IT'S...
...***AWESOM***

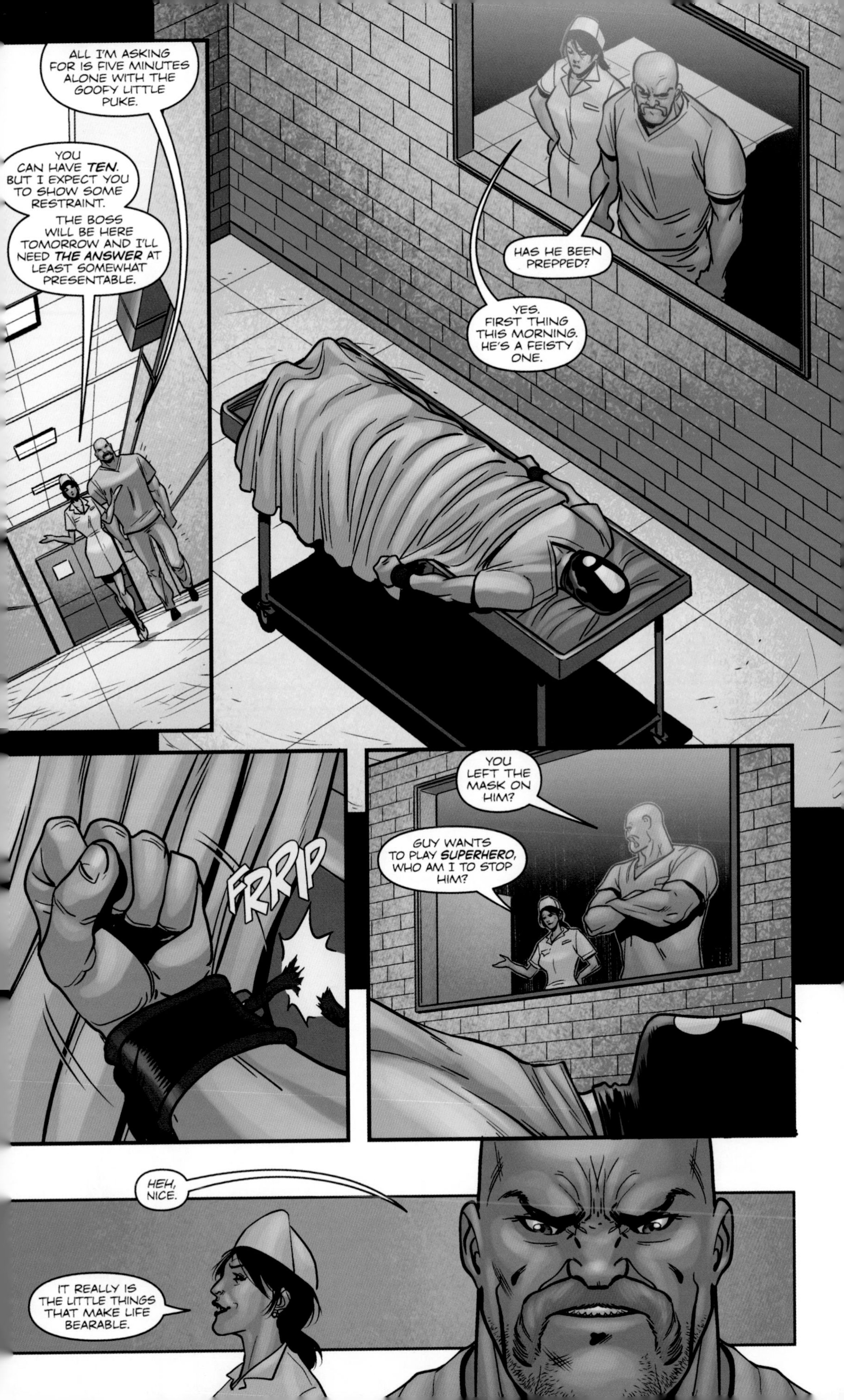
ALL I'M ASKING FOR IS FIVE MINUTES ALONE WITH THE GOOFY LITTLE PUKE.
YOU CAN HAVE TEN. BUT I EXPECT YOU TO SHOW SOME RESTRAINT.
THE BOSS WILL BE HERE TOMORROW AND I'LL NEED THE ANSWER AT LEAST SOMEWHAT PRESENTABLE.
HAS HE BEEN PREPPED?
YES. FIRST THING THIS MORNING. HE'S A FEISTY ONE.
FRRIP
YOU LEFT THE MASK ON HIM?
GUY WANTS TO PLAY SUPERHERO, WHO AM I TO STOP HIM?
HEH, NICE.
IT REALLY IS THE LITTLE THINGS THAT MAKE LIFE BEARABLE.

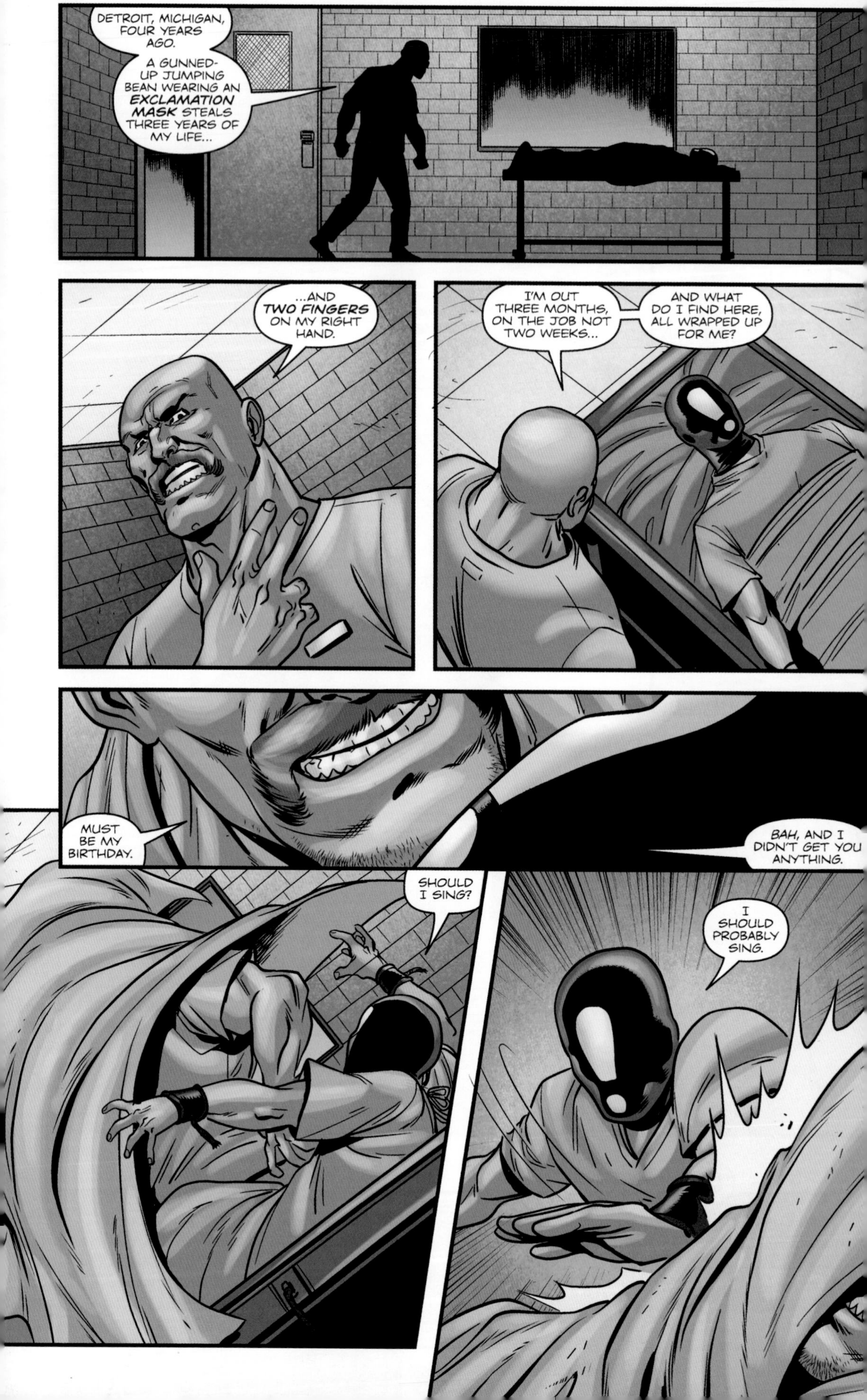
DETROIT, MICHIGAN, FOUR YEARS AGO.
A GUNNED-UP JUMPING BEAN WEARING AN **EXCLAMATION MASK** STEALS THREE YEARS OF MY LIFE...
...AND **TWO FINGERS** ON MY RIGHT HAND.
I'M OUT THREE MONTHS, ON THE JOB NOT TWO WEEKS...
AND WHAT DO I FIND HERE, ALL WRAPPED UP FOR ME?
MUST BE MY BIRTHDAY.
BAH, AND I DIDN'T GET YOU ANYTHING.
SHOULD I SING?
I SHOULD PROBABLY SING.

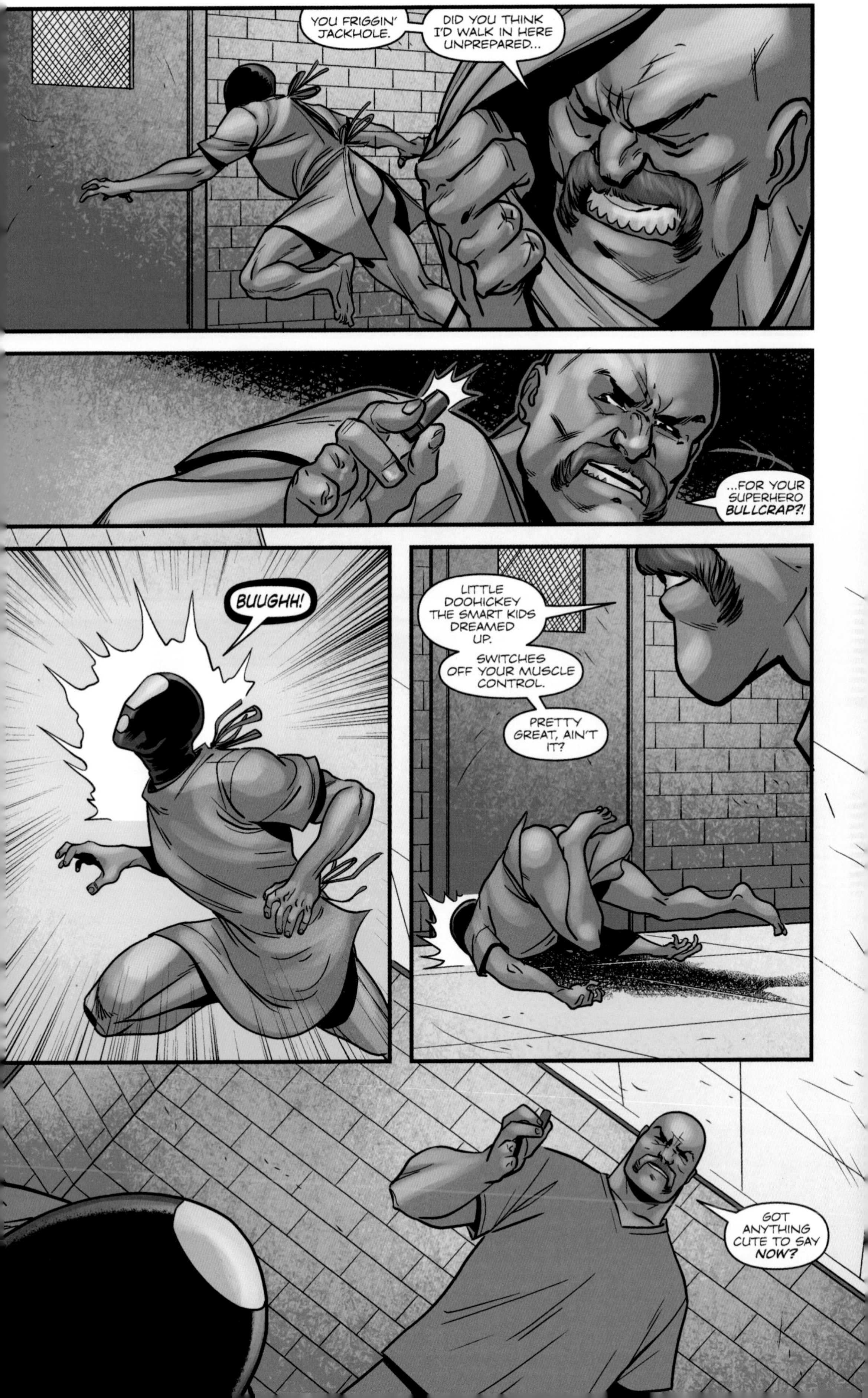

YOU FRIGGIN' JACKHOLE.
DID YOU THINK I'D WALK IN HERE UNPREPARED...
...FOR YOUR SUPERHERO *BULLCRAP?!*
BUUGHH!
LITTLE DOOHICKEY THE SMART KIDS DREAMED UP.
SWITCHES OFF YOUR MUSCLE CONTROL.
PRETTY GREAT, AIN'T IT?
GOT ANYTHING CUTE TO SAY *NOW?*

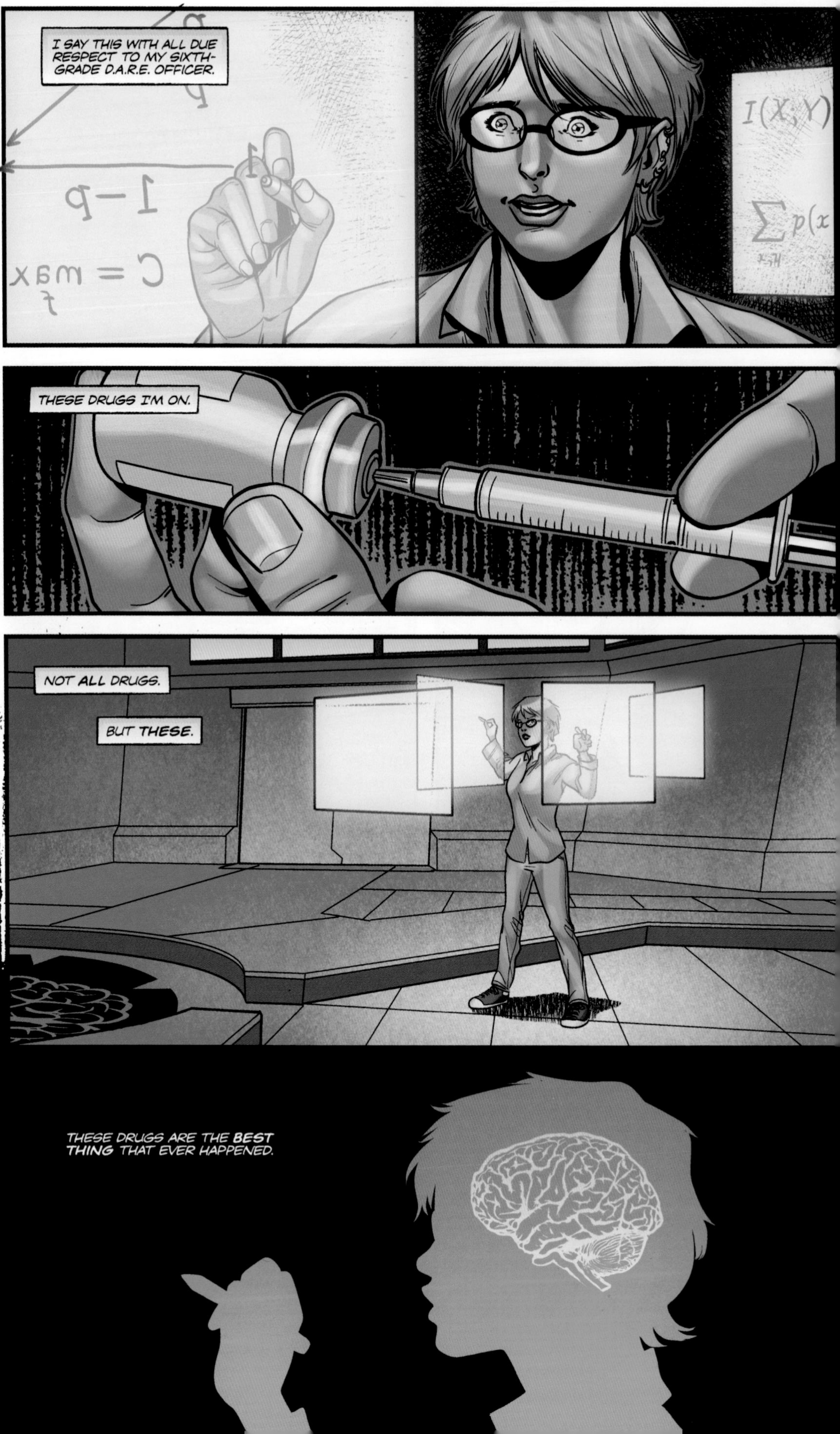
I SAY THIS WITH ALL DUE RESPECT TO MY SIXTH-GRADE D.A.R.E. OFFICER.
THESE DRUGS I'M ON.
NOT ALL DRUGS.
BUT THESE.
THESE DRUGS ARE THE BEST THING THAT EVER HAPPENED.

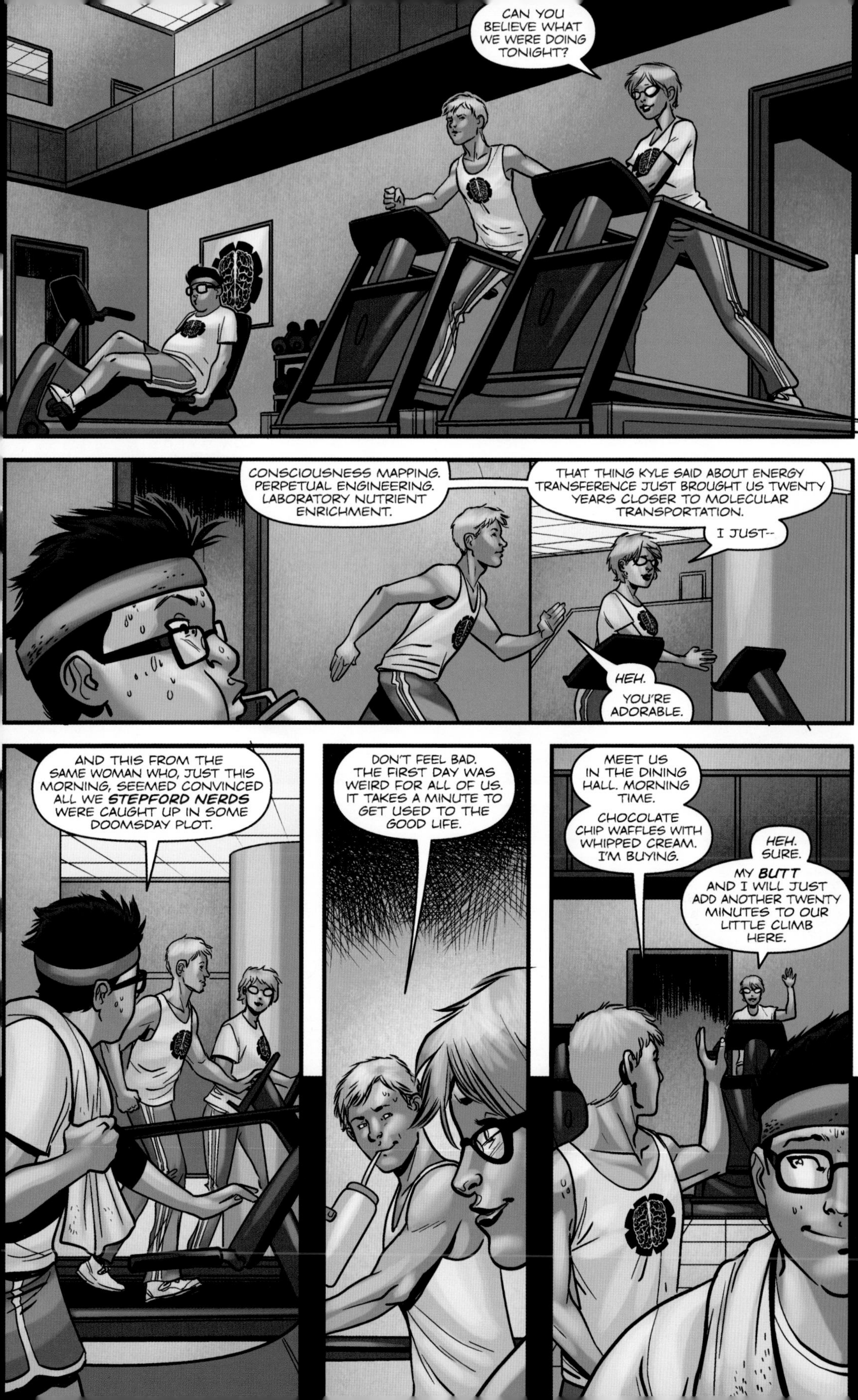
CAN YOU BELIEVE WHAT WE WERE DOING TONIGHT?
CONSCIOUSNESS MAPPING. PERPETUAL ENGINEERING. LABORATORY NUTRIENT ENRICHMENT.
THAT THING KYLE SAID ABOUT ENERGY TRANSFERENCE JUST BROUGHT US TWENTY YEARS CLOSER TO MOLECULAR TRANSPORTATION.
I JUST--
HEH.
YOU'RE ADORABLE.
AND THIS FROM THE SAME WOMAN WHO, JUST THIS MORNING, SEEMED CONVINCED ALL WE STEPFORD NERDS WERE CAUGHT UP IN SOME DOOMSDAY PLOT.
DON'T FEEL BAD. THE FIRST DAY WAS WEIRD FOR ALL OF US. IT TAKES A MINUTE TO GET USED TO THE GOOD LIFE.
MEET US IN THE DINING HALL. MORNING TIME.
CHOCOLATE CHIP WAFFLES WITH WHIPPED CREAM. I'M BUYING.
HEH. SURE.
MY BUTT AND I WILL JUST ADD ANOTHER TWENTY MINUTES TO OUR LITTLE CLIMB HERE.

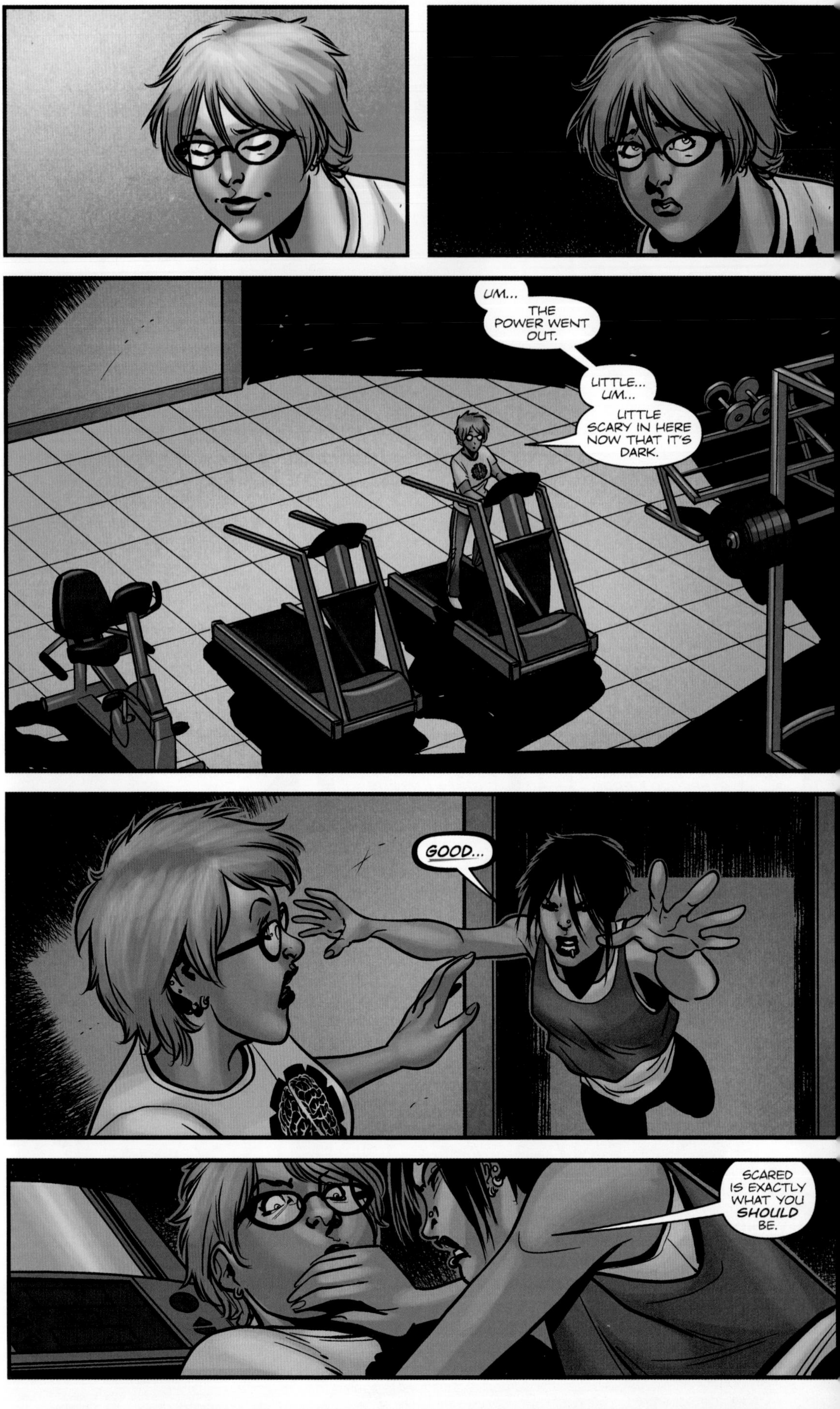
UM... THE POWER WENT OUT.
LITTLE... UM...
LITTLE SCARY IN HERE NOW THAT IT'S DARK.
GOOD...
SCARED IS EXACTLY WHAT YOU SHOULD BE.

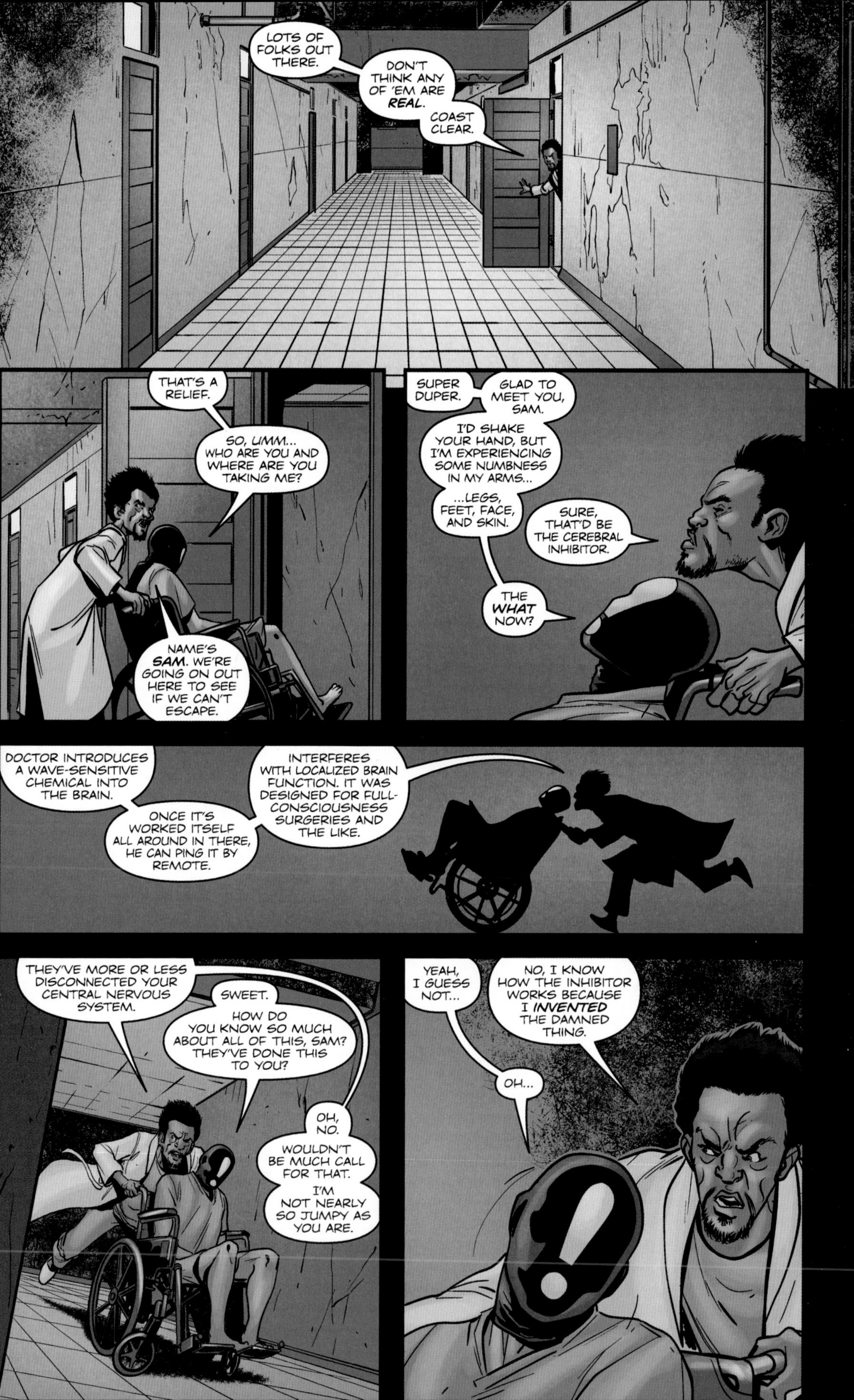
LOTS OF FOLKS OUT THERE.
DON'T THINK ANY OF 'EM ARE REAL.
COAST CLEAR.
THAT'S A RELIEF.
SO, UMM... WHO ARE YOU AND WHERE ARE YOU TAKING ME?
NAME'S SAM. WE'RE GOING ON OUT HERE TO SEE IF WE CAN'T ESCAPE.
SUPER DUPER.
GLAD TO MEET YOU, SAM.
I'D SHAKE YOUR HAND, BUT I'M EXPERIENCING SOME NUMBNESS IN MY ARMS...
...LEGS, FEET, FACE, AND SKIN.
SURE, THAT'D BE THE CEREBRAL INHIBITOR.
THE WHAT NOW?
DOCTOR INTRODUCES A WAVE-SENSITIVE CHEMICAL INTO THE BRAIN.
ONCE IT'S WORKED ITSELF ALL AROUND IN THERE, HE CAN PING IT BY REMOTE.
INTERFERES WITH LOCALIZED BRAIN FUNCTION. IT WAS DESIGNED FOR FULL-CONSCIOUSNESS SURGERIES AND THE LIKE.
THEY'VE MORE OR LESS DISCONNECTED YOUR CENTRAL NERVOUS SYSTEM.
SWEET.
HOW DO YOU KNOW SO MUCH ABOUT ALL OF THIS, SAM? THEY'VE DONE THIS TO YOU?
OH, NO.
WOULDN'T BE MUCH CALL FOR THAT.
I'M NOT NEARLY SO JUMPY AS YOU ARE.
YEAH, I GUESS NOT...
NO, I KNOW HOW THE INHIBITOR WORKS BECAUSE I INVENTED THE DAMNED THING.
OH...

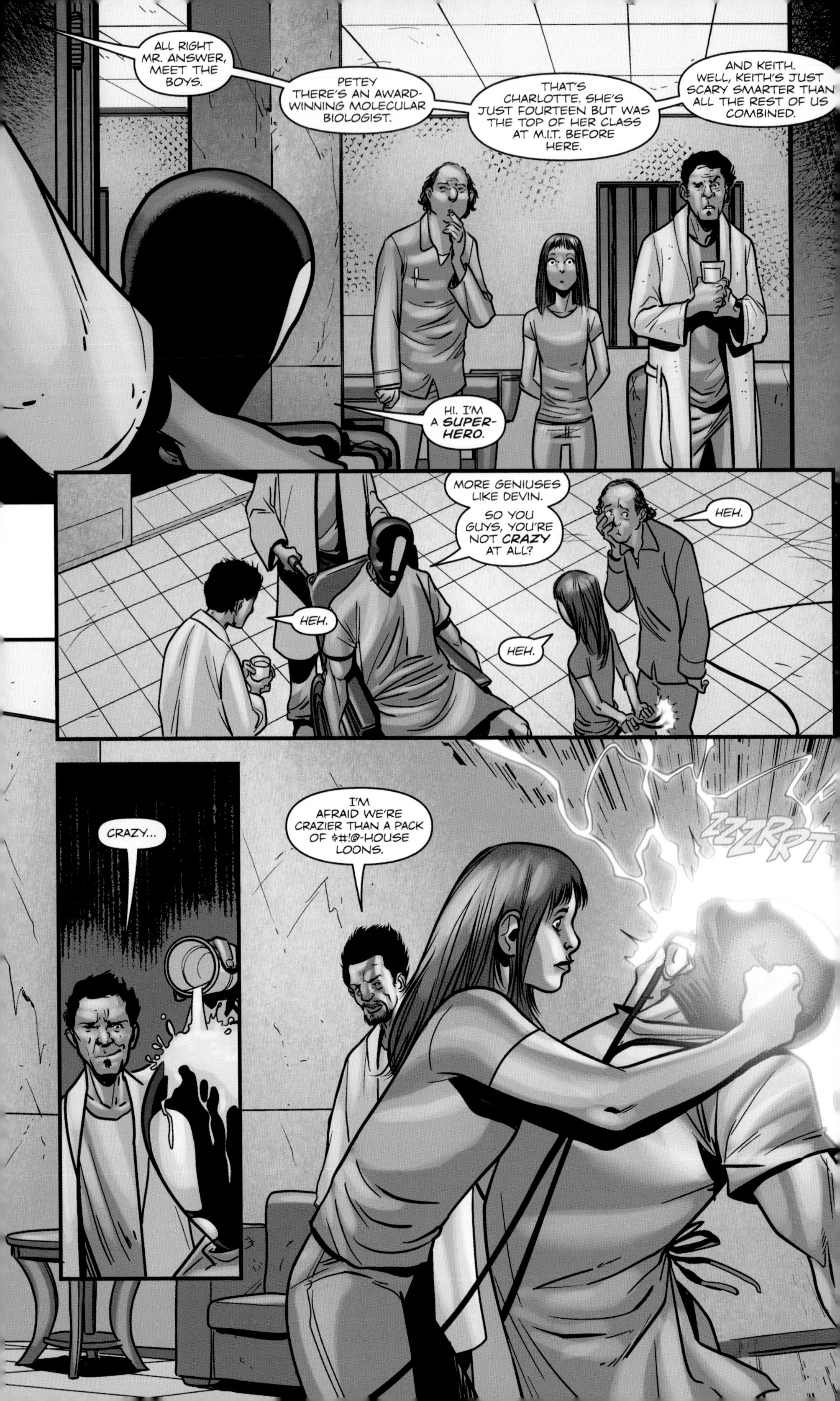
ALL RIGHT MR. ANSWER, MEET THE BOYS.
PETEY THERE'S AN AWARD-WINNING MOLECULAR BIOLOGIST.
THAT'S CHARLOTTE. SHE'S JUST FOURTEEN BUT WAS THE TOP OF HER CLASS AT M.I.T. BEFORE HERE.
AND KEITH. WELL, KEITH'S JUST SCARY SMARTER THAN ALL THE REST OF US COMBINED.
HI. I'M A **SUPER-HERO**.
MORE GENIUSES LIKE DEVIN.
SO YOU GUYS, YOU'RE NOT ***CRAZY*** AT ALL?
HEH.
HEH.
HEH.
CRAZY...
I'M AFRAID WE'RE CRAZIER THAN A PACK OF $#!@-HOUSE LOONS.
ZZZRRRT

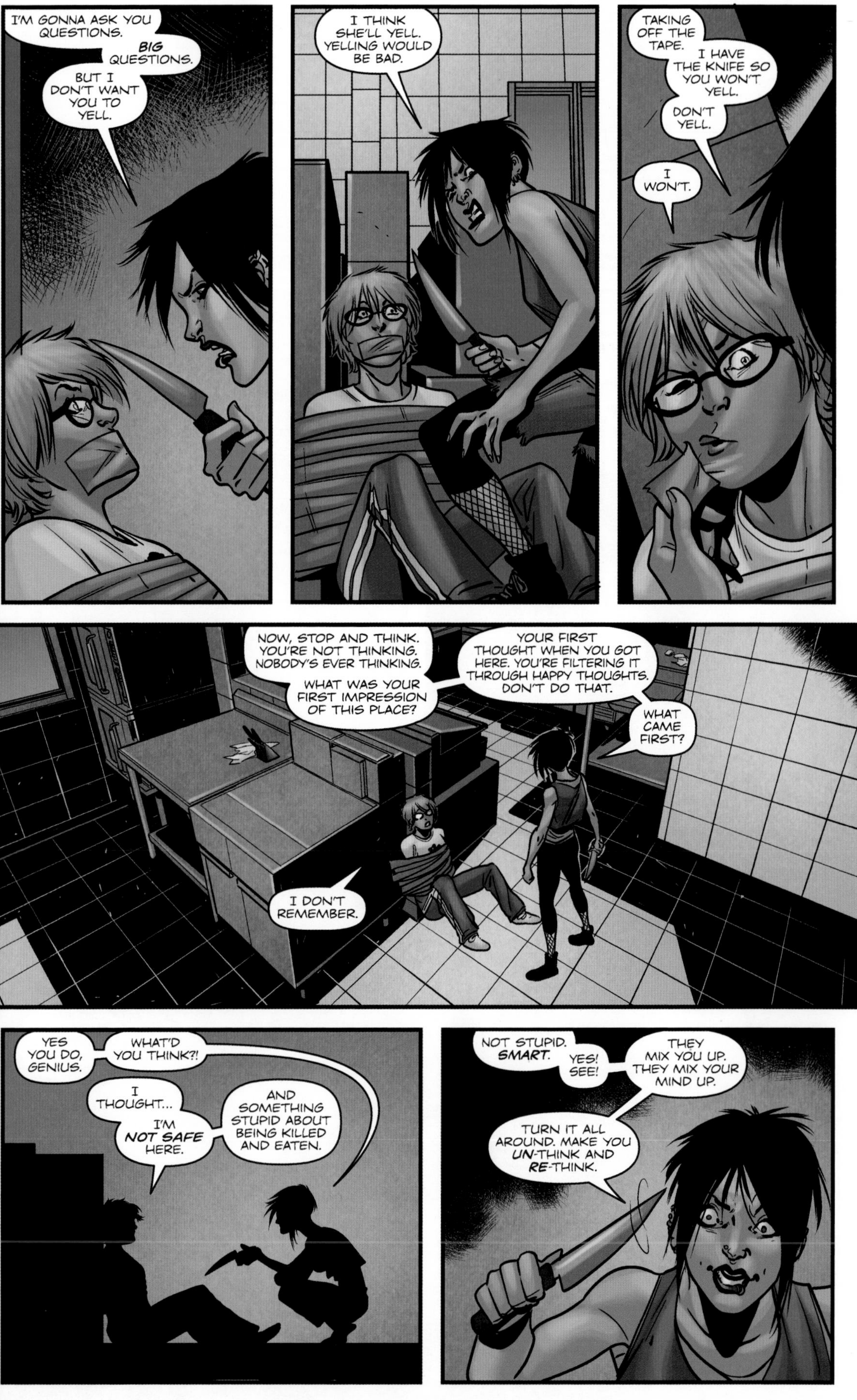
I'M GONNA ASK YOU QUESTIONS.
BIG QUESTIONS.
BUT I DON'T WANT YOU TO YELL.
I THINK SHE'LL YELL. YELLING WOULD BE BAD.
TAKING OFF THE TAPE.
I HAVE THE KNIFE SO YOU WON'T YELL.
DON'T YELL.
I WON'T.
NOW, STOP AND THINK. YOU'RE NOT THINKING. NOBODY'S EVER THINKING.
WHAT WAS YOUR FIRST IMPRESSION OF THIS PLACE?
YOUR FIRST THOUGHT WHEN YOU GOT HERE. YOU'RE FILTERING IT THROUGH HAPPY THOUGHTS. DON'T DO THAT.
WHAT CAME FIRST?
I DON'T REMEMBER.
YES YOU DO, GENIUS.
WHAT'D YOU THINK?!
I THOUGHT...
I'M NOT SAFE HERE.
AND SOMETHING STUPID ABOUT BEING KILLED AND EATEN.
NOT STUPID. SMART.
YES! SEE!
THEY MIX YOU UP. THEY MIX YOUR MIND UP.
TURN IT ALL AROUND. MAKE YOU UN-THINK AND RE-THINK.

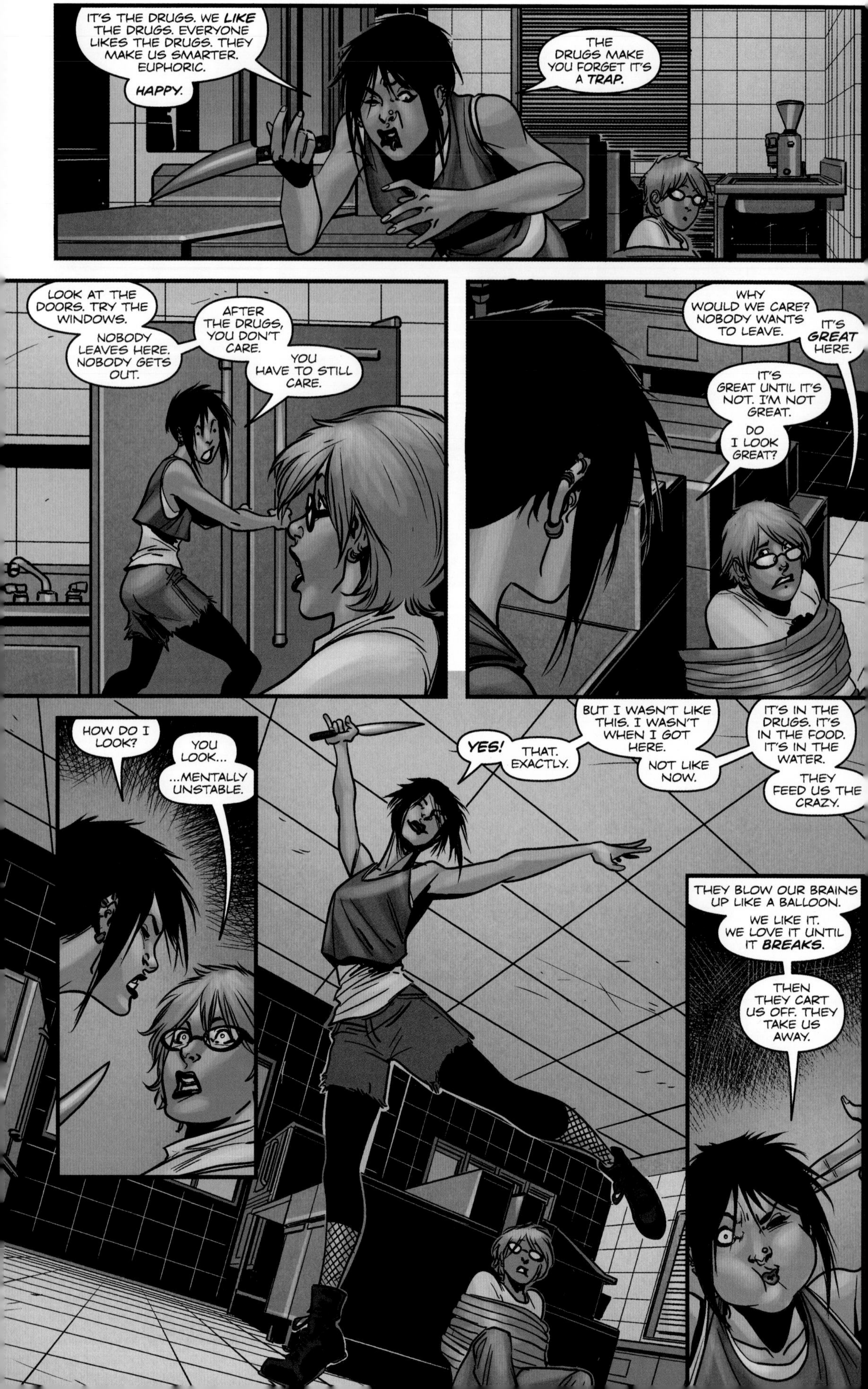
IT'S THE DRUGS. WE LIKE THE DRUGS. EVERYONE LIKES THE DRUGS. THEY MAKE US SMARTER. EUPHORIC.
HAPPY.
THE DRUGS MAKE YOU FORGET IT'S A TRAP.
LOOK AT THE DOORS. TRY THE WINDOWS.
NOBODY LEAVES HERE. NOBODY GETS OUT.
AFTER THE DRUGS, YOU DON'T CARE.
YOU HAVE TO STILL CARE.
WHY WOULD WE CARE? NOBODY WANTS TO LEAVE.
IT'S GREAT HERE.
IT'S GREAT UNTIL IT'S NOT. I'M NOT GREAT.
DO I LOOK GREAT?
HOW DO I LOOK?
YOU LOOK...
...MENTALLY UNSTABLE.
YES!
THAT. EXACTLY.
BUT I WASN'T LIKE THIS. I WASN'T WHEN I GOT HERE.
NOT LIKE NOW.
IT'S IN THE DRUGS. IT'S IN THE FOOD. IT'S IN THE WATER.
THEY FEED US THE CRAZY.
THEY BLOW OUR BRAINS UP LIKE A BALLOON.
WE LIKE IT. WE LOVE IT UNTIL IT BREAKS.
THEN THEY CART US OFF. THEY TAKE US AWAY.

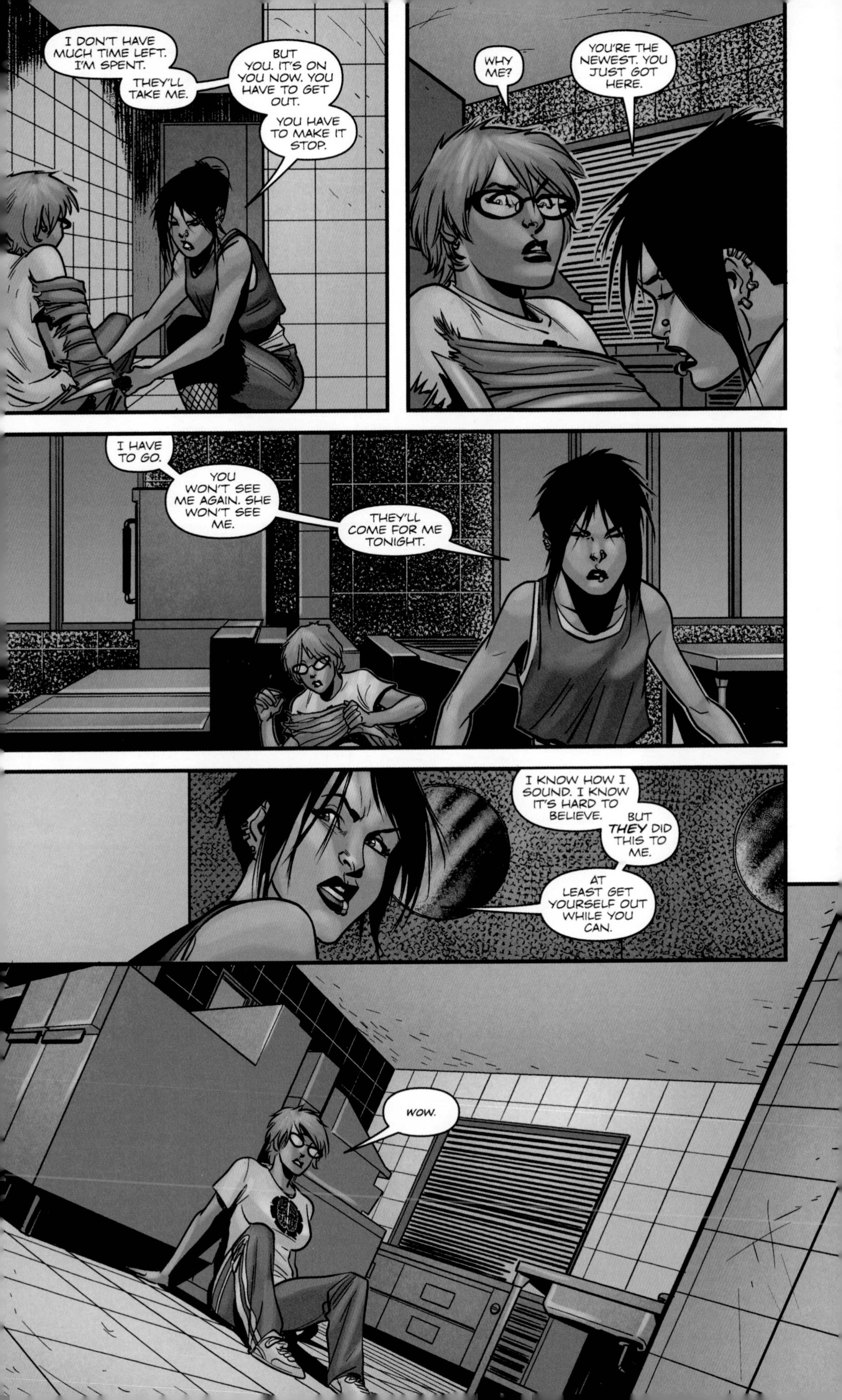
I DON'T HAVE MUCH TIME LEFT. I'M SPENT.
THEY'LL TAKE ME.
BUT YOU. IT'S ON YOU NOW. YOU HAVE TO GET OUT.
YOU HAVE TO MAKE IT STOP.
WHY ME?
YOU'RE THE NEWEST. YOU JUST GOT HERE.
I HAVE TO GO.
YOU WON'T SEE ME AGAIN. SHE WON'T SEE ME.
THEY'LL COME FOR ME TONIGHT.
I KNOW HOW I SOUND. I KNOW IT'S HARD TO BELIEVE.
BUT *THEY* DID THIS TO ME.
AT LEAST GET YOURSELF OUT WHILE YOU CAN.
WOW.

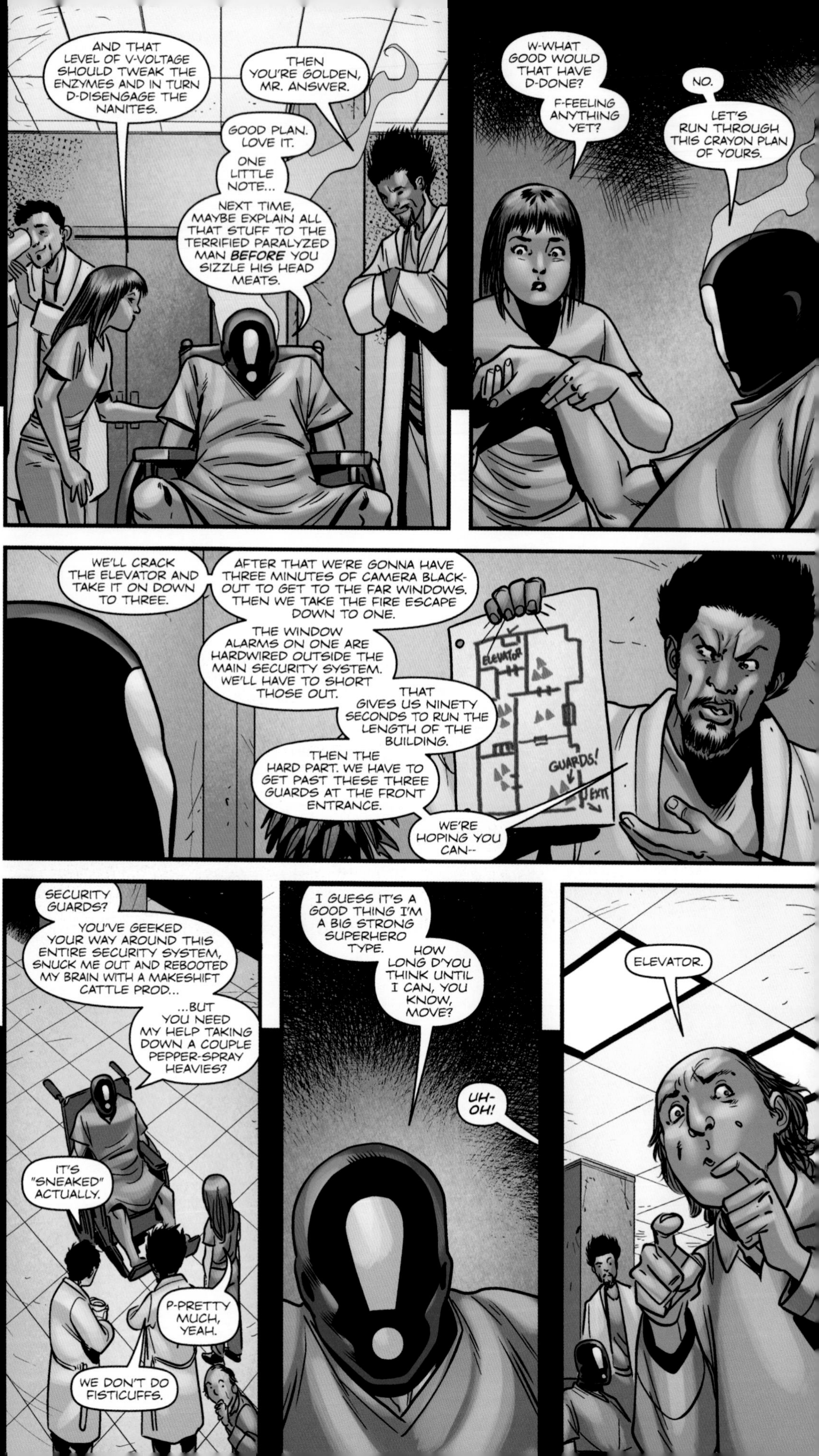
AND THAT LEVEL OF V-VOLTAGE SHOULD TWEAK THE ENZYMES AND IN TURN D-DISENGAGE THE NANITES.
THEN YOU'RE GOLDEN, MR. ANSWER.
GOOD PLAN. LOVE IT.
ONE LITTLE NOTE...
NEXT TIME, MAYBE EXPLAIN ALL THAT STUFF TO THE TERRIFIED PARALYZED MAN BEFORE YOU SIZZLE HIS HEAD MEATS.
W-WHAT GOOD WOULD THAT HAVE D-DONE?
F-FEELING ANYTHING YET?
NO.
LET'S RUN THROUGH THIS CRAYON PLAN OF YOURS.
WE'LL CRACK THE ELEVATOR AND TAKE IT ON DOWN TO THREE.
AFTER THAT WE'RE GONNA HAVE THREE MINUTES OF CAMERA BLACK-OUT TO GET TO THE FAR WINDOWS. THEN WE TAKE THE FIRE ESCAPE DOWN TO ONE.
THE WINDOW ALARMS ON ONE ARE HARDWIRED OUTSIDE THE MAIN SECURITY SYSTEM. WE'LL HAVE TO SHORT THOSE OUT.
THAT GIVES US NINETY SECONDS TO RUN THE LENGTH OF THE BUILDING.
THEN THE HARD PART. WE HAVE TO GET PAST THESE THREE GUARDS AT THE FRONT ENTRANCE.
WE'RE HOPING YOU CAN--
ELEVATOR
GUARDS!
EXIT
SECURITY GUARDS?
YOU'VE GEEKED YOUR WAY AROUND THIS ENTIRE SECURITY SYSTEM, SNUCK ME OUT AND REBOOTED MY BRAIN WITH A MAKESHIFT CATTLE PROD...
...BUT YOU NEED MY HELP TAKING DOWN A COUPLE PEPPER-SPRAY HEAVIES?
IT'S "SNEAKED" ACTUALLY.
P-PRETTY MUCH, YEAH.
WE DON'T DO FISTICUFFS.
I GUESS IT'S A GOOD THING I'M A BIG STRONG SUPERHERO TYPE.
HOW LONG D'YOU THINK UNTIL I CAN, YOU KNOW, MOVE?
UH-OH!
ELEVATOR.

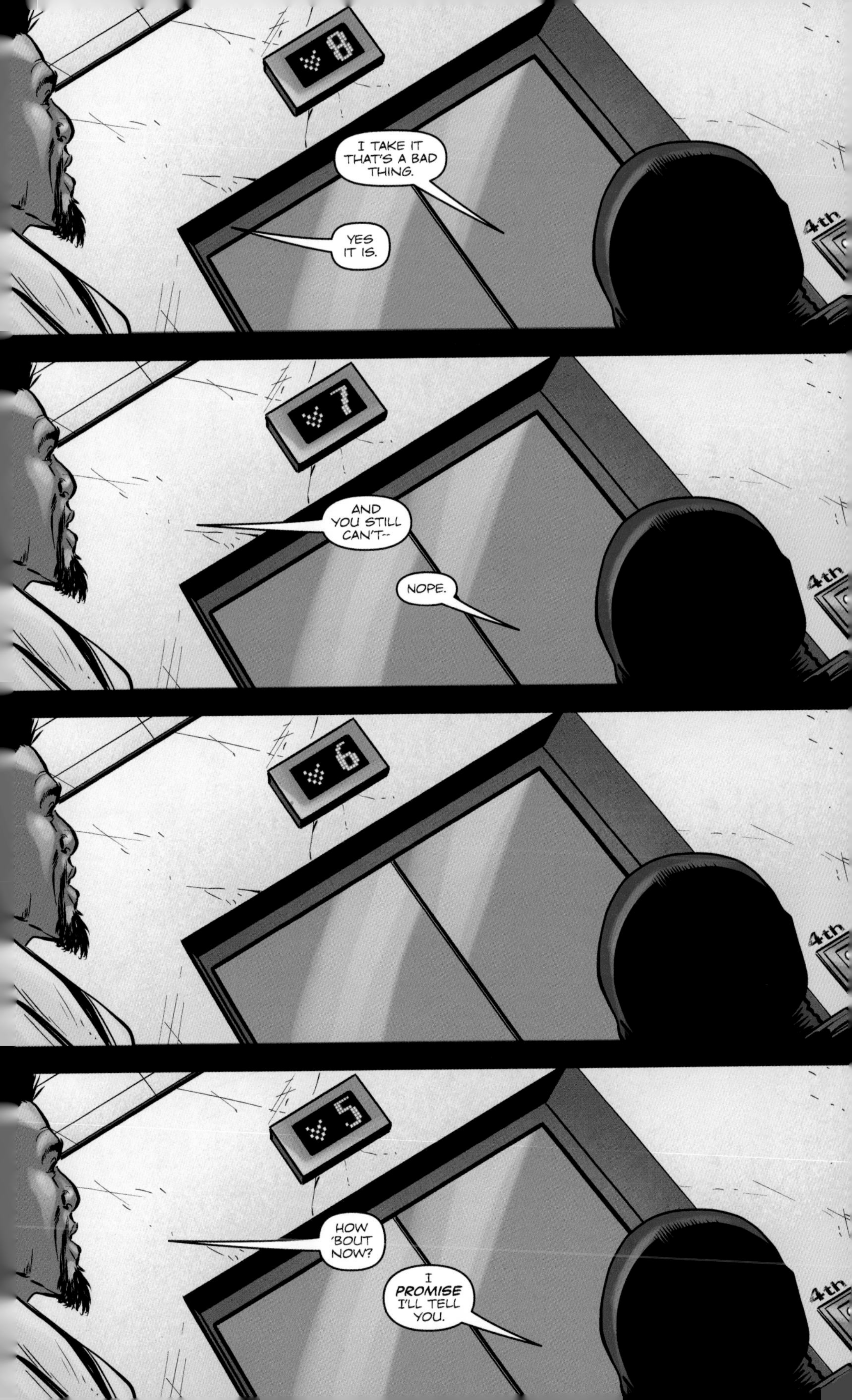
I TAKE IT THAT'S A BAD THING.
YES IT IS.
AND YOU STILL CAN'T--
NOPE.
HOW 'BOUT NOW?
I *PROMISE* I'LL TELL YOU.

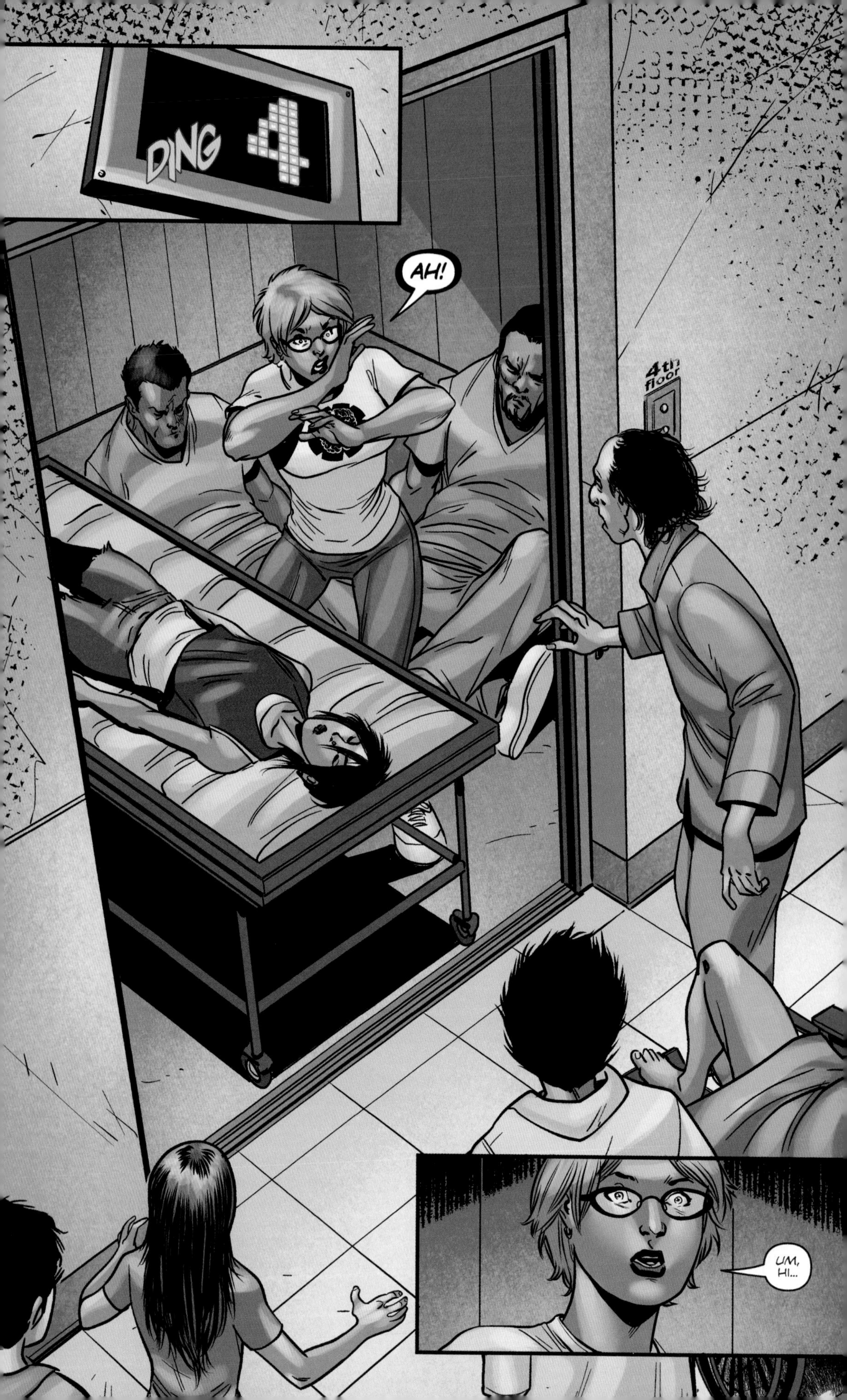
DING
4
AH!
4th floor
UM, HI...

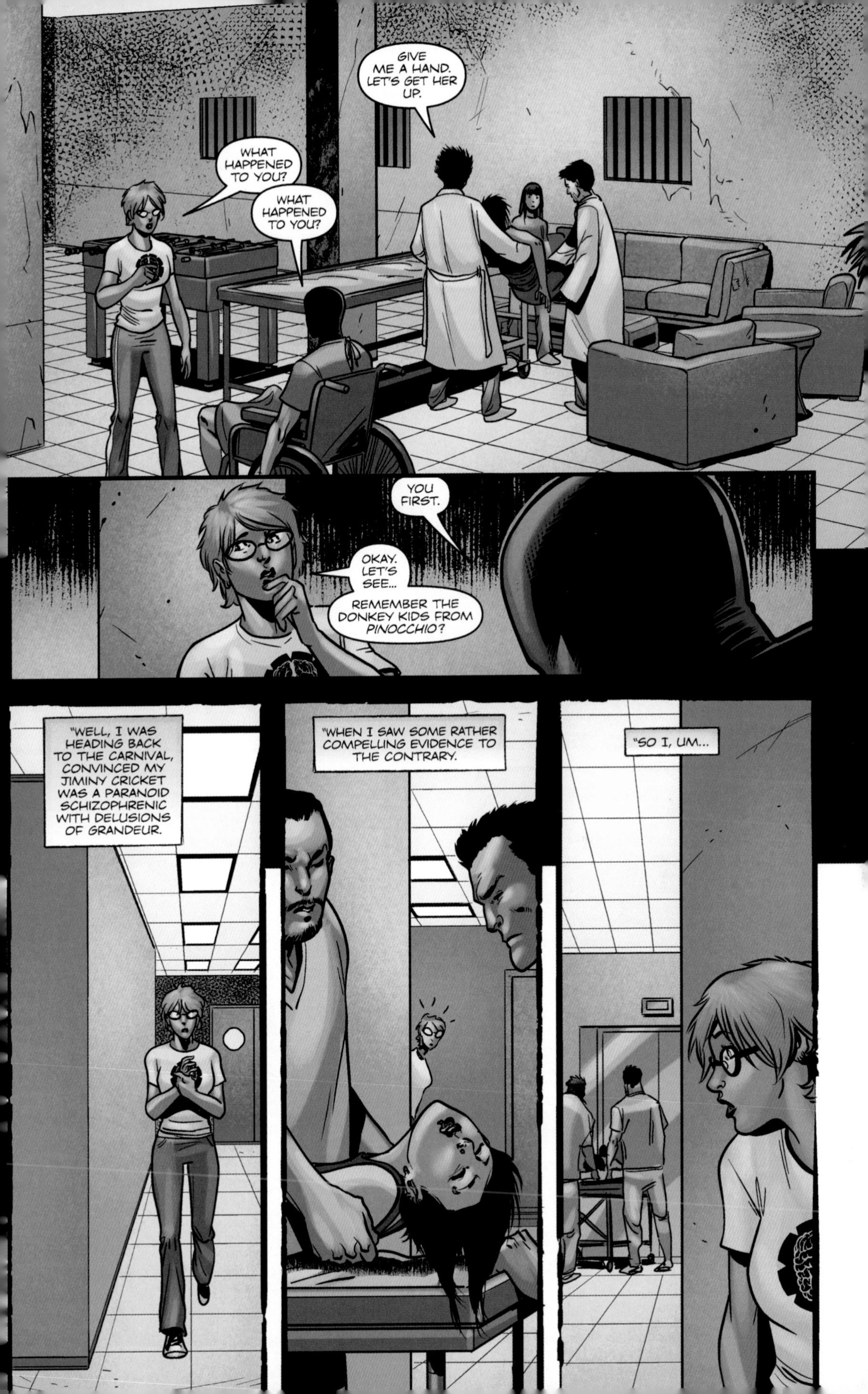
GIVE ME A HAND. LET'S GET HER UP.
WHAT HAPPENED TO YOU?
WHAT HAPPENED TO YOU?
YOU FIRST.
OKAY. LET'S SEE...
REMEMBER THE DONKEY KIDS FROM *PINOCCHIO*?
"WELL, I WAS HEADING BACK TO THE CARNIVAL, CONVINCED MY JIMINY CRICKET WAS A PARANOID SCHIZOPHRENIC WITH DELUSIONS OF GRANDEUR.
"WHEN I SAW SOME RATHER COMPELLING EVIDENCE TO THE CONTRARY.
"SO I, UM...

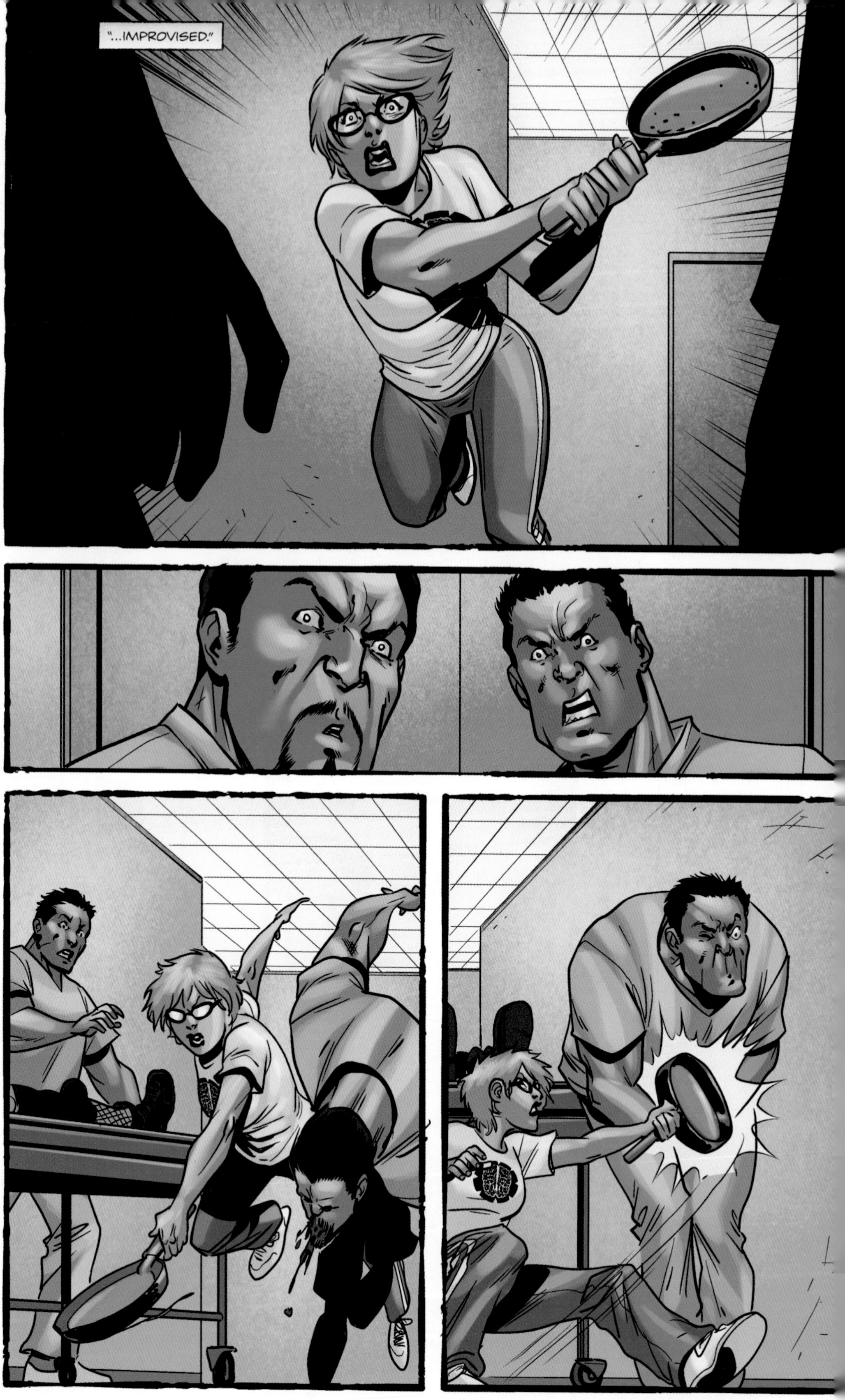
"...IMPROVISED."

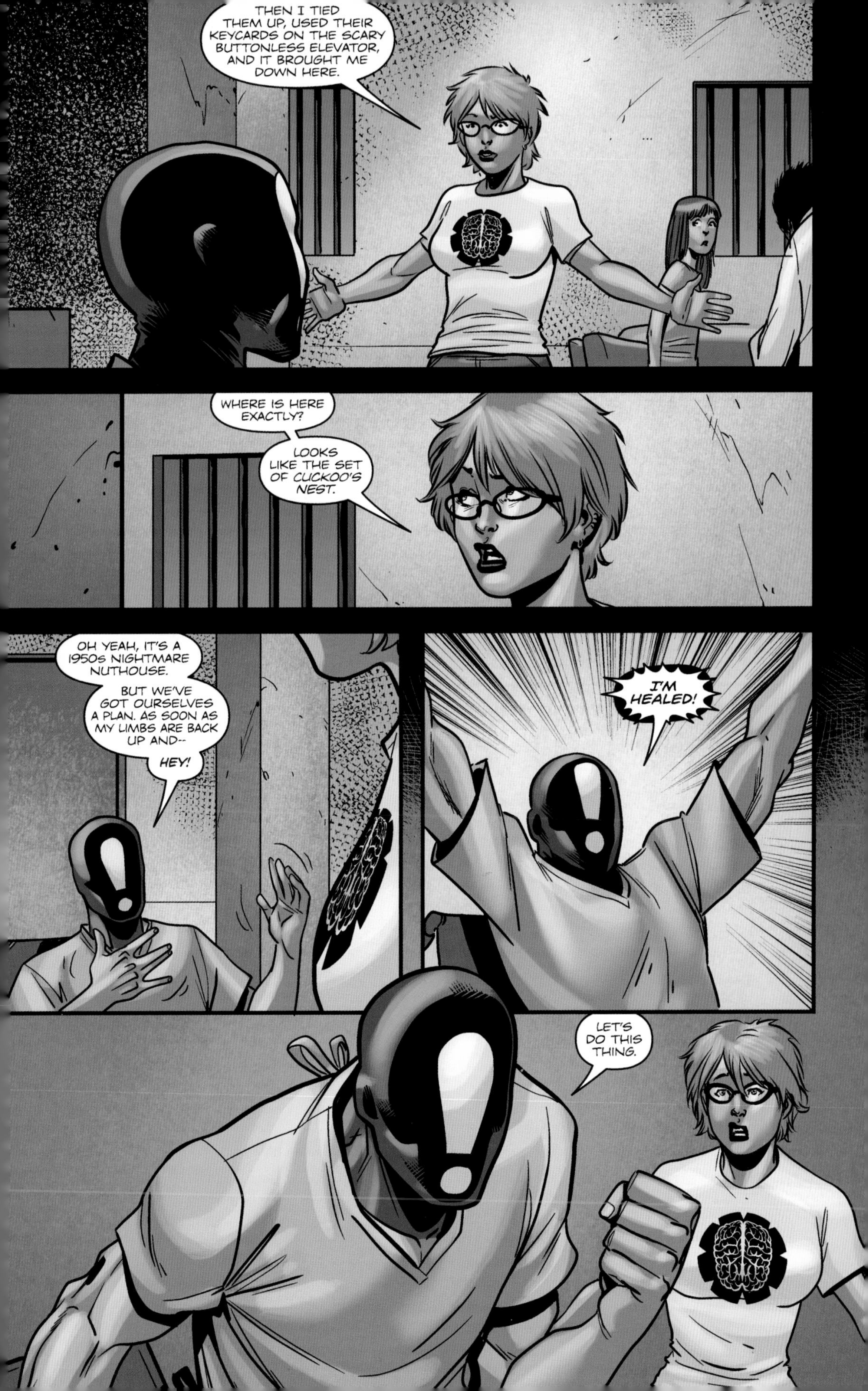
THEN I TIED THEM UP, USED THEIR KEYCARDS ON THE SCARY BUTTONLESS ELEVATOR, AND IT BROUGHT ME DOWN HERE.
WHERE IS HERE EXACTLY?
LOOKS LIKE THE SET OF CUCKOO'S NEST.
OH YEAH, IT'S A 1950s NIGHTMARE NUTHOUSE.
BUT WE'VE GOT OURSELVES A PLAN. AS SOON AS MY LIMBS ARE BACK UP AND--
HEY!
I'M HEALED!
LET'S DO THIS THING.

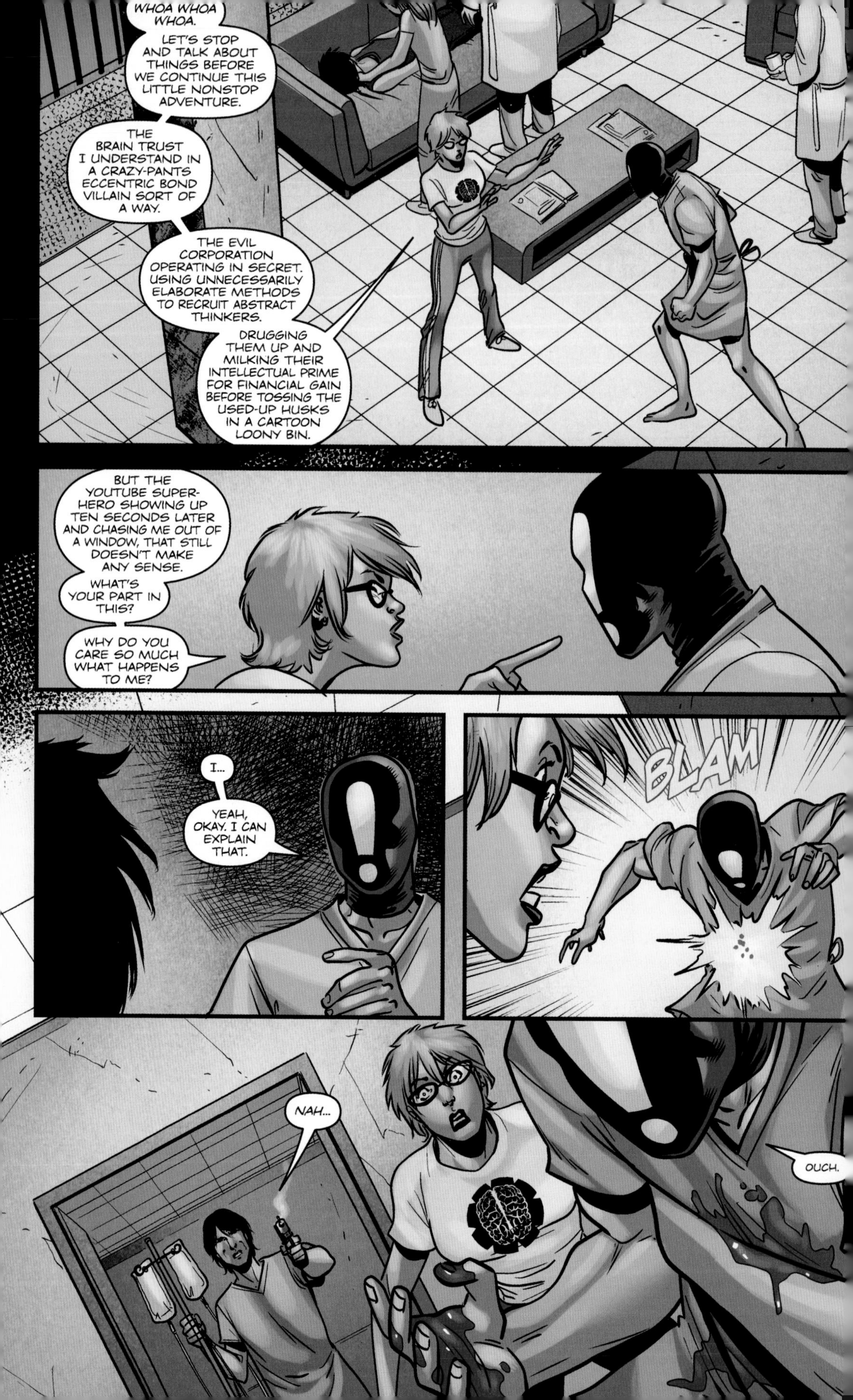
WHOA WHOA WHOA.
LET'S STOP AND TALK ABOUT THINGS BEFORE WE CONTINUE THIS LITTLE NONSTOP ADVENTURE.
THE BRAIN TRUST I UNDERSTAND IN A CRAZY-PANTS ECCENTRIC BOND VILLAIN SORT OF A WAY.
THE EVIL CORPORATION OPERATING IN SECRET. USING UNNECESSARILY ELABORATE METHODS TO RECRUIT ABSTRACT THINKERS.
DRUGGING THEM UP AND MILKING THEIR INTELLECTUAL PRIME FOR FINANCIAL GAIN BEFORE TOSSING THE USED-UP HUSKS IN A CARTOON LOONY BIN.
BUT THE YOUTUBE SUPER-HERO SHOWING UP TEN SECONDS LATER AND CHASING ME OUT OF A WINDOW, THAT STILL DOESN'T MAKE ANY SENSE.
WHAT'S YOUR PART IN THIS?
WHY DO YOU CARE SO MUCH WHAT HAPPENS TO ME?
I...
YEAH, OKAY. I CAN EXPLAIN THAT.
BLAM
NAH...
OUCH.

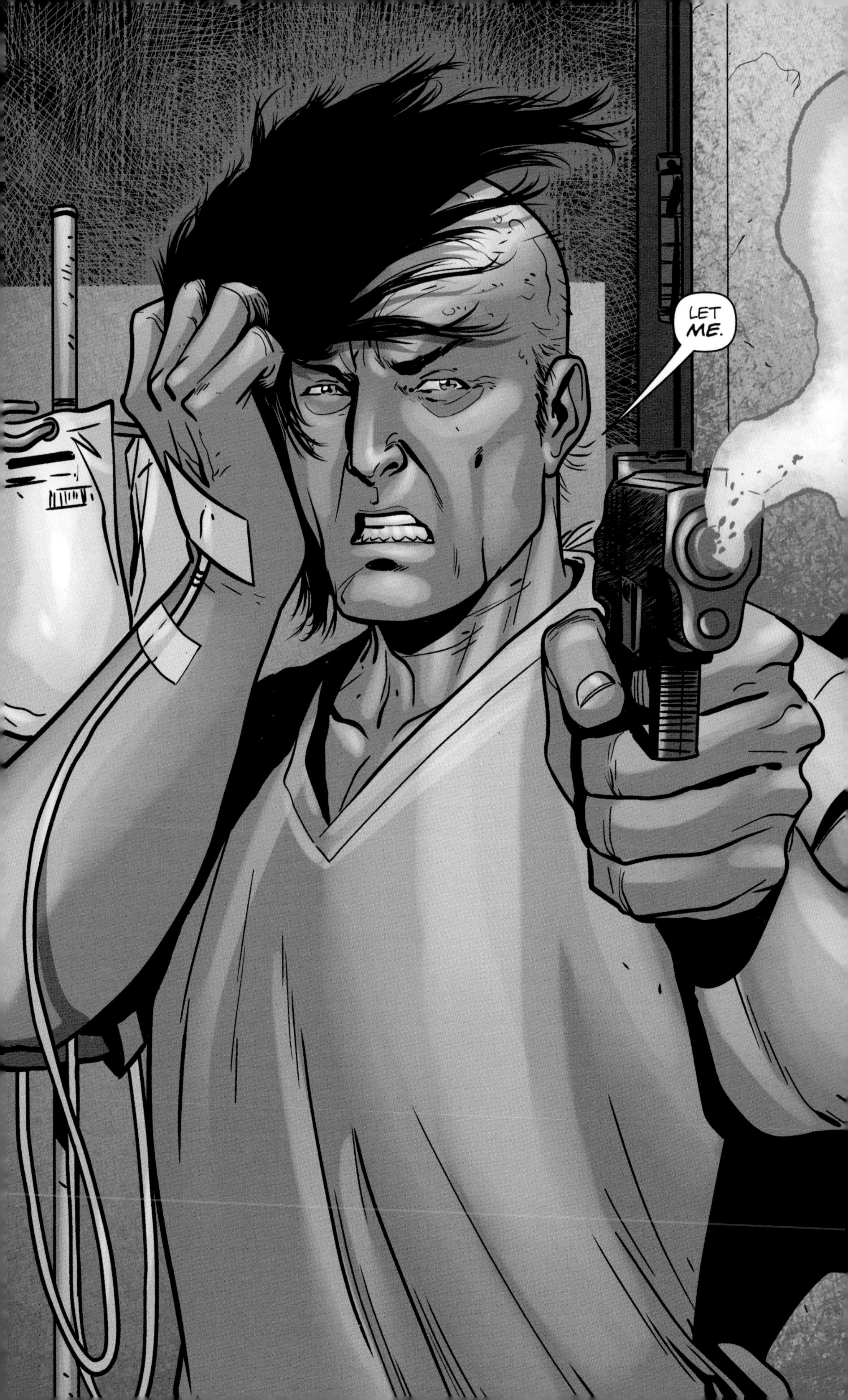
LET ME.

CHAPTER 4

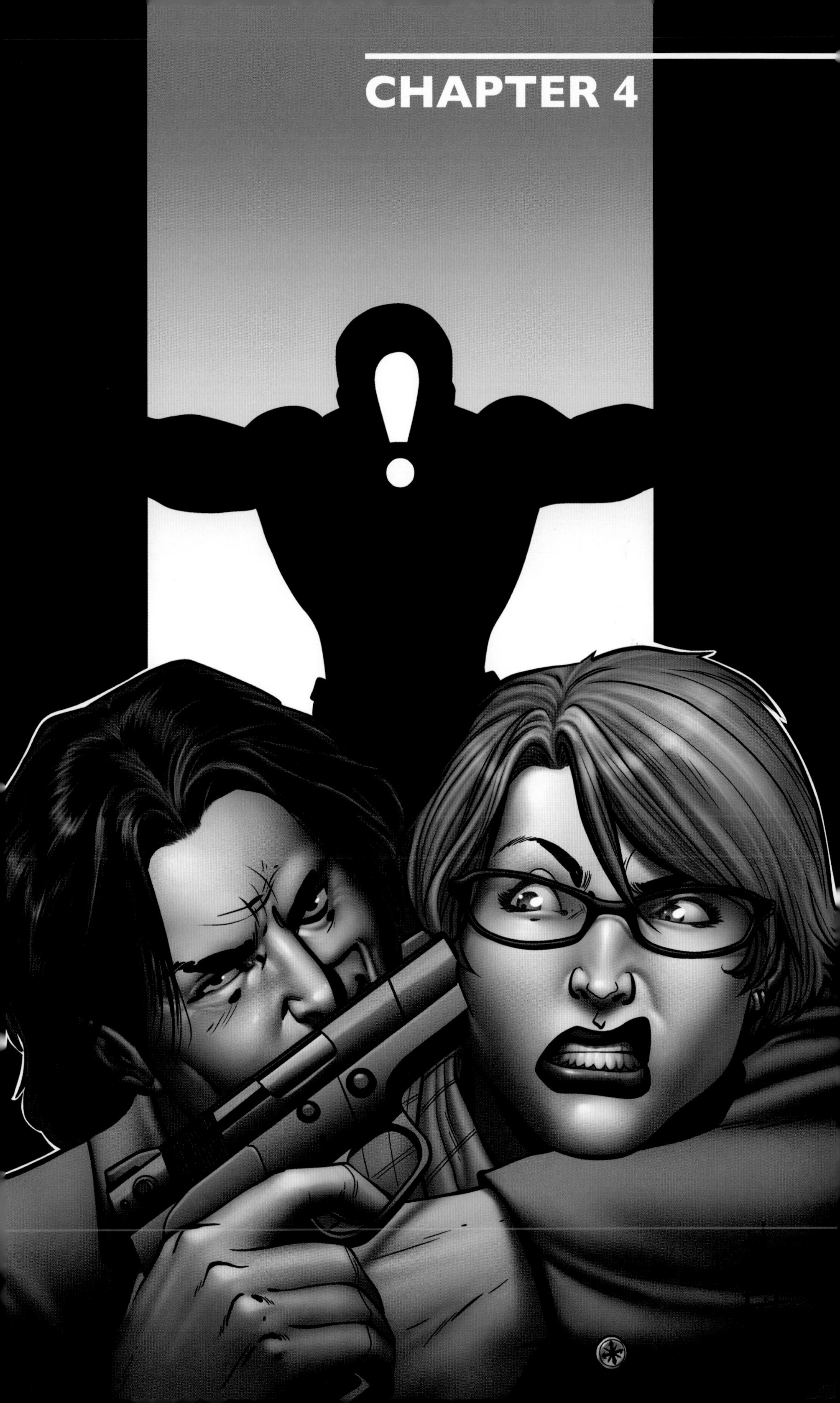

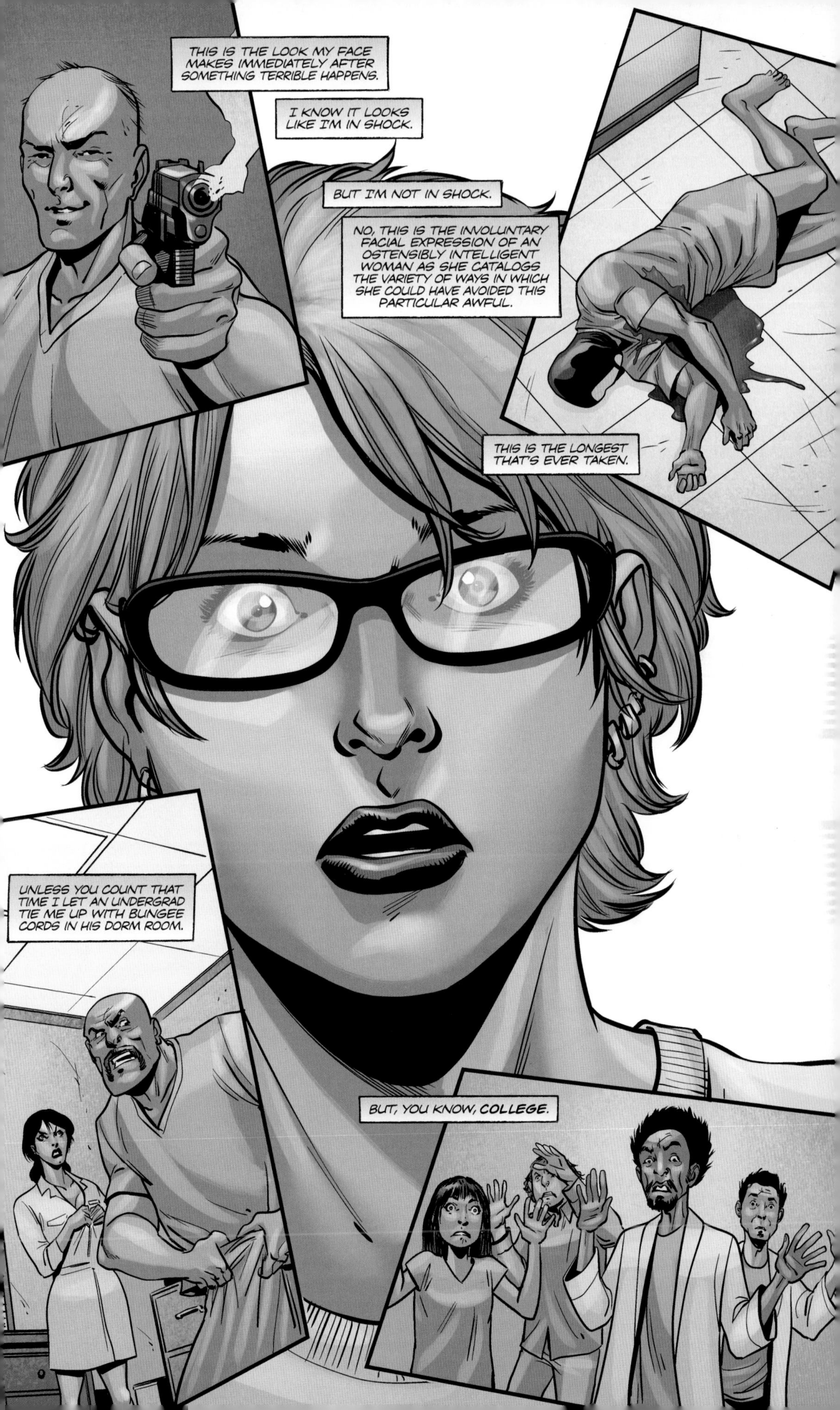
THIS IS THE LOOK MY FACE MAKES IMMEDIATELY AFTER SOMETHING TERRIBLE HAPPENS.
I KNOW IT LOOKS LIKE I'M IN SHOCK.
BUT I'M NOT IN SHOCK.
NO, THIS IS THE INVOLUNTARY FACIAL EXPRESSION OF AN OSTENSIBLY INTELLIGENT WOMAN AS SHE CATALOGS THE VARIETY OF WAYS IN WHICH SHE COULD HAVE AVOIDED THIS PARTICULAR AWFUL.
THIS IS THE LONGEST THAT'S EVER TAKEN.
UNLESS YOU COUNT THAT TIME I LET AN UNDERGRAD TIE ME UP WITH BUNGEE CORDS IN HIS DORM ROOM.
BUT, YOU KNOW, COLLEGE.

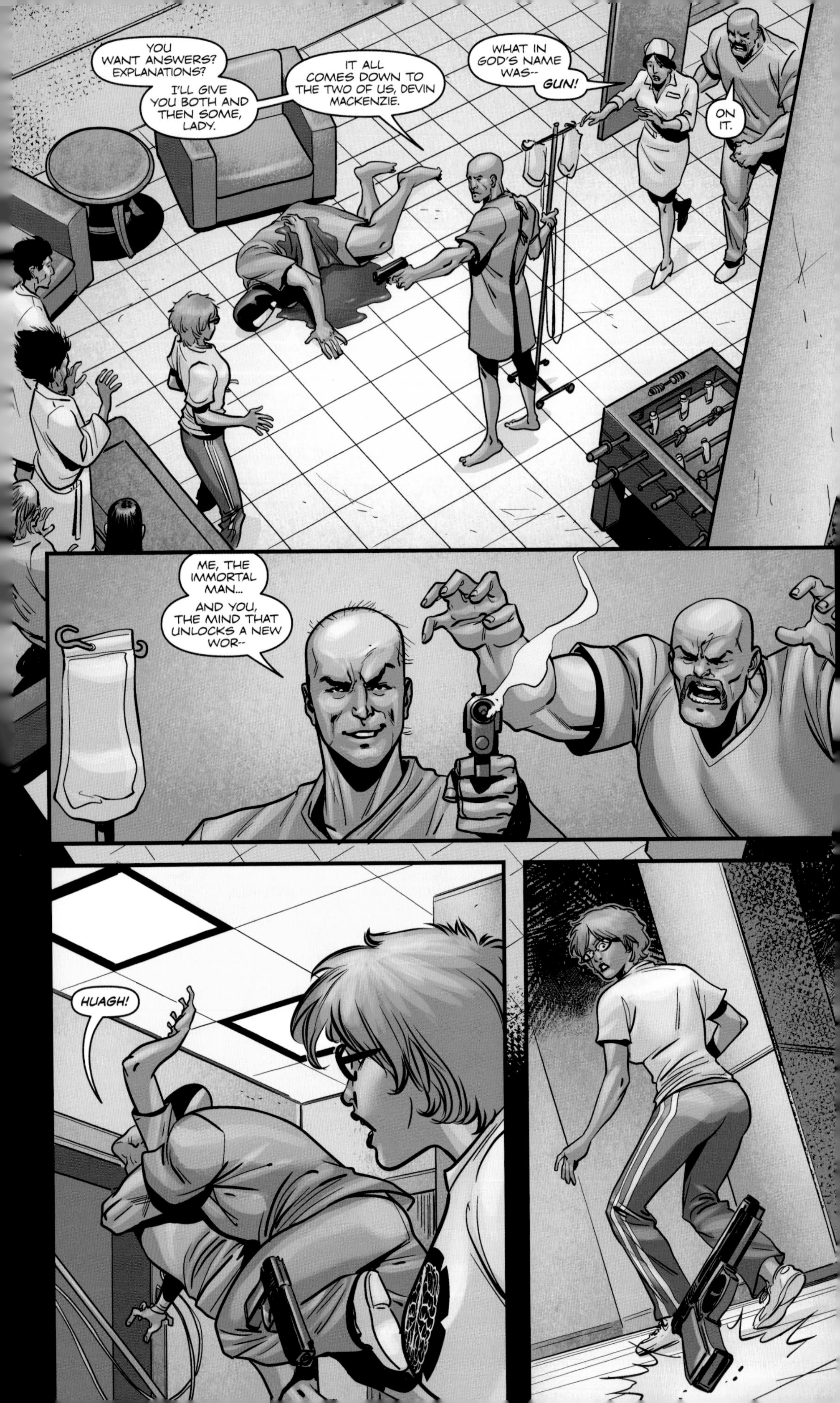
YOU WANT ANSWERS? EXPLANATIONS?
I'LL GIVE YOU BOTH AND THEN SOME, LADY.
IT ALL COMES DOWN TO THE TWO OF US, DEVIN MACKENZIE.
WHAT IN GOD'S NAME WAS--
GUN!
ON IT.
ME, THE IMMORTAL MAN...
AND YOU, THE MIND THAT UNLOCKS A NEW WOR--
HUAGH!

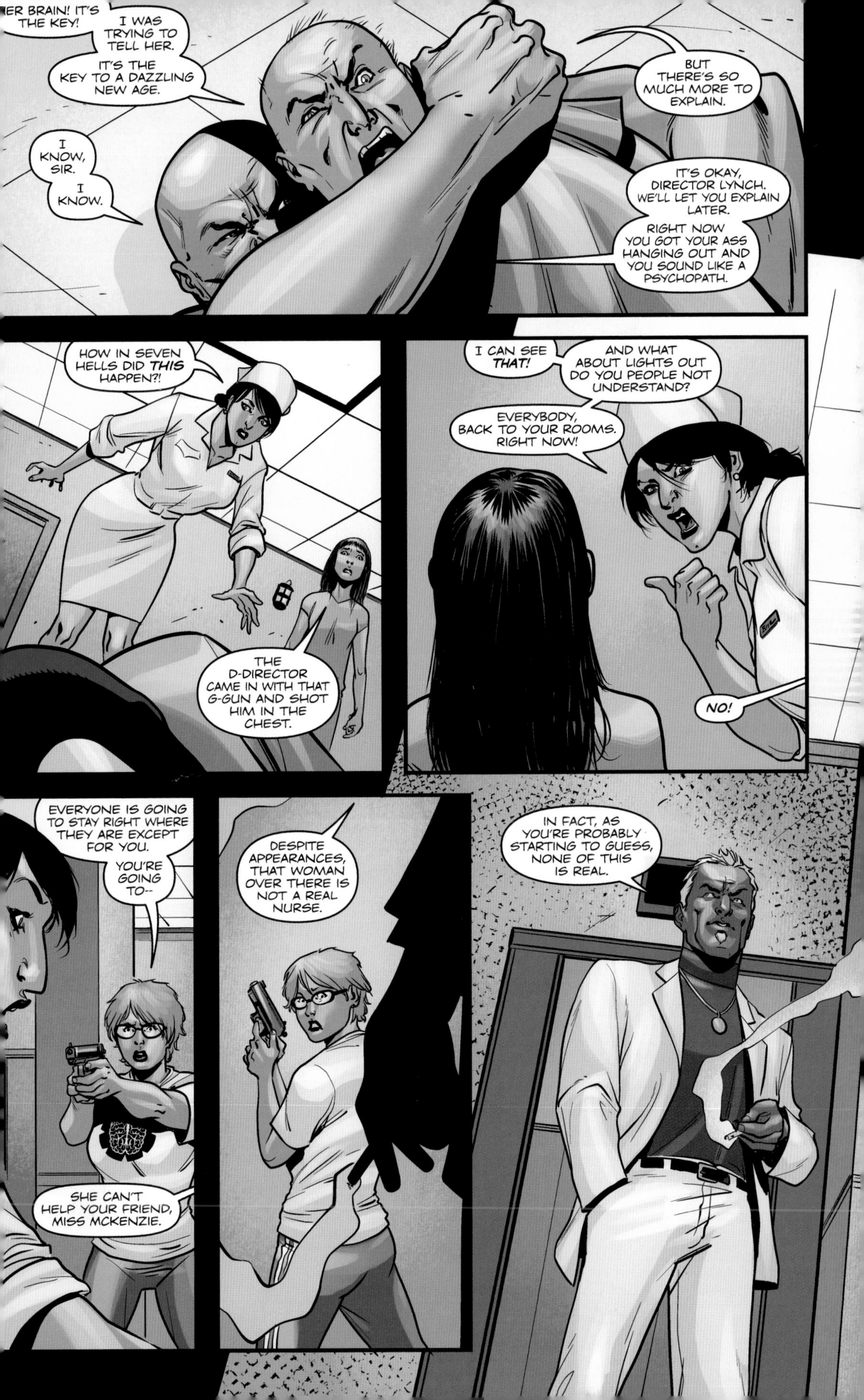
ER BRAIN! IT'S THE KEY!
I WAS TRYING TO TELL HER.
IT'S THE KEY TO A DAZZLING NEW AGE.
BUT THERE'S SO MUCH MORE TO EXPLAIN.
I KNOW, SIR.
I KNOW.
IT'S OKAY, DIRECTOR LYNCH. WE'LL LET YOU EXPLAIN LATER.
RIGHT NOW YOU GOT YOUR ASS HANGING OUT AND YOU SOUND LIKE A PSYCHOPATH.
HOW IN SEVEN HELLS DID THIS HAPPEN?!
THE D-DIRECTOR CAME IN WITH THAT G-GUN AND SHOT HIM IN THE CHEST.
I CAN SEE THAT!
AND WHAT ABOUT LIGHTS OUT DO YOU PEOPLE NOT UNDERSTAND?
EVERYBODY, BACK TO YOUR ROOMS. RIGHT NOW!
NO!
EVERYONE IS GOING TO STAY RIGHT WHERE THEY ARE EXCEPT FOR YOU.
YOU'RE GOING TO--
SHE CAN'T HELP YOUR FRIEND, MISS MCKENZIE.
DESPITE APPEARANCES, THAT WOMAN OVER THERE IS NOT A REAL NURSE.
IN FACT, AS YOU'RE PROBABLY STARTING TO GUESS, NONE OF THIS IS REAL.

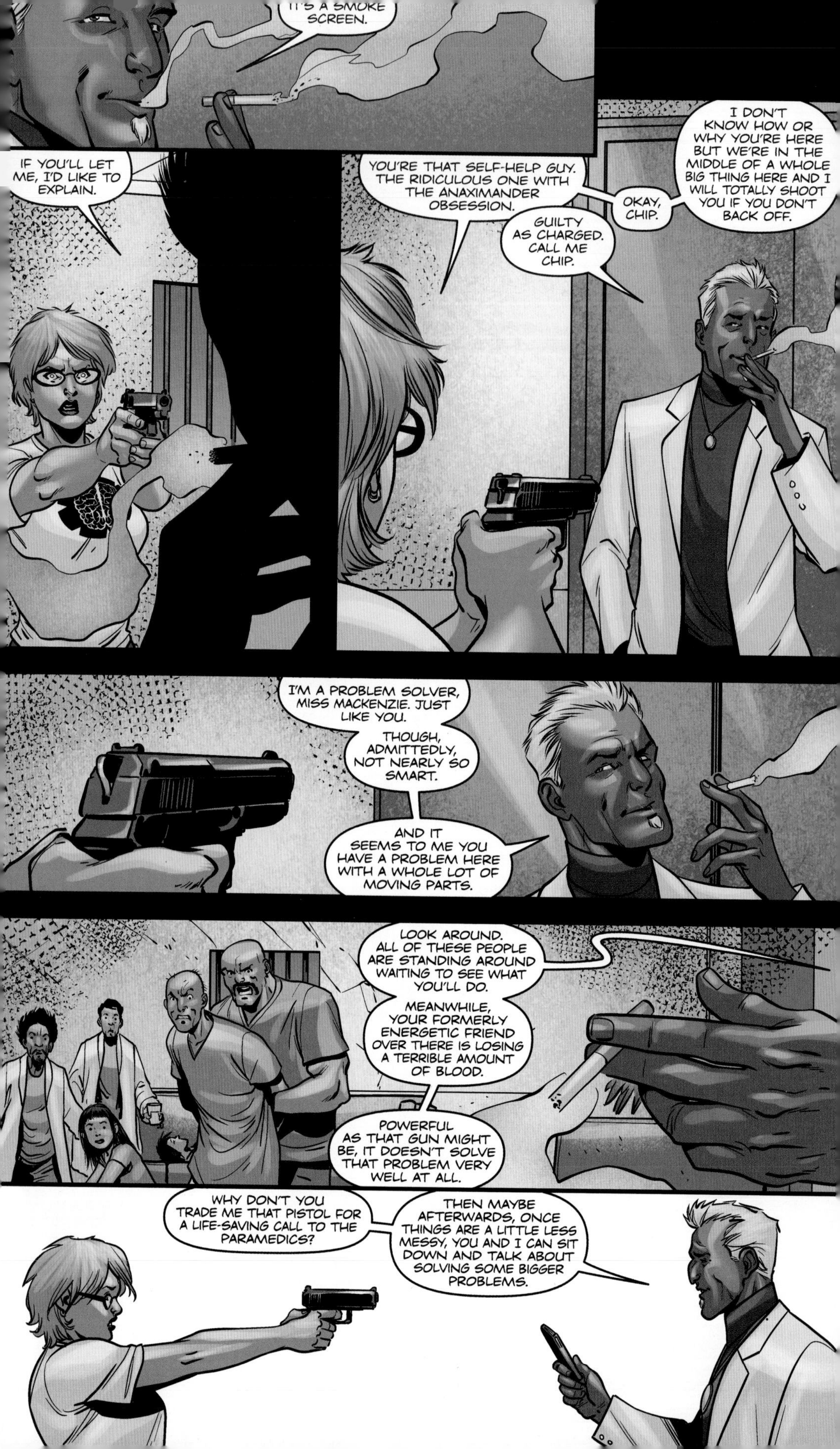
IT'S A SMOKE SCREEN.
IF YOU'LL LET ME, I'D LIKE TO EXPLAIN.
YOU'RE THAT SELF-HELP GUY. THE RIDICULOUS ONE WITH THE ANAXIMANDER OBSESSION.
GUILTY AS CHARGED. CALL ME CHIP.
OKAY, CHIP.
I DON'T KNOW HOW OR WHY YOU'RE HERE BUT WE'RE IN THE MIDDLE OF A WHOLE BIG THING HERE AND I WILL TOTALLY SHOOT YOU IF YOU DON'T BACK OFF.
I'M A PROBLEM SOLVER, MISS MACKENZIE. JUST LIKE YOU.
THOUGH, ADMITTEDLY, NOT NEARLY SO SMART.
AND IT SEEMS TO ME YOU HAVE A PROBLEM HERE WITH A WHOLE LOT OF MOVING PARTS.
LOOK AROUND. ALL OF THESE PEOPLE ARE STANDING AROUND WAITING TO SEE WHAT YOU'LL DO.
MEANWHILE, YOUR FORMERLY ENERGETIC FRIEND OVER THERE IS LOSING A TERRIBLE AMOUNT OF BLOOD.
POWERFUL AS THAT GUN MIGHT BE, IT DOESN'T SOLVE THAT PROBLEM VERY WELL AT ALL.
WHY DON'T YOU TRADE ME THAT PISTOL FOR A LIFE-SAVING CALL TO THE PARAMEDICS?
THEN MAYBE AFTERWARDS, ONCE THINGS ARE A LITTLE LESS MESSY, YOU AND I CAN SIT DOWN AND TALK ABOUT SOLVING SOME BIGGER PROBLEMS.

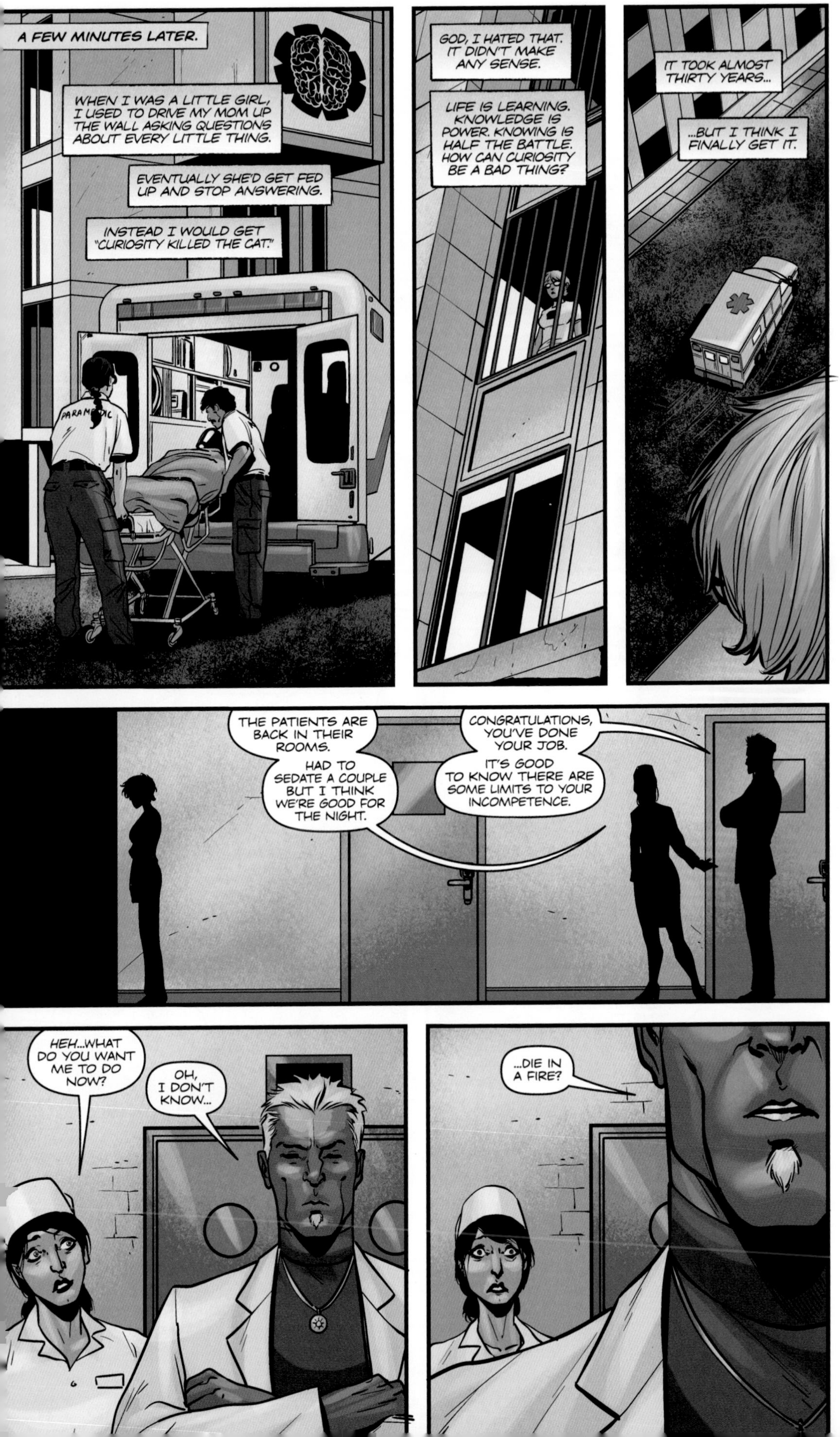
A FEW MINUTES LATER.
WHEN I WAS A LITTLE GIRL, I USED TO DRIVE MY MOM UP THE WALL ASKING QUESTIONS ABOUT EVERY LITTLE THING.
EVENTUALLY SHE'D GET FED UP AND STOP ANSWERING.
INSTEAD I WOULD GET "CURIOSITY KILLED THE CAT."
PARAMEDIC
GOD, I HATED THAT. IT DIDN'T MAKE ANY SENSE.
LIFE IS LEARNING. KNOWLEDGE IS POWER. KNOWING IS HALF THE BATTLE. HOW CAN CURIOSITY BE A BAD THING?
IT TOOK ALMOST THIRTY YEARS...
...BUT I THINK I FINALLY GET IT.
THE PATIENTS ARE BACK IN THEIR ROOMS.
HAD TO SEDATE A COUPLE BUT I THINK WE'RE GOOD FOR THE NIGHT.
CONGRATULATIONS, YOU'VE DONE YOUR JOB.
IT'S GOOD TO KNOW THERE ARE SOME LIMITS TO YOUR INCOMPETENCE.
HEH...WHAT DO YOU WANT ME TO DO NOW?
OH, I DON'T KNOW...
...DIE IN A FIRE?

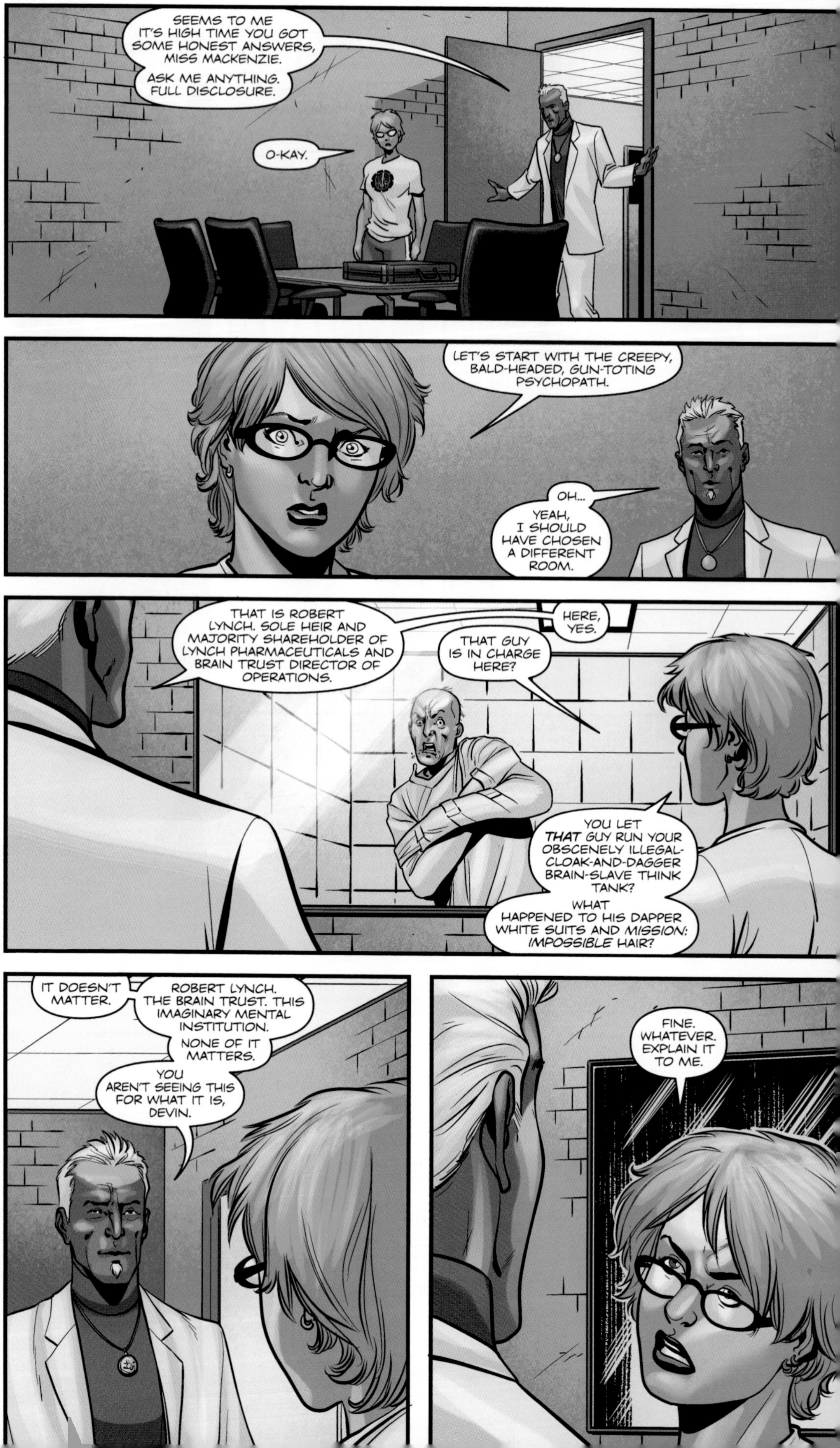
SEEMS TO ME IT'S HIGH TIME YOU GOT SOME HONEST ANSWERS, MISS MACKENZIE.
ASK ME ANYTHING. FULL DISCLOSURE.
O-KAY.
LET'S START WITH THE CREEPY, BALD-HEADED, GUN-TOTING PSYCHOPATH.
OH...
YEAH, I SHOULD HAVE CHOSEN A DIFFERENT ROOM.
THAT IS ROBERT LYNCH. SOLE HEIR AND MAJORITY SHAREHOLDER OF LYNCH PHARMACEUTICALS AND BRAIN TRUST DIRECTOR OF OPERATIONS.
THAT GUY IS IN CHARGE HERE?
HERE, YES.
YOU LET THAT GUY RUN YOUR OBSCENELY ILLEGAL-CLOAK-AND-DAGGER BRAIN-SLAVE THINK TANK?
WHAT HAPPENED TO HIS DAPPER WHITE SUITS AND MISSION: IMPOSSIBLE HAIR?
IT DOESN'T MATTER.
ROBERT LYNCH. THE BRAIN TRUST. THIS IMAGINARY MENTAL INSTITUTION.
NONE OF IT MATTERS.
YOU AREN'T SEEING THIS FOR WHAT IT IS, DEVIN.
FINE. WHATEVER. EXPLAIN IT TO ME.

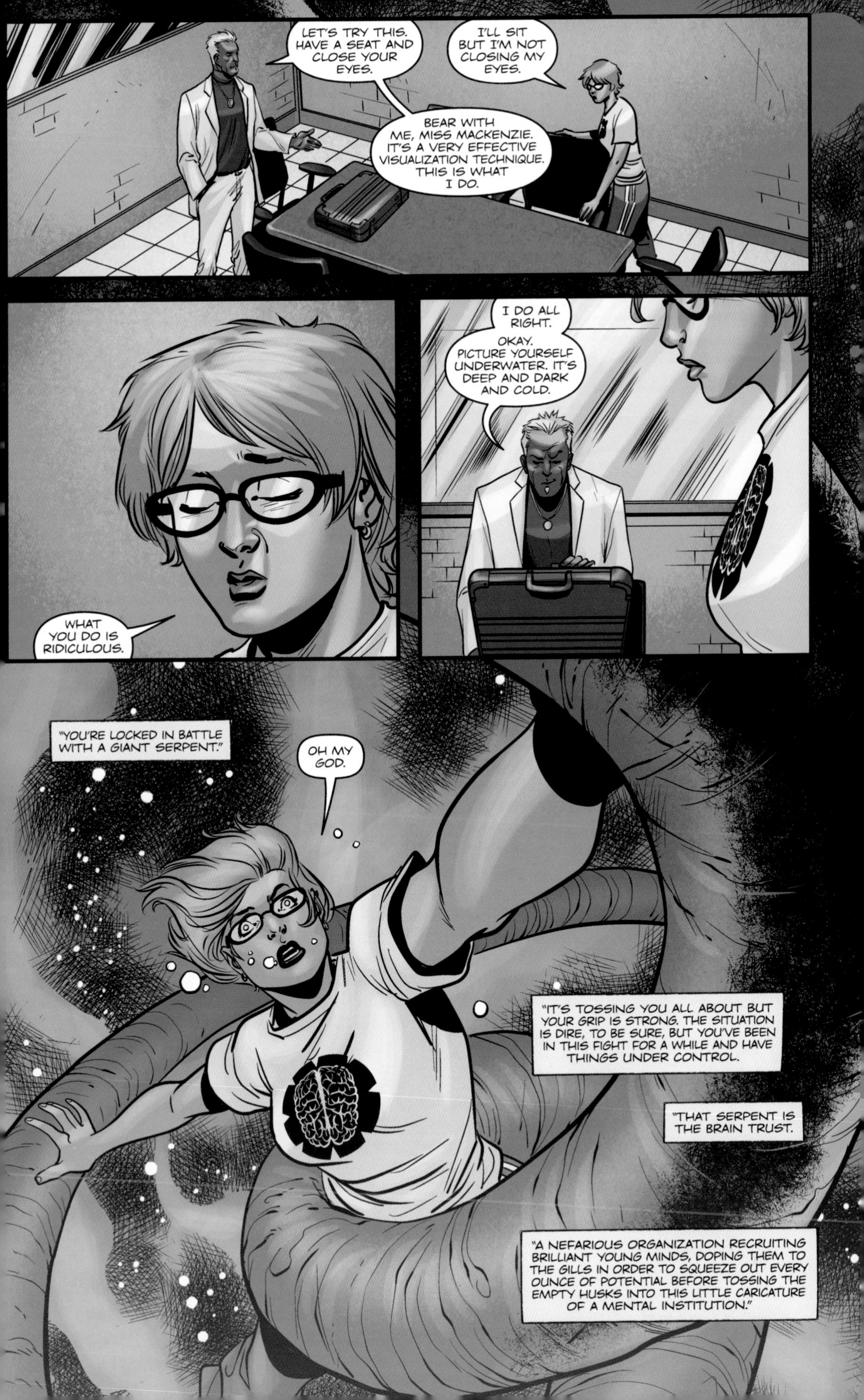
LET'S TRY THIS. HAVE A SEAT AND CLOSE YOUR EYES.
I'LL SIT BUT I'M NOT CLOSING MY EYES.
BEAR WITH ME, MISS MACKENZIE. IT'S A VERY EFFECTIVE VISUALIZATION TECHNIQUE. THIS IS WHAT I DO.
WHAT YOU DO IS RIDICULOUS.
I DO ALL RIGHT.
OKAY. PICTURE YOURSELF UNDERWATER. IT'S DEEP AND DARK AND COLD.
"YOU'RE LOCKED IN BATTLE WITH A GIANT SERPENT."
OH MY GOD.
"IT'S TOSSING YOU ALL ABOUT BUT YOUR GRIP IS STRONG. THE SITUATION IS DIRE, TO BE SURE, BUT YOU'VE BEEN IN THIS FIGHT FOR A WHILE AND HAVE THINGS UNDER CONTROL.
"THAT SERPENT IS THE BRAIN TRUST.
"A NEFARIOUS YOUNG ORGANIZATION RECRUITING BRILLIANT YOUNG MINDS, DOPING THEM TO THE GILLS IN ORDER TO SQUEEZE OUT EVERY OUNCE OF POTENTIAL BEFORE TOSSING THE EMPTY HUSKS INTO THIS LITTLE CARICATURE OF A MENTAL INSTITUTION."

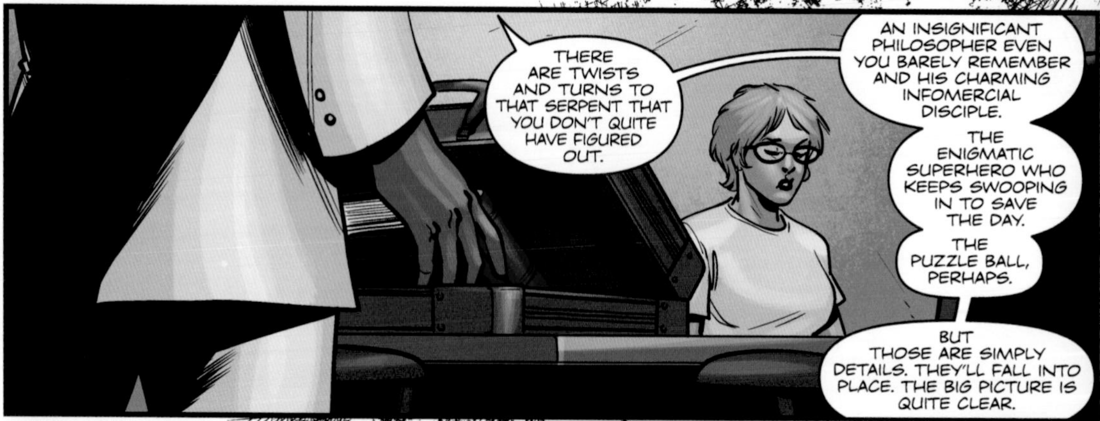
THERE ARE TWISTS AND TURNS TO THAT SERPENT THAT YOU DON'T QUITE HAVE FIGURED OUT.
AN INSIGNIFICANT PHILOSOPHER EVEN YOU BARELY REMEMBER AND HIS CHARMING INFOMERCIAL DISCIPLE.
THE ENIGMATIC SUPERHERO WHO KEEPS SWOOPING IN TO SAVE THE DAY.
THE PUZZLE BALL, PERHAPS.
BUT THOSE ARE SIMPLY DETAILS. THEY'LL FALL INTO PLACE. THE BIG PICTURE IS QUITE CLEAR.

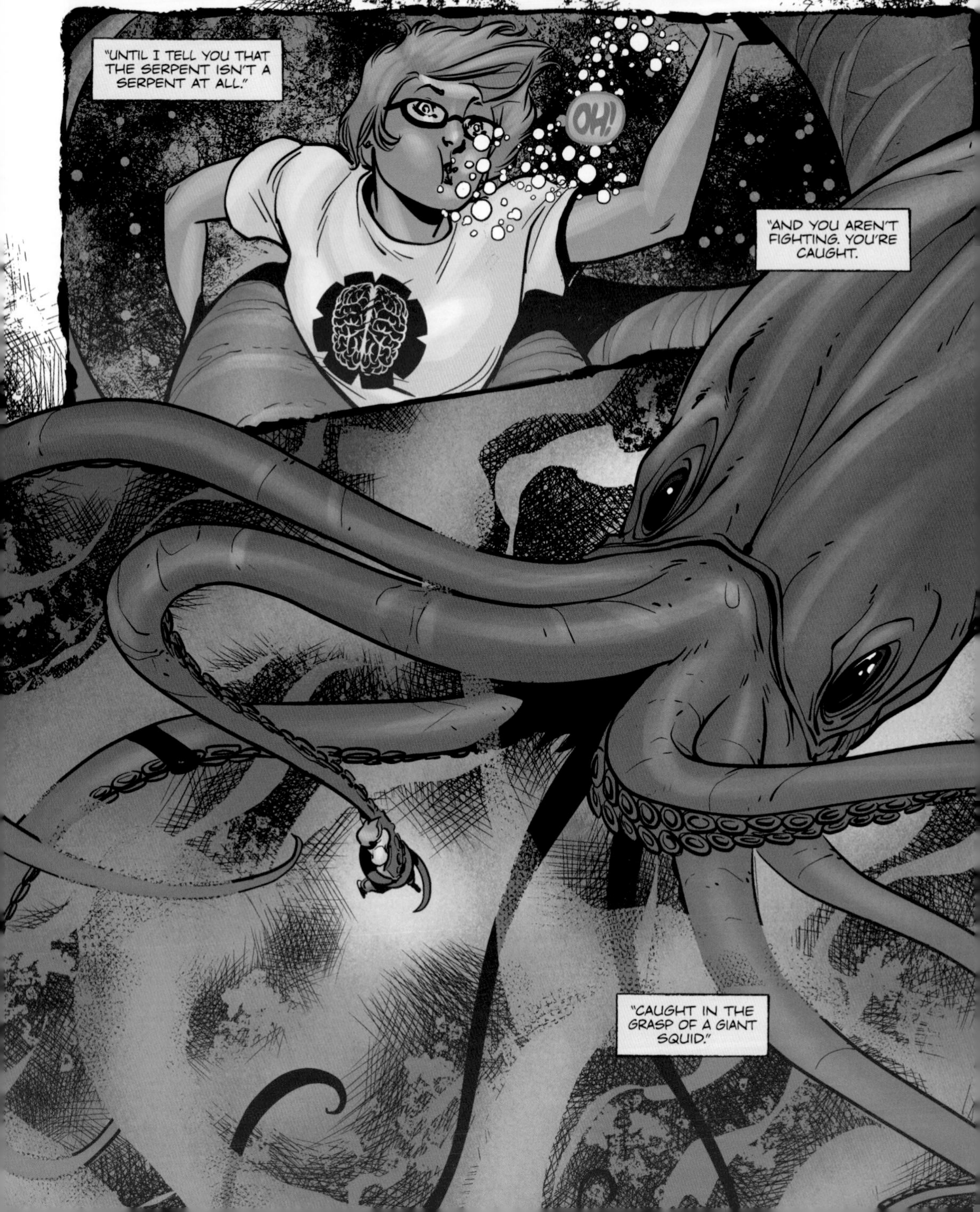
"UNTIL I TELL YOU THAT THE SERPENT ISN'T A SERPENT AT ALL."
OH!
"AND YOU AREN'T FIGHTING. YOU'RE CAUGHT.
"CAUGHT IN THE GRASP OF A GIANT SQUID."

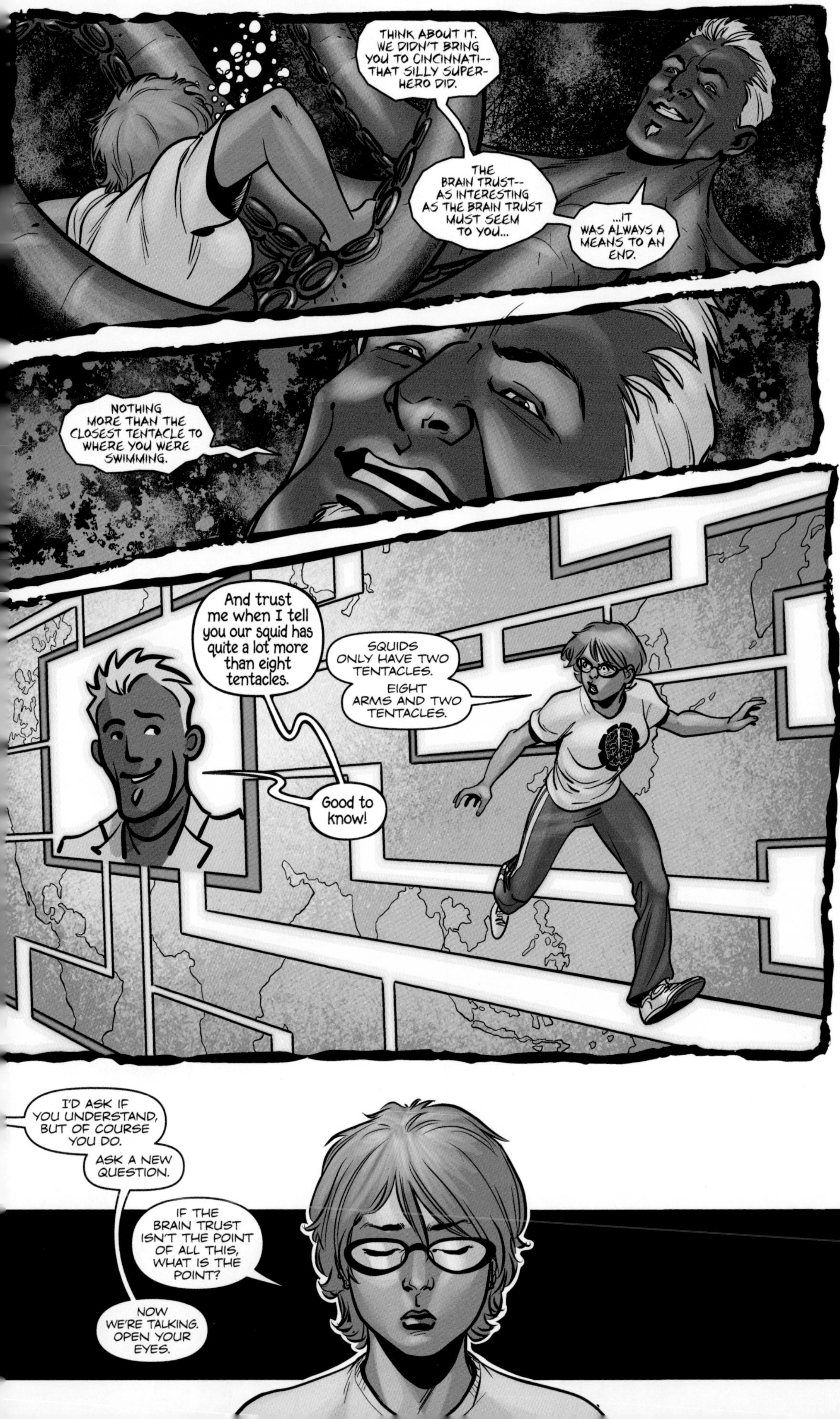
THINK ABOUT IT. WE DIDN'T BRING YOU TO CINCINNATI-- THAT SILLY SUPER-HERO DID.
THE BRAIN TRUST-- AS INTERESTING AS THE BRAIN TRUST MUST SEEM TO YOU...
...IT WAS ALWAYS A MEANS TO AN END.
NOTHING MORE THAN THE CLOSEST TENTACLE TO WHERE YOU WERE SWIMMING.
And trust me when I tell you our squid has quite a lot more than eight tentacles.
SQUIDS ONLY HAVE TWO TENTACLES.
EIGHT ARMS AND TWO TENTACLES.
Good to know!
I'D ASK IF YOU UNDERSTAND, BUT OF COURSE YOU DO.
ASK A NEW QUESTION.
IF THE BRAIN TRUST ISN'T THE POINT OF ALL THIS, WHAT IS THE POINT?
NOW WE'RE TALKING. OPEN YOUR EYES.

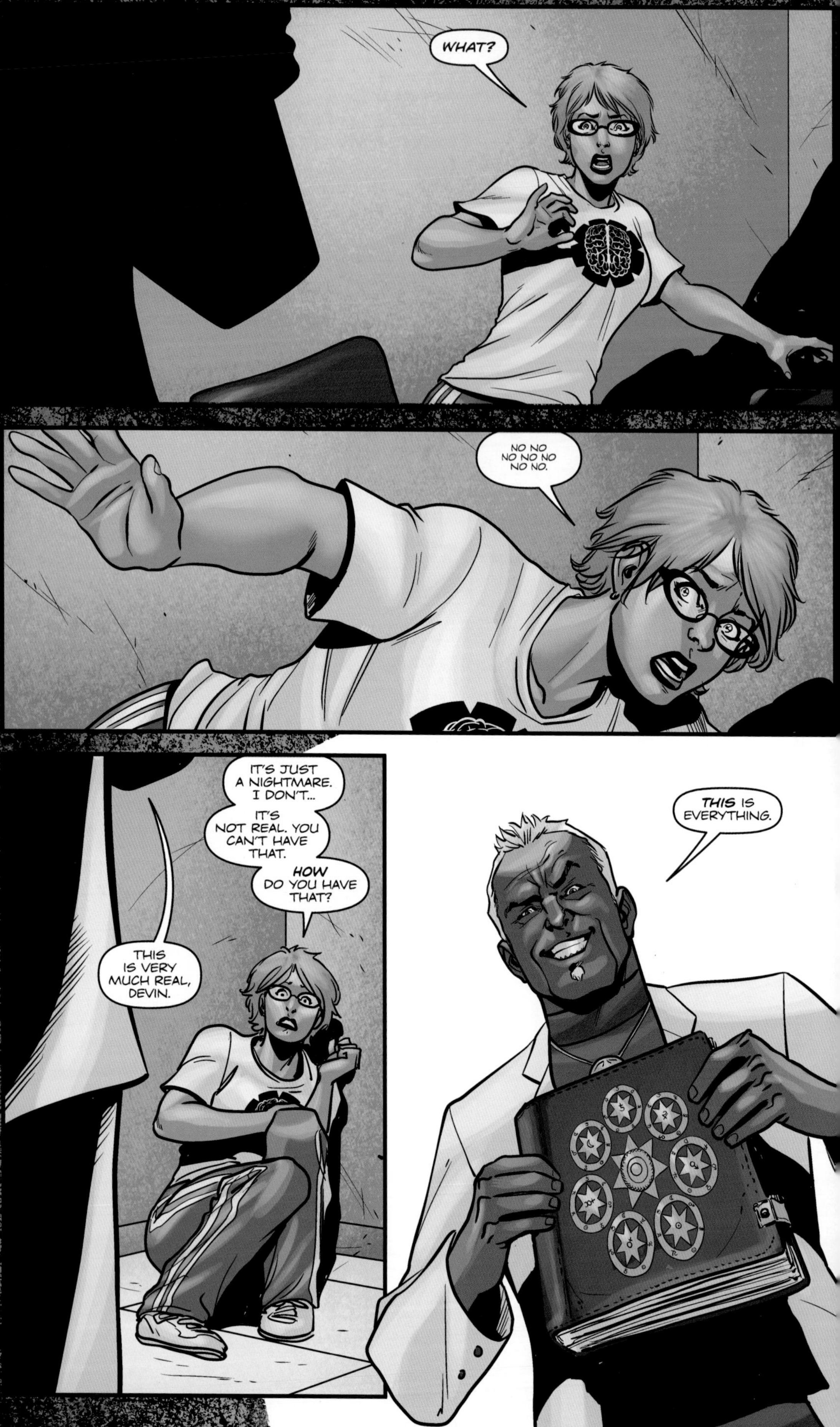
WHAT?
NO NO NO NO NO NO NO.
IT'S JUST A NIGHTMARE. I DON'T...
IT'S NOT REAL. YOU CAN'T HAVE THAT.
HOW DO YOU HAVE THAT?
THIS IS VERY MUCH REAL, DEVIN.
THIS IS EVERYTHING.

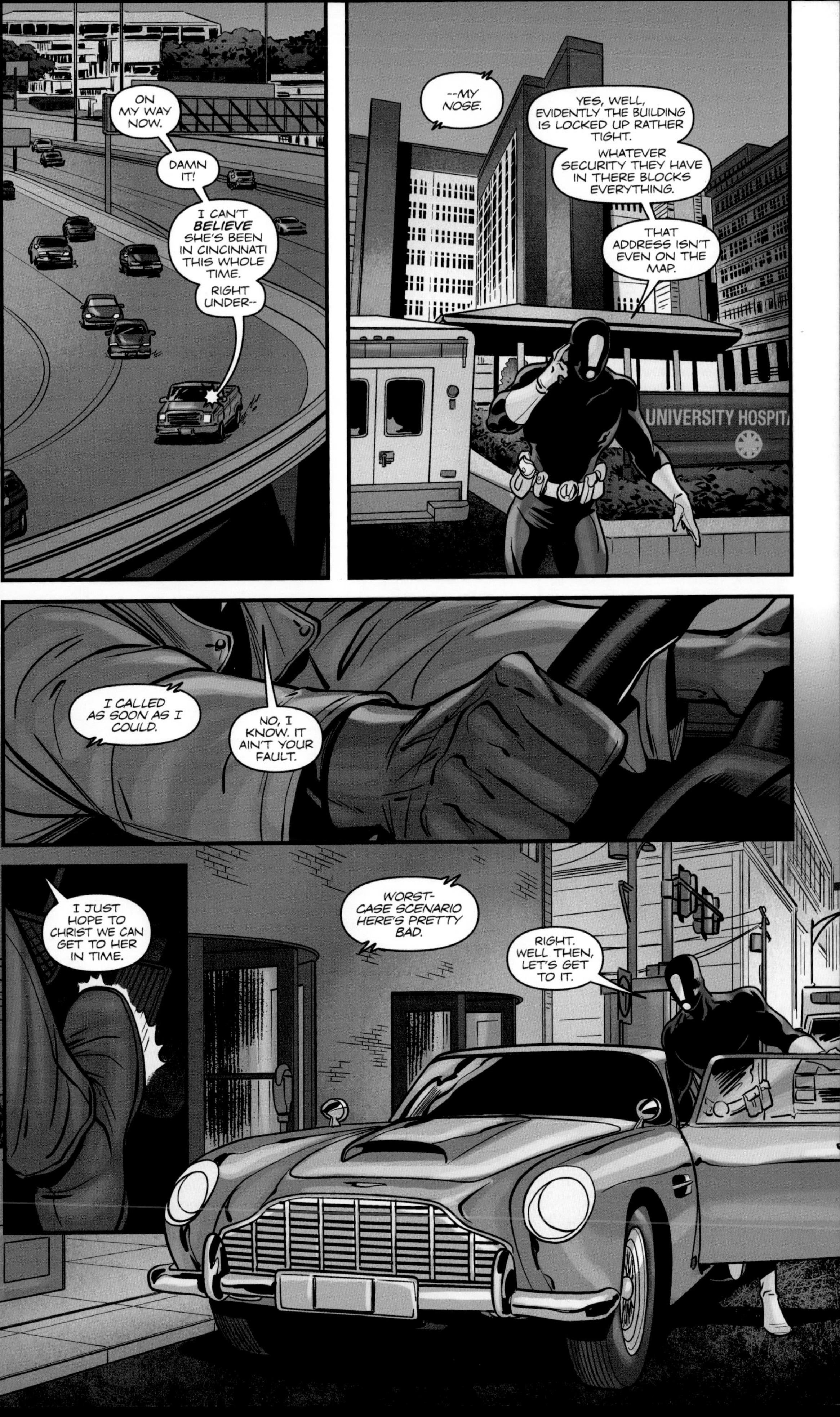
ON MY WAY NOW.
DAMN IT!
I CAN'T **BELIEVE** SHE'S BEEN IN CINCINNATI THIS WHOLE TIME.
RIGHT UNDER--
--MY NOSE.
YES, WELL, EVIDENTLY THE BUILDING IS LOCKED UP RATHER TIGHT.
WHATEVER SECURITY THEY HAVE IN THERE BLOCKS EVERYTHING.
THAT ADDRESS ISN'T EVEN ON THE MAP.
UNIVERSITY HOSPIT
I CALLED AS SOON AS I COULD.
NO, I KNOW. IT AIN'T YOUR FAULT.
I JUST HOPE TO CHRIST WE CAN GET TO HER IN TIME.
WORST-CASE SCENARIO HERE'S PRETTY BAD.
RIGHT. WELL THEN, LET'S GET TO IT.

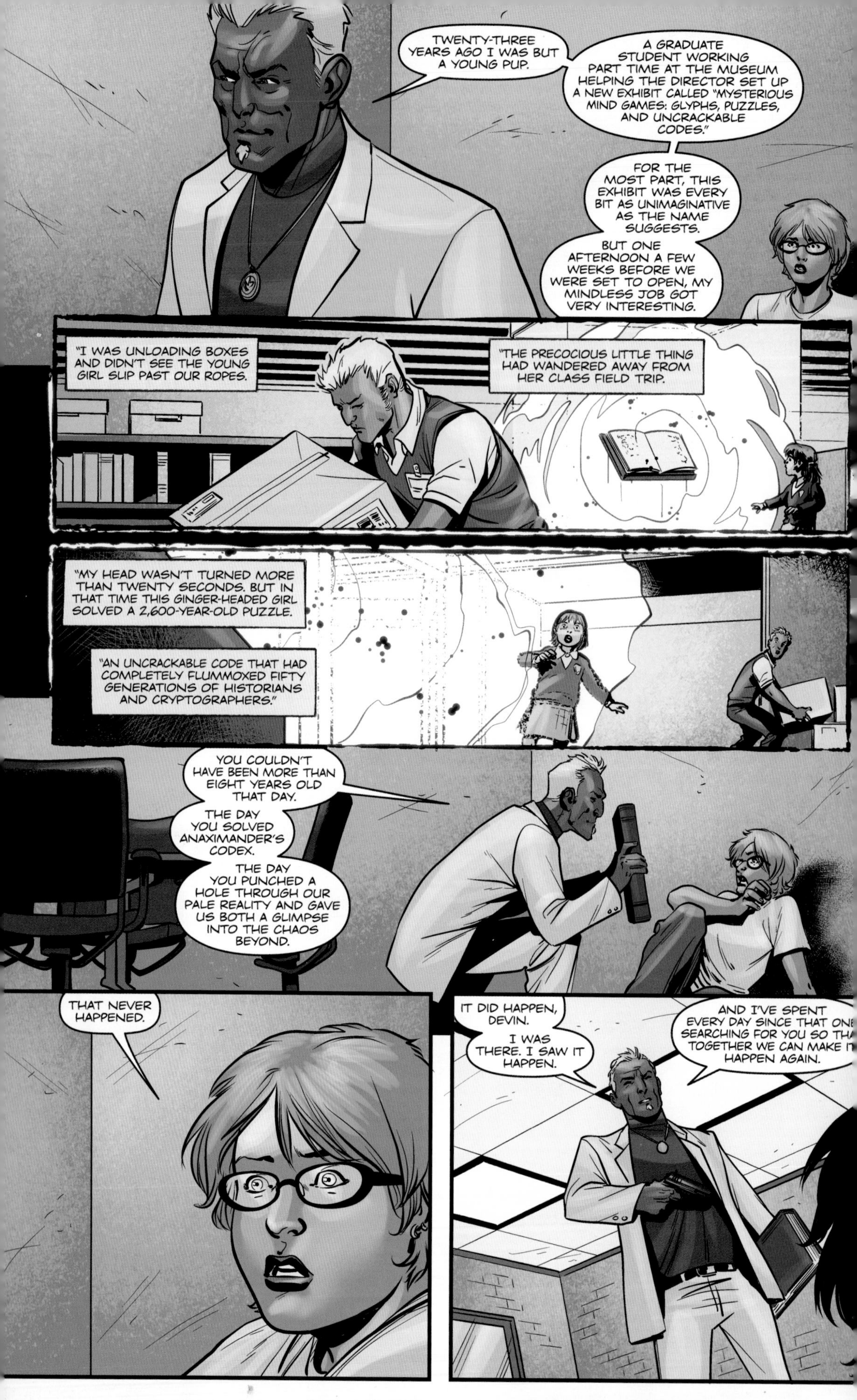

TWENTY-THREE YEARS AGO I WAS BUT A YOUNG PUP.
A GRADUATE STUDENT WORKING PART TIME AT THE MUSEUM HELPING THE DIRECTOR SET UP A NEW EXHIBIT CALLED "MYSTERIOUS MIND GAMES: GLYPHS, PUZZLES, AND UNCRACKABLE CODES."
FOR THE MOST PART, THIS EXHIBIT WAS EVERY BIT AS UNIMAGINATIVE AS THE NAME SUGGESTS.
BUT ONE AFTERNOON A FEW WEEKS BEFORE WE WERE SET TO OPEN, MY MINDLESS JOB GOT VERY INTERESTING.
"I WAS UNLOADING BOXES AND DIDN'T SEE THE YOUNG GIRL SLIP PAST OUR ROPES.
"THE PRECOCIOUS LITTLE THING HAD WANDERED AWAY FROM HER CLASS FIELD TRIP.
"MY HEAD WASN'T TURNED MORE THAN TWENTY SECONDS. BUT IN THAT TIME THIS GINGER-HEADED GIRL SOLVED A 2,600-YEAR-OLD PUZZLE.
"AN UNCRACKABLE CODE THAT HAD COMPLETELY FLUMMOXED FIFTY GENERATIONS OF HISTORIANS AND CRYPTOGRAPHERS."
YOU COULDN'T HAVE BEEN MORE THAN EIGHT YEARS OLD THAT DAY.
THE DAY YOU SOLVED ANAXIMANDER'S CODEX.
THE DAY YOU PUNCHED A HOLE THROUGH OUR PALE REALITY AND GAVE US BOTH A GLIMPSE INTO THE CHAOS BEYOND.
THAT NEVER HAPPENED.
IT DID HAPPEN, DEVIN.
I WAS THERE. I SAW IT HAPPEN.
AND I'VE SPENT EVERY DAY SINCE THAT ONE SEARCHING FOR YOU SO THAT TOGETHER WE CAN MAKE IT HAPPEN AGAIN.

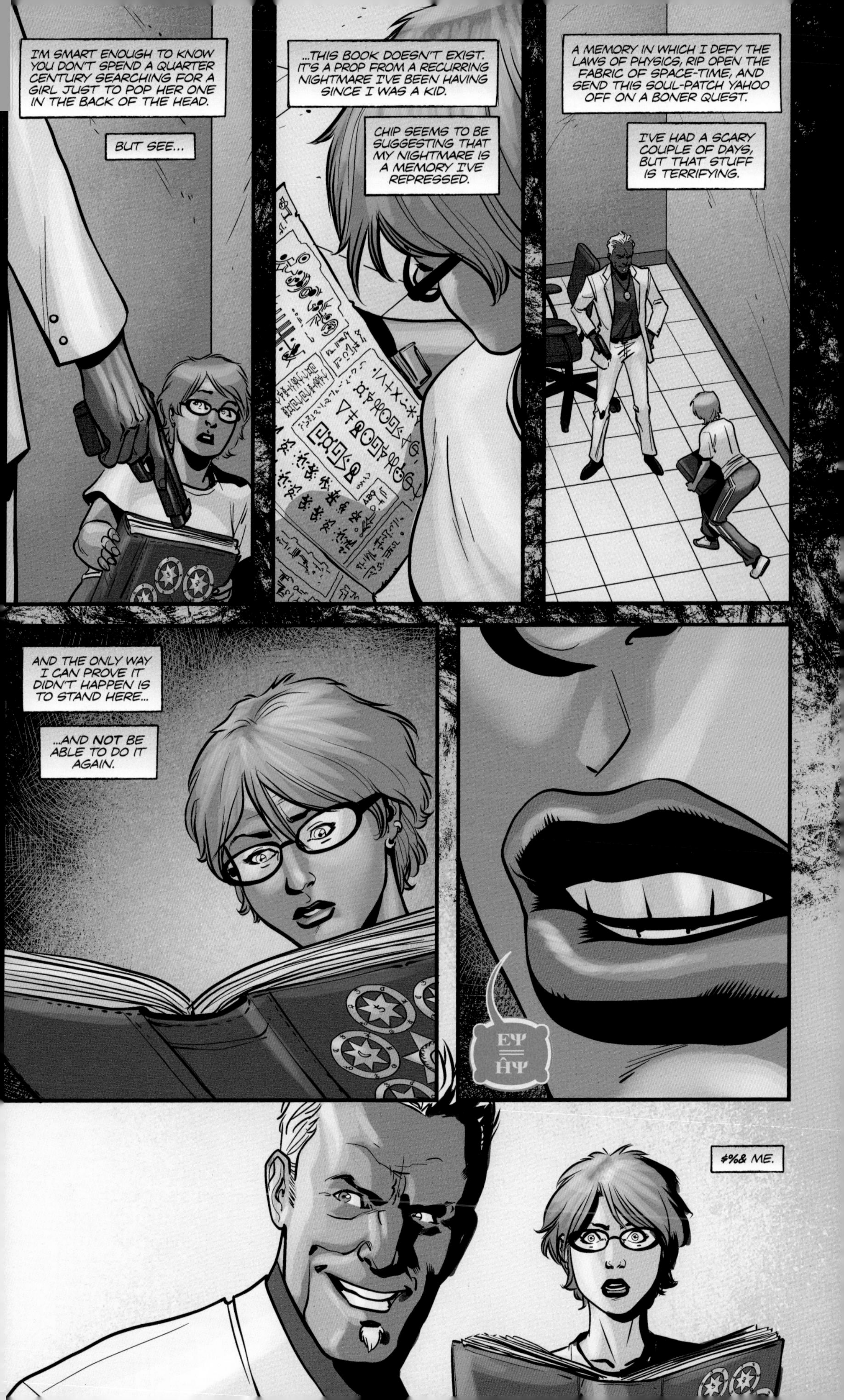
I'M SMART ENOUGH TO KNOW YOU DON'T SPEND A QUARTER CENTURY SEARCHING FOR A GIRL JUST TO POP HER ONE IN THE BACK OF THE HEAD.
BUT SEE...
...THIS BOOK DOESN'T EXIST. IT'S A PROP FROM A RECURRING NIGHTMARE I'VE BEEN HAVING SINCE I WAS A KID.
CHIP SEEMS TO BE SUGGESTING THAT MY NIGHTMARE IS A MEMORY I'VE REPRESSED.
A MEMORY IN WHICH I DEFY THE LAWS OF PHYSICS, RIP OPEN THE FABRIC OF SPACE-TIME, AND SEND THIS SOUL-PATCH YAHOO OFF ON A BONER QUEST.
I'VE HAD A SCARY COUPLE OF DAYS, BUT THAT STUFF IS TERRIFYING.
AND THE ONLY WAY I CAN PROVE IT DIDN'T HAPPEN IS TO STAND HERE...
...AND NOT BE ABLE TO DO IT AGAIN.
EΨ = ĤΨ
$%& ME.

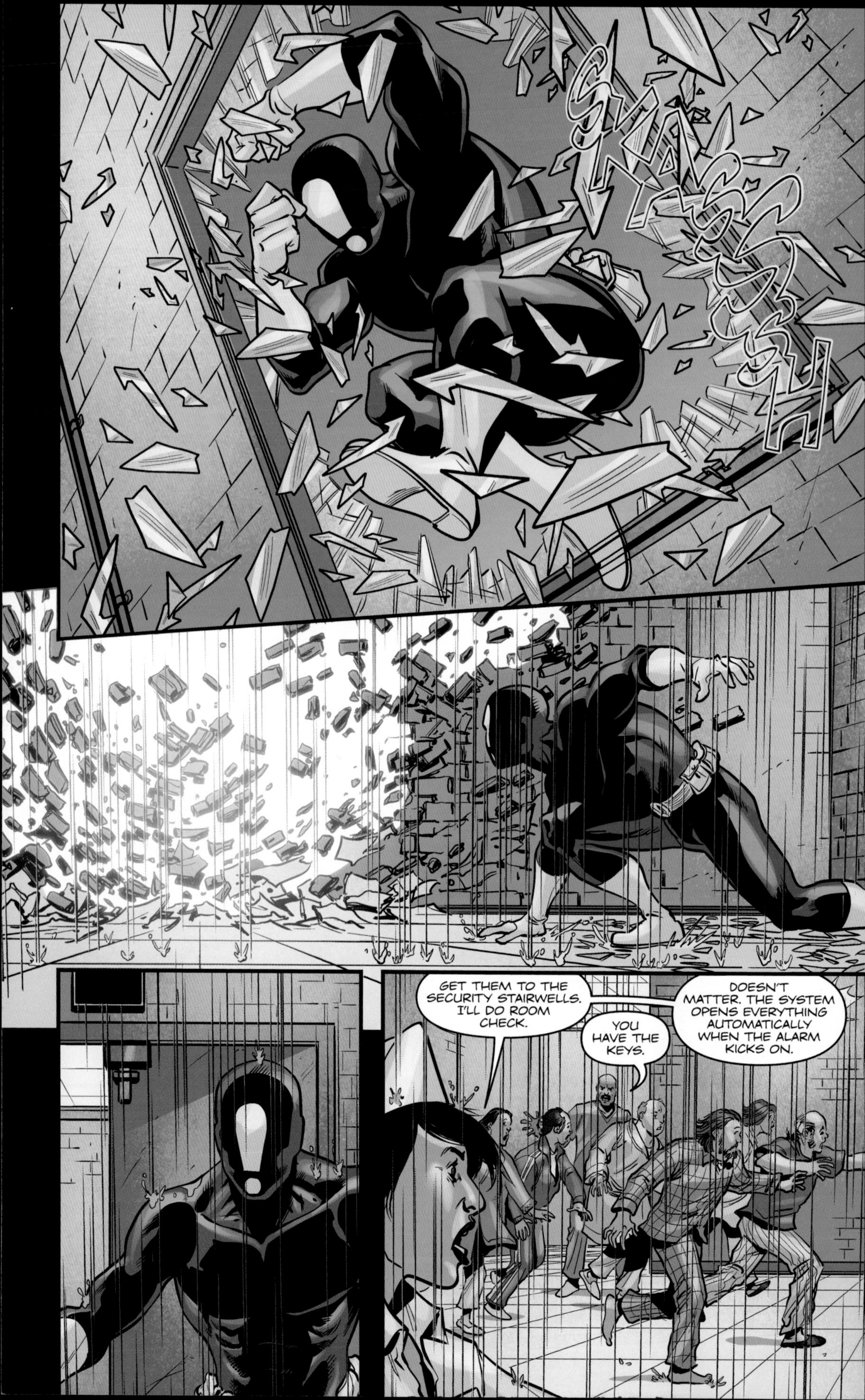
SHASSSSHH
GET THEM TO THE SECURITY STAIRWELLS. I'LL DO ROOM CHECK.
YOU HAVE THE KEYS.
DOESN'T MATTER. THE SYSTEM OPENS EVERYTHING AUTOMATICALLY WHEN THE ALARM KICKS ON.

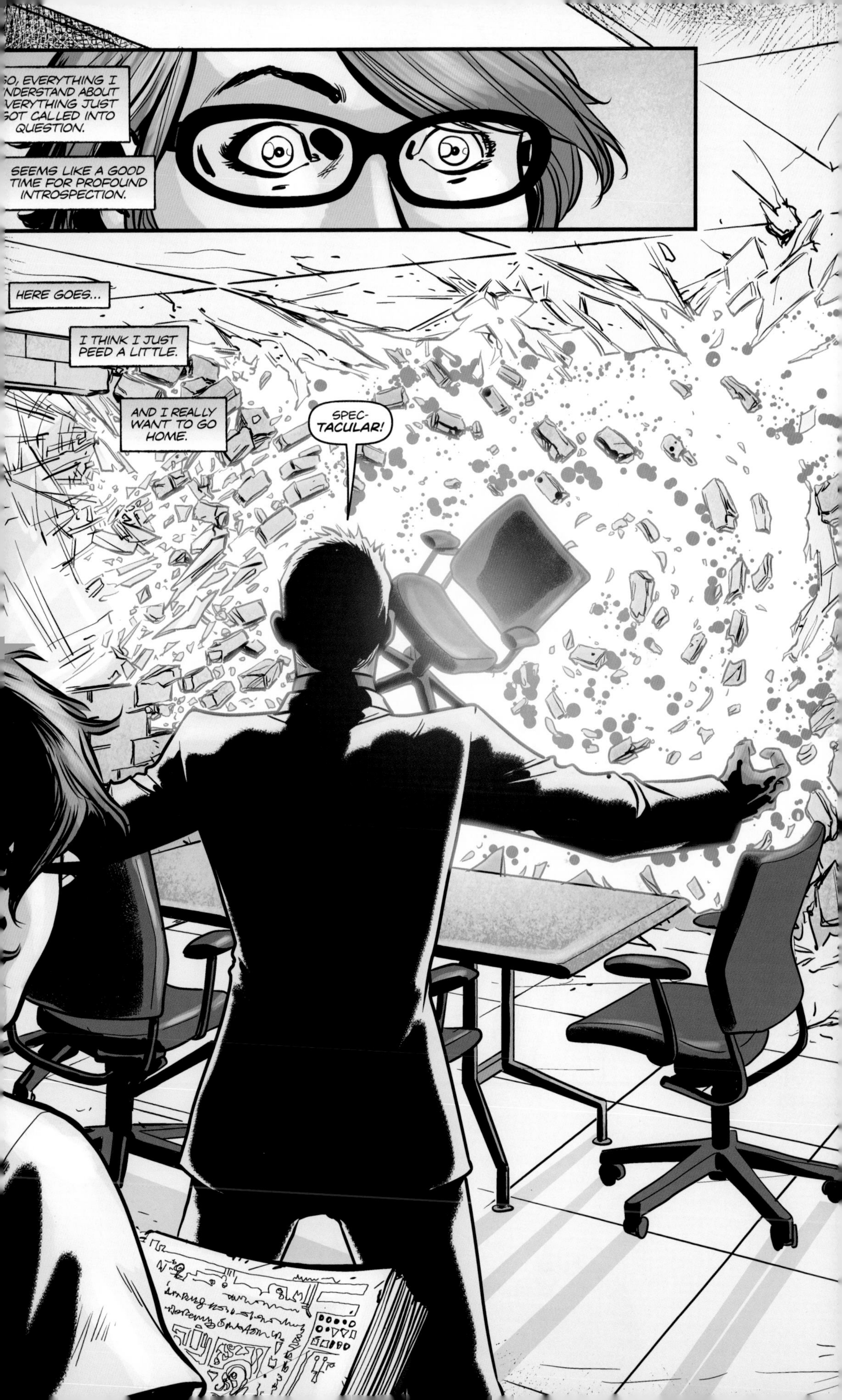
SO, EVERYTHING I UNDERSTAND ABOUT EVERYTHING JUST GOT CALLED INTO QUESTION.
SEEMS LIKE A GOOD TIME FOR PROFOUND INTROSPECTION.
HERE GOES...
I THINK I JUST PEED A LITTLE.
AND I REALLY WANT TO GO HOME.
SPEC-TACULAR!

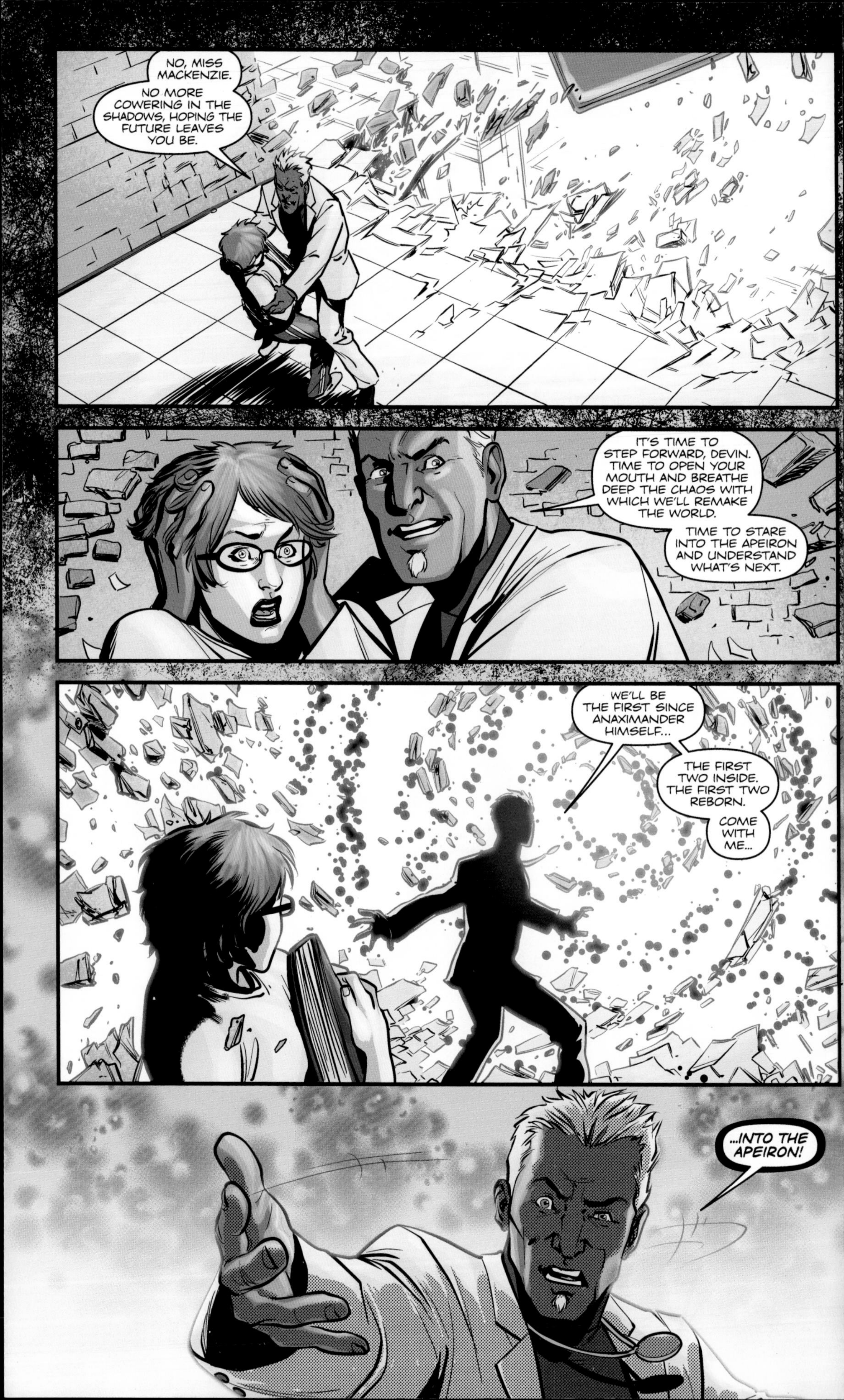
NO, MISS MACKENZIE.
NO MORE COWERING IN THE SHADOWS, HOPING THE FUTURE LEAVES YOU BE.
IT'S TIME TO STEP FORWARD, DEVIN. TIME TO OPEN YOUR MOUTH AND BREATHE DEEP THE CHAOS WITH WHICH WE'LL REMAKE THE WORLD.
TIME TO STARE INTO THE APEIRON AND UNDERSTAND WHAT'S NEXT.
WE'LL BE THE FIRST SINCE ANAXIMANDER HIMSELF...
THE FIRST TWO INSIDE. THE FIRST TWO REBORN.
COME WITH ME...
...INTO THE APEIRON!

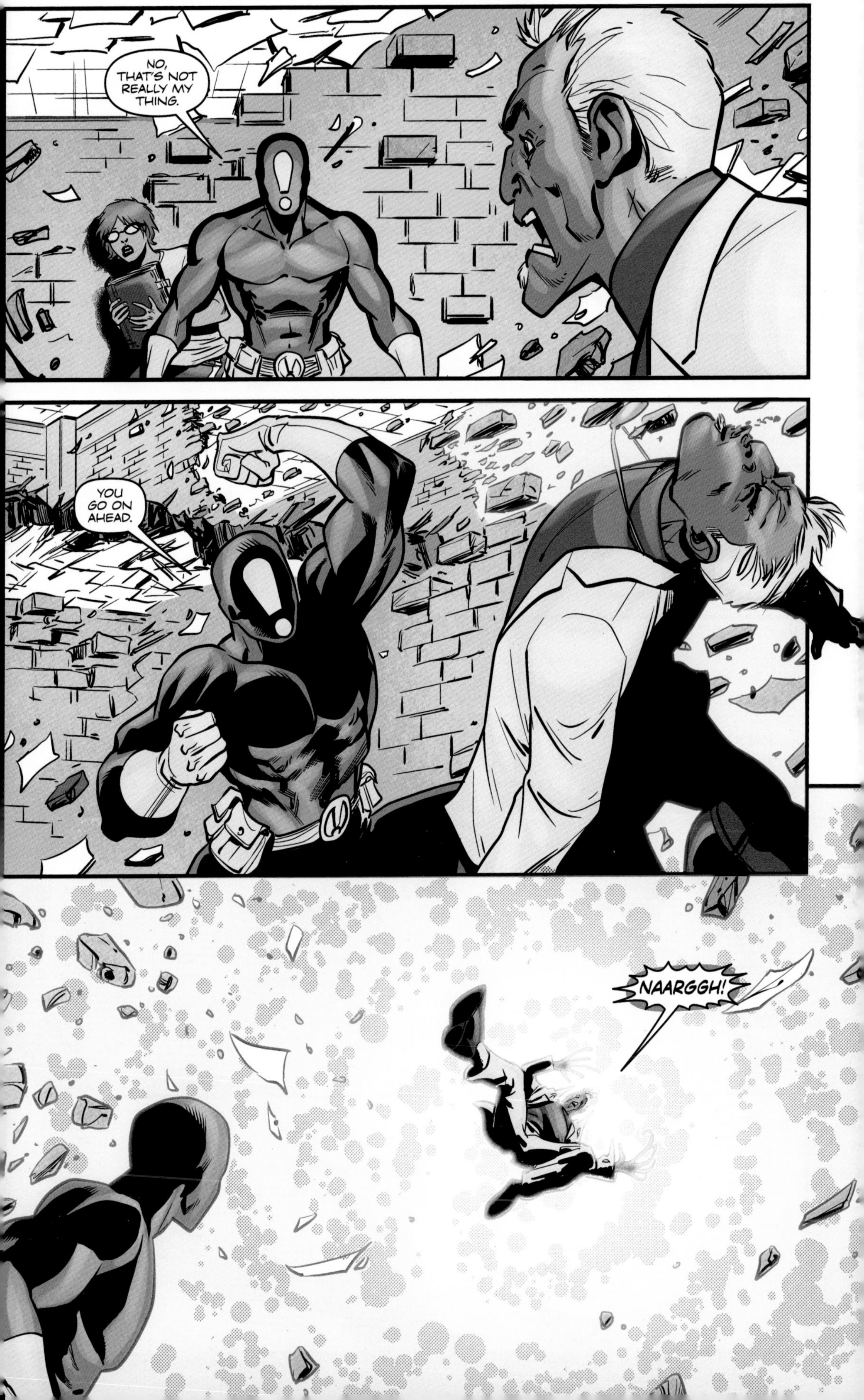
NO, THAT'S NOT REALLY MY THING.
YOU GO ON AHEAD.
NAARGGH!

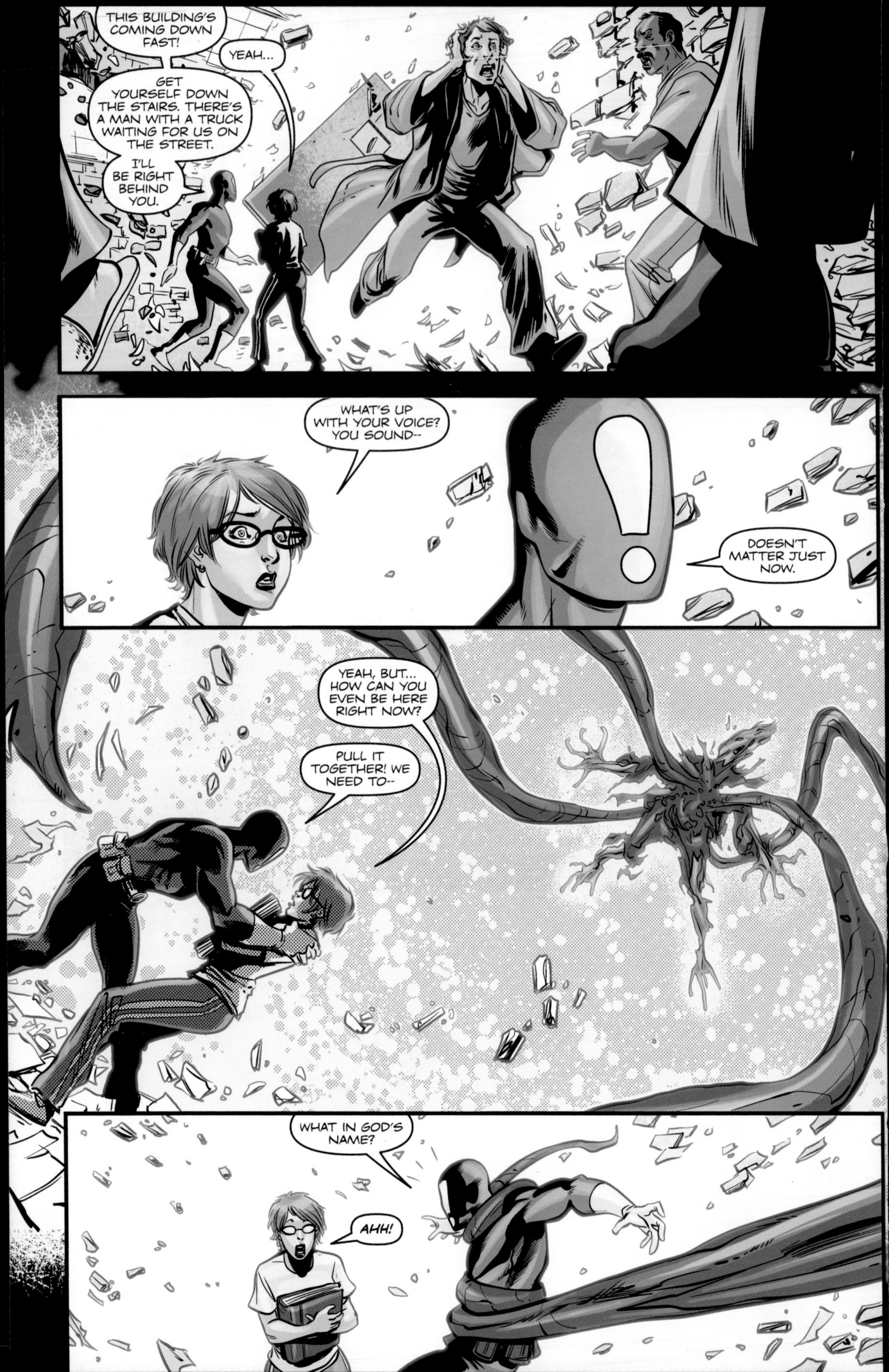
THIS BUILDING'S COMING DOWN FAST!
YEAH...
GET YOURSELF DOWN THE STAIRS. THERE'S A MAN WITH A TRUCK WAITING FOR US ON THE STREET.
I'LL BE RIGHT BEHIND YOU.
WHAT'S UP WITH YOUR VOICE? YOU SOUND--
DOESN'T MATTER JUST NOW.
YEAH, BUT... HOW CAN YOU EVEN BE HERE RIGHT NOW?
PULL IT TOGETHER! WE NEED TO--
WHAT IN GOD'S NAME?
AHH!

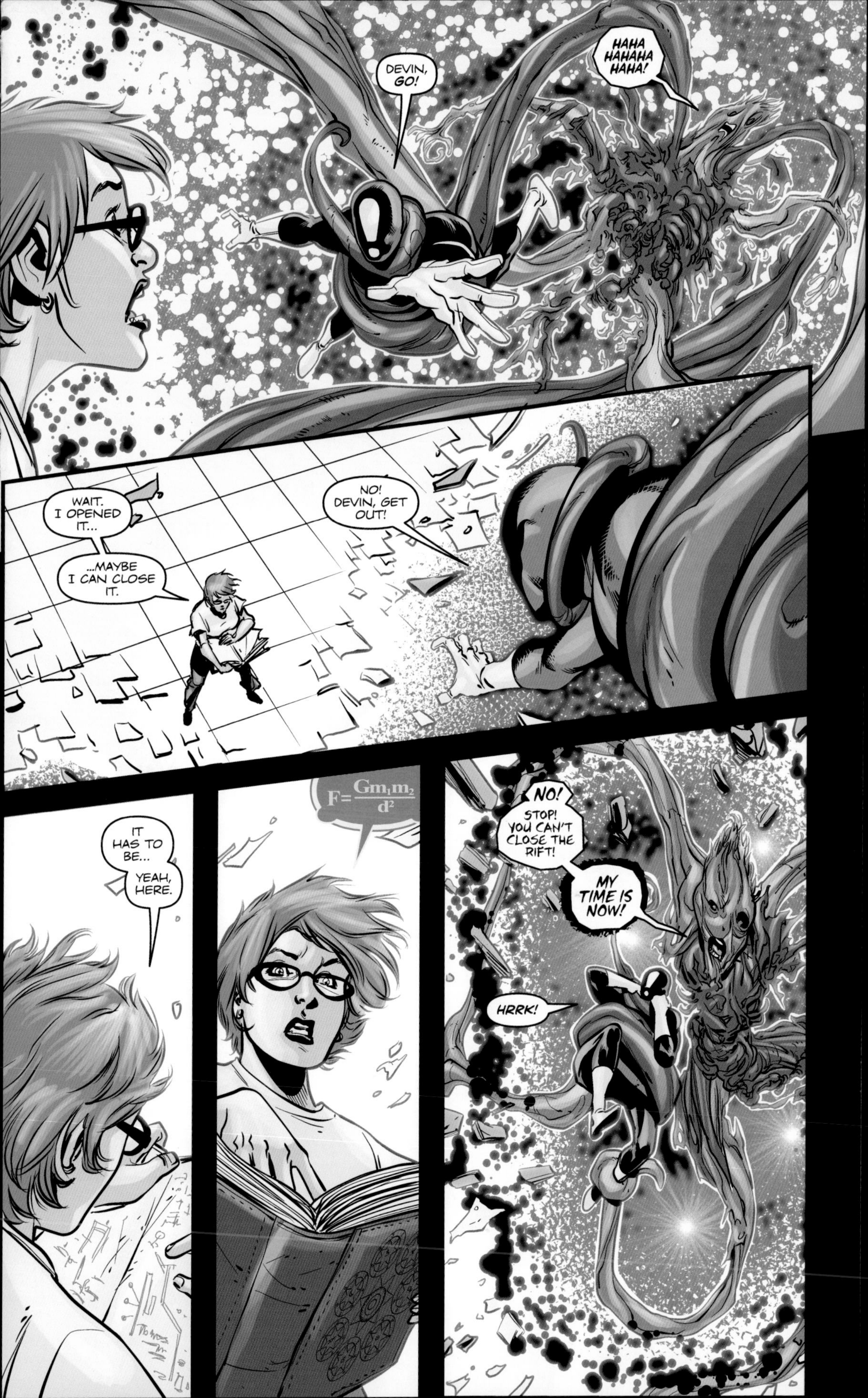
DEVIN, GO!
HAHA HAHAHA HAHA!
WAIT. I OPENED IT...
...MAYBE I CAN CLOSE IT.
NO! DEVIN, GET OUT!
IT HAS TO BE...
YEAH, HERE.
$F=\frac{Gm_1m_2}{d^2}$
NO!
STOP! YOU CAN'T CLOSE THE RIFT!
MY TIME IS NOW!
HRRK!

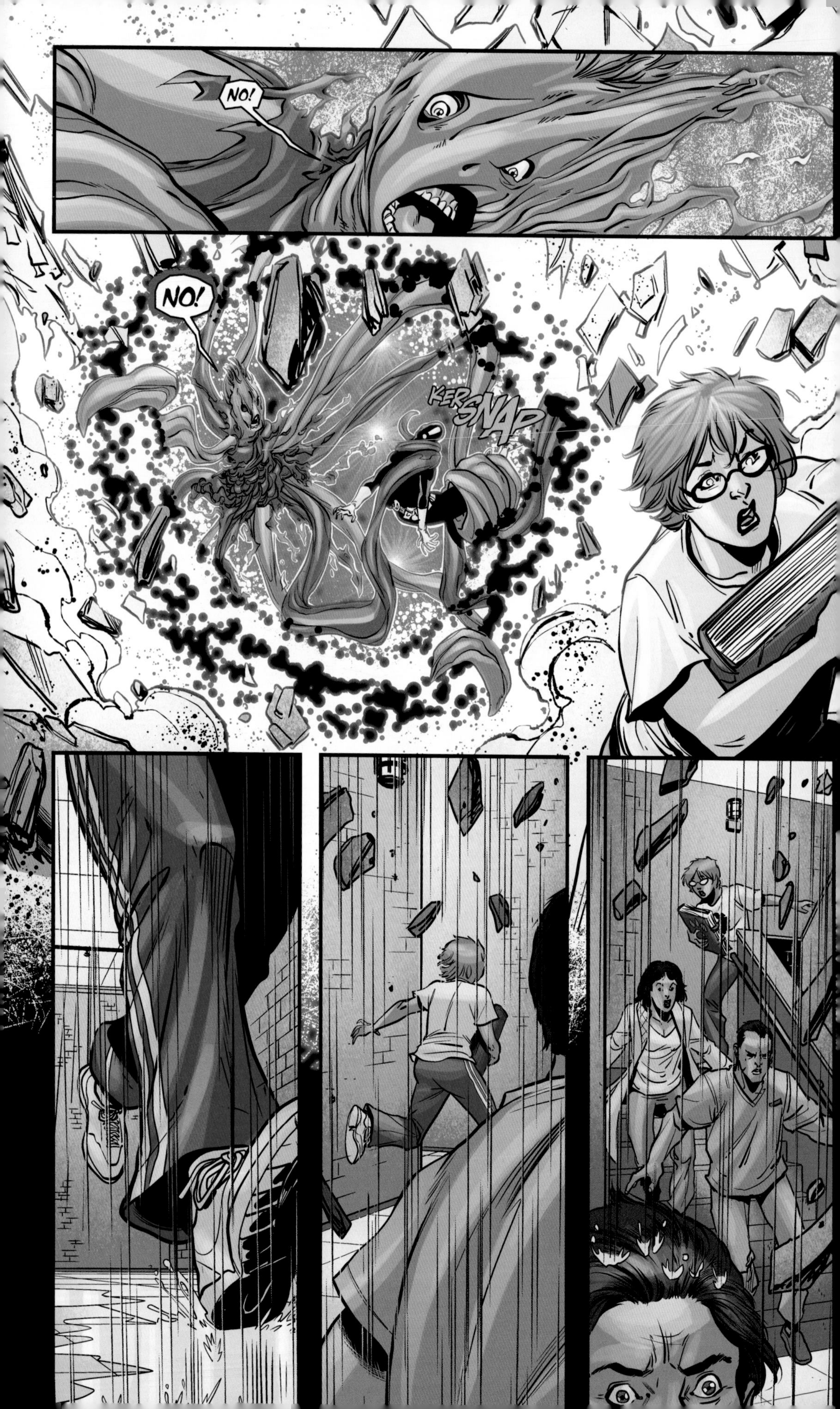
NO!
NO!
KERSNAP

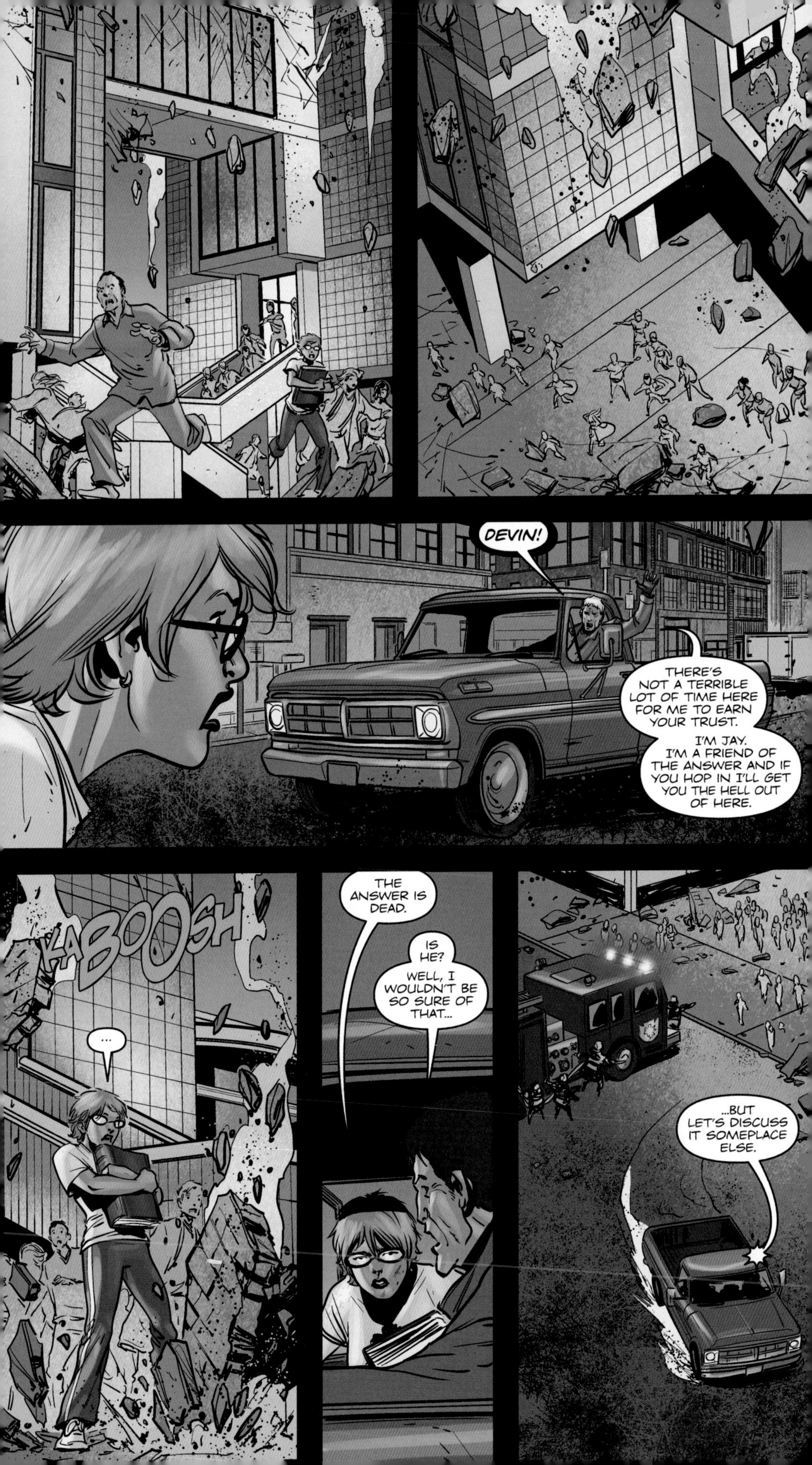
DEVIN!
THERE'S NOT A TERRIBLE LOT OF TIME HERE FOR ME TO EARN YOUR TRUST.
I'M JAY. I'M A FRIEND OF THE ANSWER AND IF YOU HOP IN I'LL GET YOU THE HELL OUT OF HERE.
KABOOSH
...
THE ANSWER IS DEAD.
IS HE?
WELL, I WOULDN'T BE SO SURE OF THAT...
...BUT LET'S DISCUSS IT SOMEPLACE ELSE.

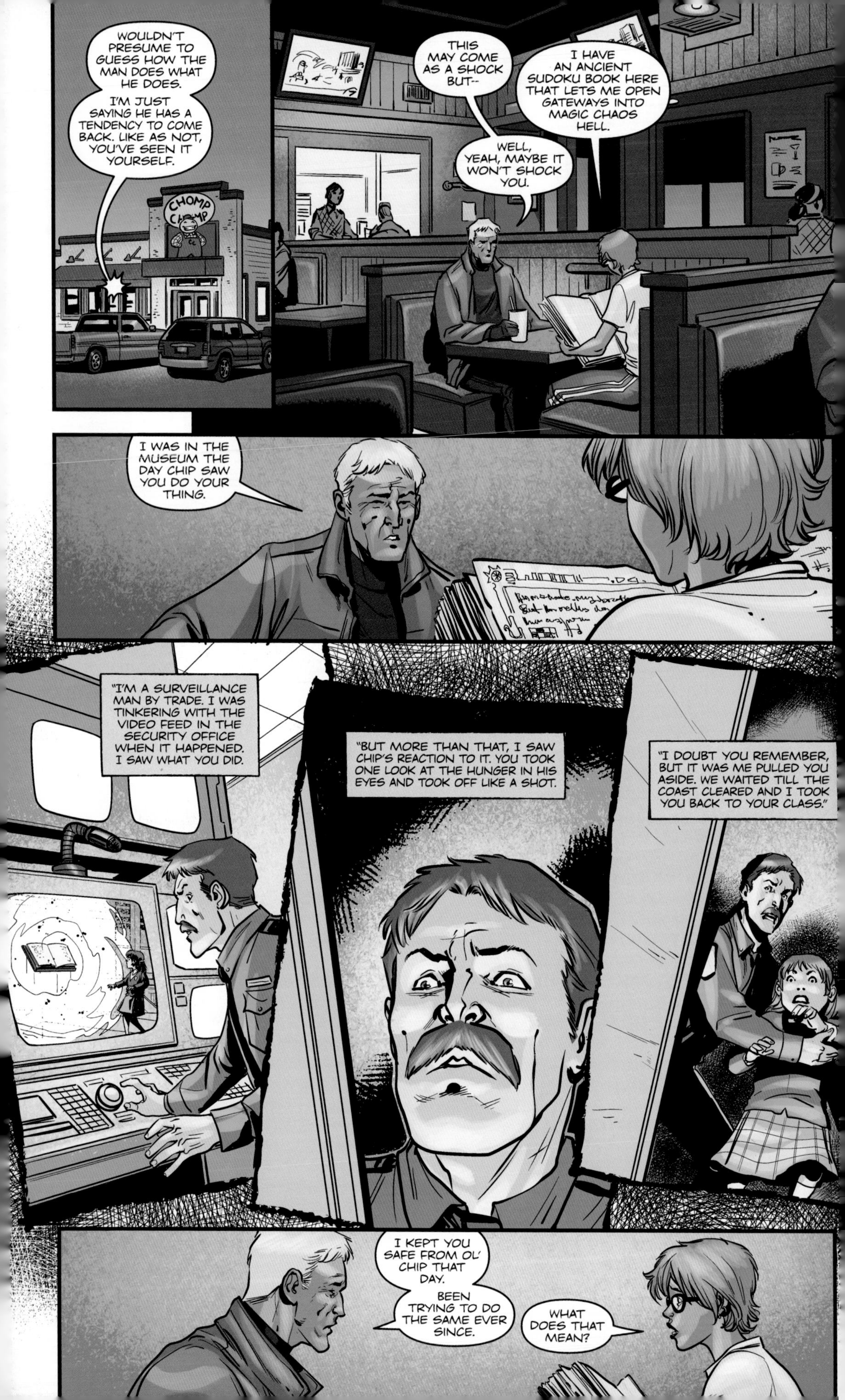
WOULDN'T PRESUME TO GUESS HOW THE MAN DOES WHAT HE DOES.
I'M JUST SAYING HE HAS A TENDENCY TO COME BACK. LIKE AS NOT, YOU'VE SEEN IT YOURSELF.
CHOMP CHOMP
THIS MAY COME AS A SHOCK BUT--
I HAVE AN ANCIENT SUDOKU BOOK HERE THAT LETS ME OPEN GATEWAYS INTO MAGIC CHAOS HELL.
WELL, YEAH, MAYBE IT WON'T SHOCK YOU.
I WAS IN THE MUSEUM THE DAY CHIP SAW YOU DO YOUR THING.
"I'M A SURVEILLANCE MAN BY TRADE. I WAS TINKERING WITH THE VIDEO FEED IN THE SECURITY OFFICE WHEN IT HAPPENED. I SAW WHAT YOU DID.
"BUT MORE THAN THAT, I SAW CHIP'S REACTION TO IT. YOU TOOK ONE LOOK AT THE HUNGER IN HIS EYES AND TOOK OFF LIKE A SHOT.
"I DOUBT YOU REMEMBER, BUT IT WAS ME PULLED YOU ASIDE. WE WAITED TILL THE COAST CLEARED AND I TOOK YOU BACK TO YOUR CLASS."
I KEPT YOU SAFE FROM OL' CHIP THAT DAY.
BEEN TRYING TO DO THE SAME EVER SINCE.
WHAT DOES THAT MEAN?

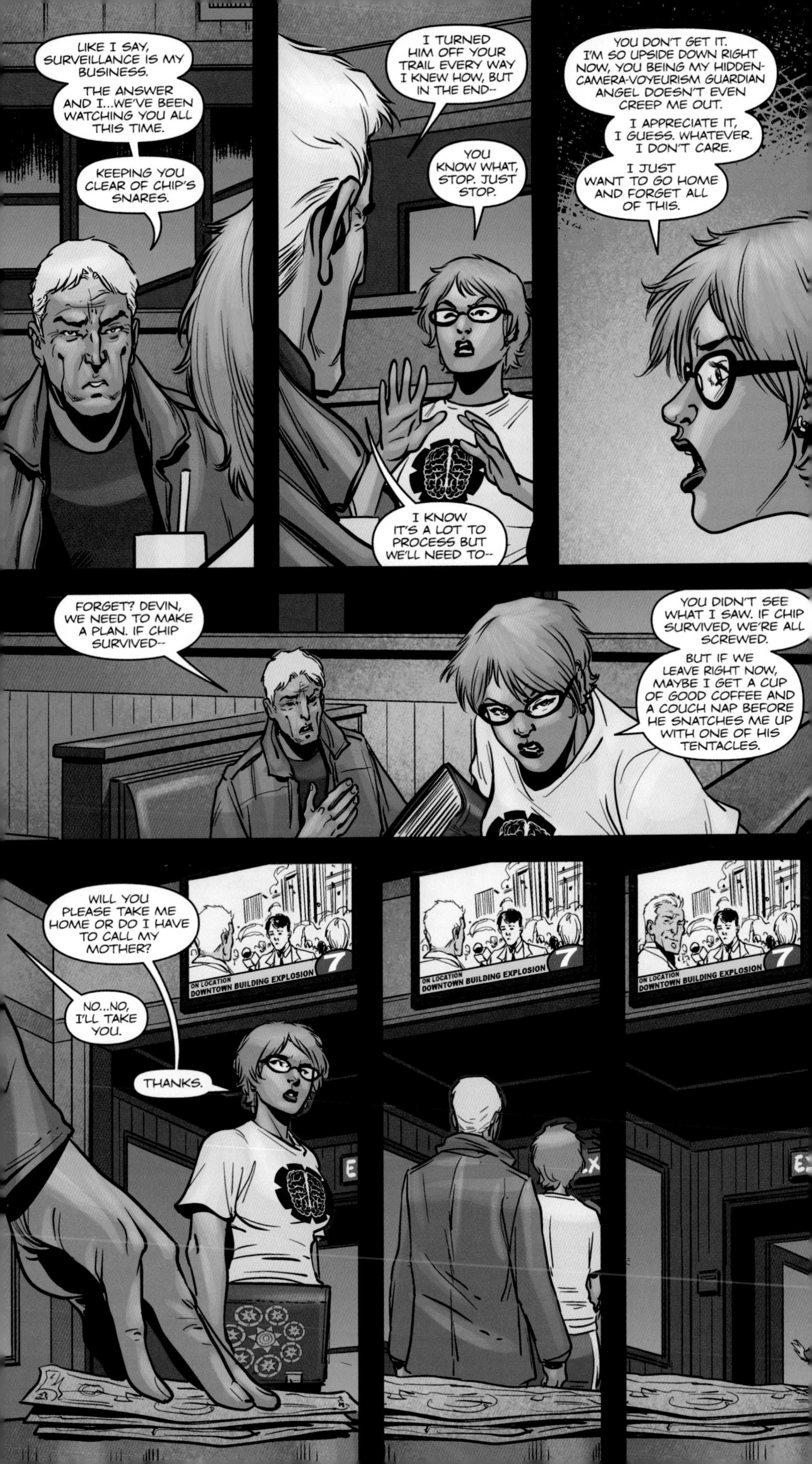
LIKE I SAY, SURVEILLANCE IS MY BUSINESS.
THE ANSWER AND I...WE'VE BEEN WATCHING YOU ALL THIS TIME.
KEEPING YOU CLEAR OF CHIP'S SNARES.
I TURNED HIM OFF YOUR TRAIL EVERY WAY I KNEW HOW, BUT IN THE END--
YOU KNOW WHAT, STOP. JUST STOP.
I KNOW IT'S A LOT TO PROCESS BUT WE'LL NEED TO--
YOU DON'T GET IT. I'M SO UPSIDE DOWN RIGHT NOW, YOU BEING MY HIDDEN-CAMERA-VOYEURISM GUARDIAN ANGEL DOESN'T EVEN CREEP ME OUT.
I APPRECIATE IT, I GUESS. WHATEVER. I DON'T CARE.
I JUST WANT TO GO HOME AND FORGET ALL OF THIS.
FORGET? DEVIN, WE NEED TO MAKE A PLAN. IF CHIP SURVIVED--
YOU DIDN'T SEE WHAT I SAW. IF CHIP SURVIVED, WE'RE ALL SCREWED.
BUT IF WE LEAVE RIGHT NOW, MAYBE I GET A CUP OF GOOD COFFEE AND A COUCH NAP BEFORE HE SNATCHES ME UP WITH ONE OF HIS TENTACLES.
ON LOCATION DOWNTOWN BUILDING EXPLOSION
7
WILL YOU PLEASE TAKE ME HOME OR DO I HAVE TO CALL MY MOTHER?
NO...NO, I'LL TAKE YOU.
THANKS.
ON LOCATION DOWNTOWN BUILDING EXPLOSION
7
ON LOCATION DOWNTOWN BUILDING EXPLOSION
7

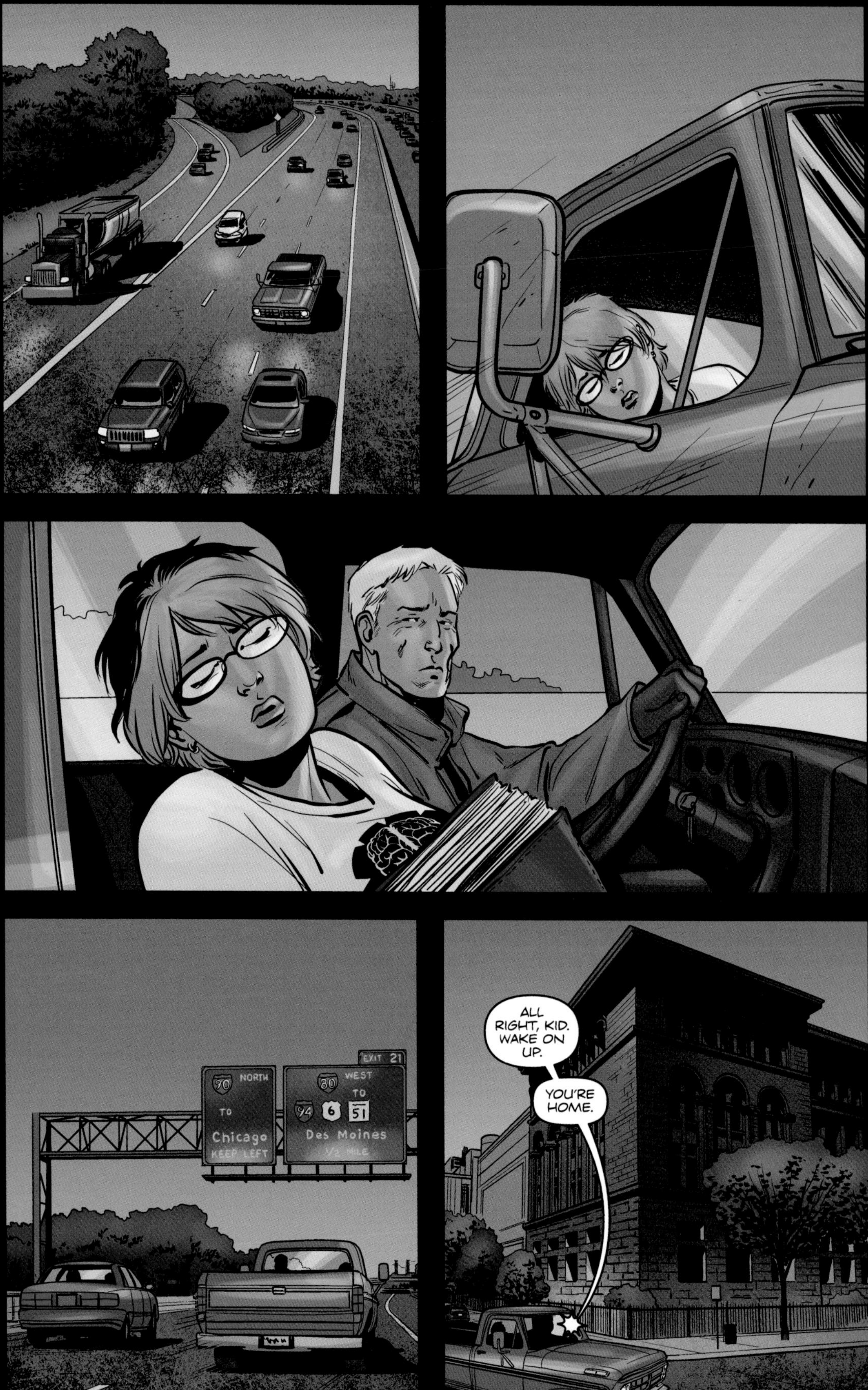
90 NORTH
TO
Chicago
KEEP LEFT
EXIT 21
80 WEST
TO
94 6 51
Des Moines
1/2 MILE
ALL RIGHT, KID. WAKE ON UP.
YOU'RE HOME.

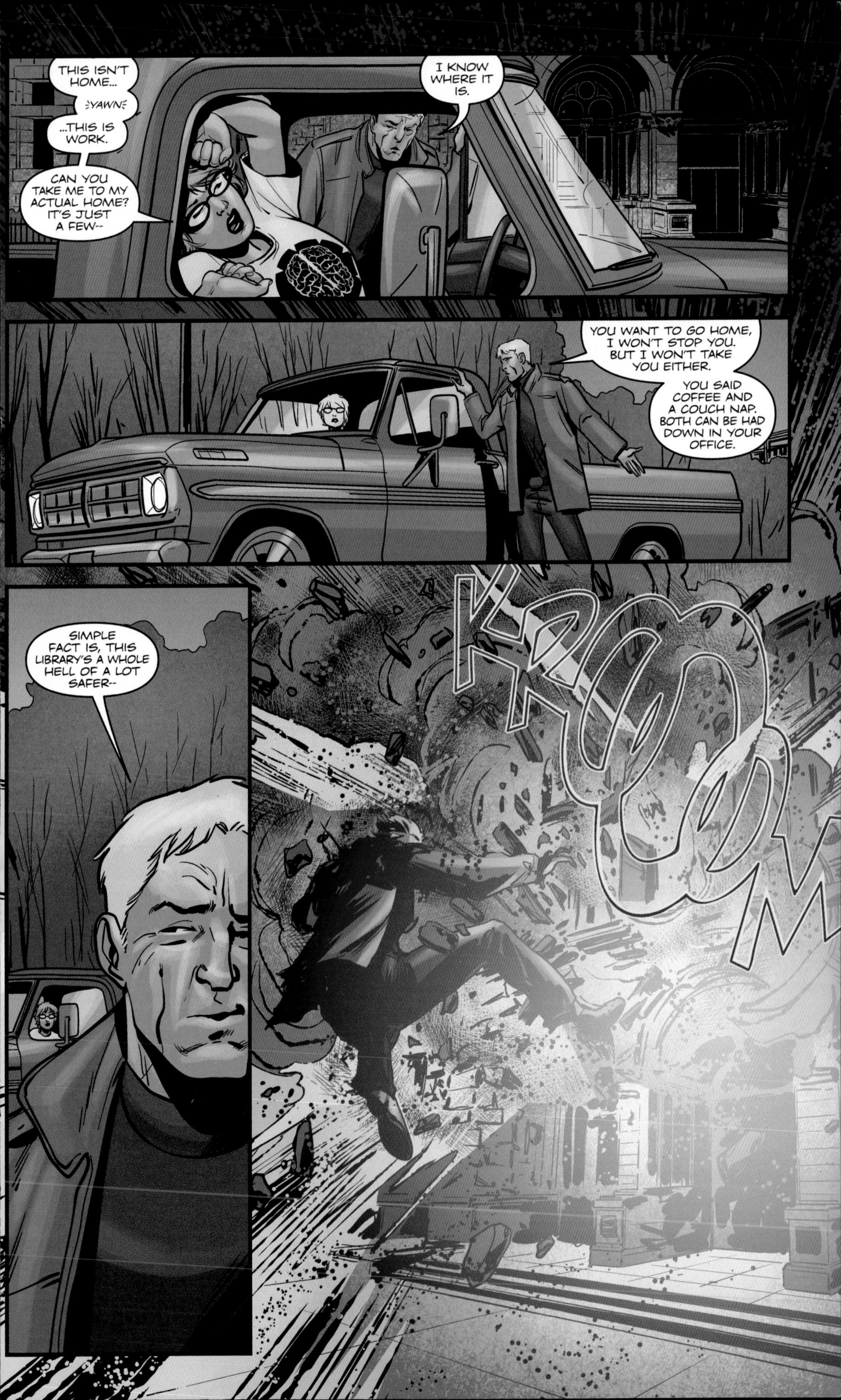

THIS ISN'T HOME...
YAWN
...THIS IS WORK.
CAN YOU TAKE ME TO MY ACTUAL HOME? IT'S JUST A FEW--
I KNOW WHERE IT IS.
YOU WANT TO GO HOME, I WON'T STOP YOU. BUT I WON'T TAKE YOU EITHER.
YOU SAID COFFEE AND A COUCH NAP. BOTH CAN BE HAD DOWN IN YOUR OFFICE.
SIMPLE FACT IS, THIS LIBRARY'S A WHOLE HELL OF A LOT SAFER--
KROOOM

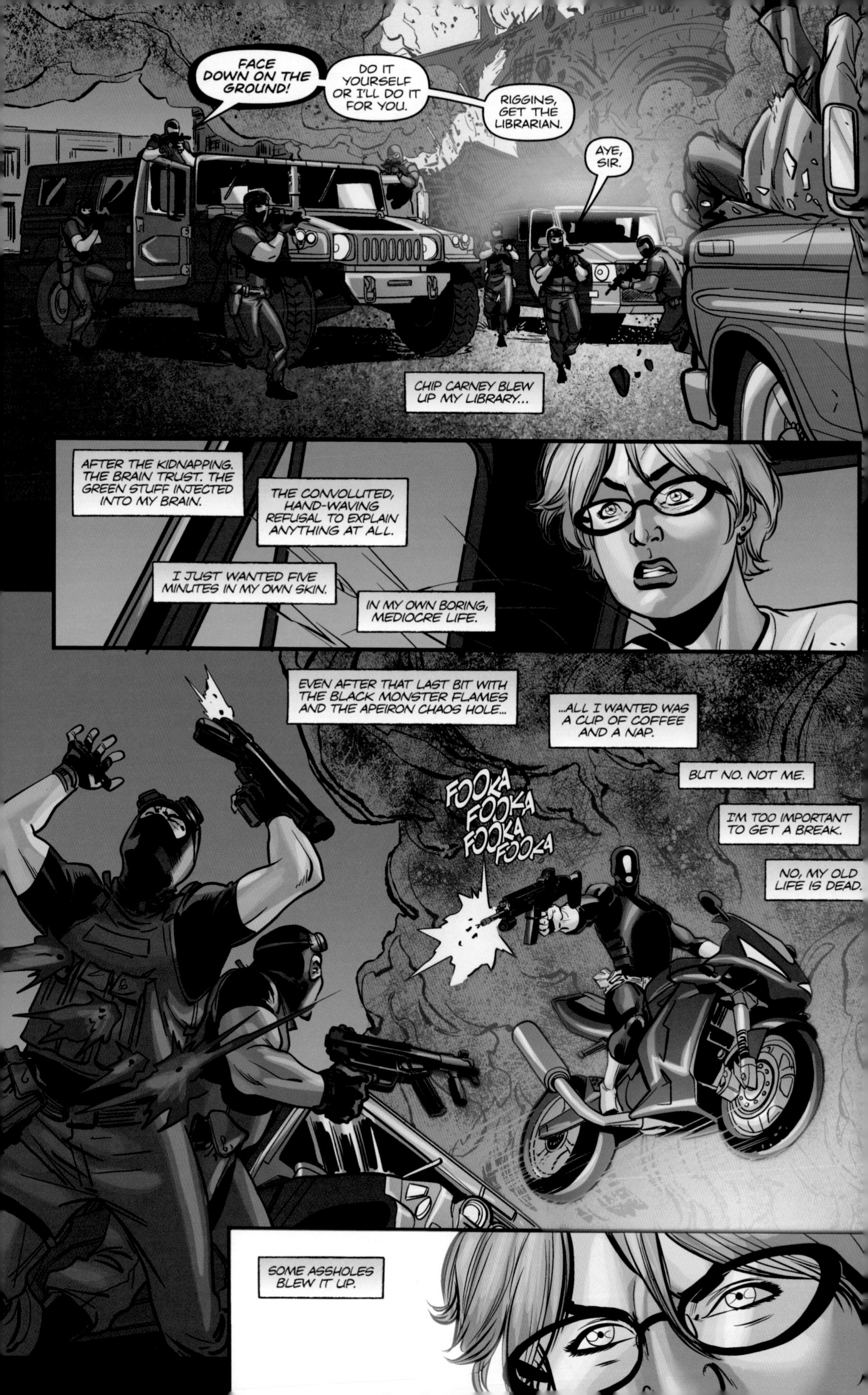
FACE DOWN ON THE GROUND!
DO IT YOURSELF OR I'LL DO IT FOR YOU.
RIGGINS, GET THE LIBRARIAN.
AYE, SIR.
CHIP CARNEY BLEW UP MY LIBRARY...
AFTER THE KIDNAPPING. THE BRAIN TRUST. THE GREEN STUFF INJECTED INTO MY BRAIN.
THE CONVOLUTED, HAND-WAVING REFUSAL TO EXPLAIN ANYTHING AT ALL.
I JUST WANTED FIVE MINUTES IN MY OWN SKIN.
IN MY OWN BORING, MEDIOCRE LIFE.
EVEN AFTER THAT LAST BIT WITH THE BLACK MONSTER FLAMES AND THE APEIRON CHAOS HOLE...
...ALL I WANTED WAS A CUP OF COFFEE AND A NAP.
BUT NO. NOT ME.
I'M TOO IMPORTANT TO GET A BREAK.
NO, MY OLD LIFE IS DEAD.
FOOKA FOOKA FOOKA FOOKA
SOME ASSHOLES BLEW IT UP.

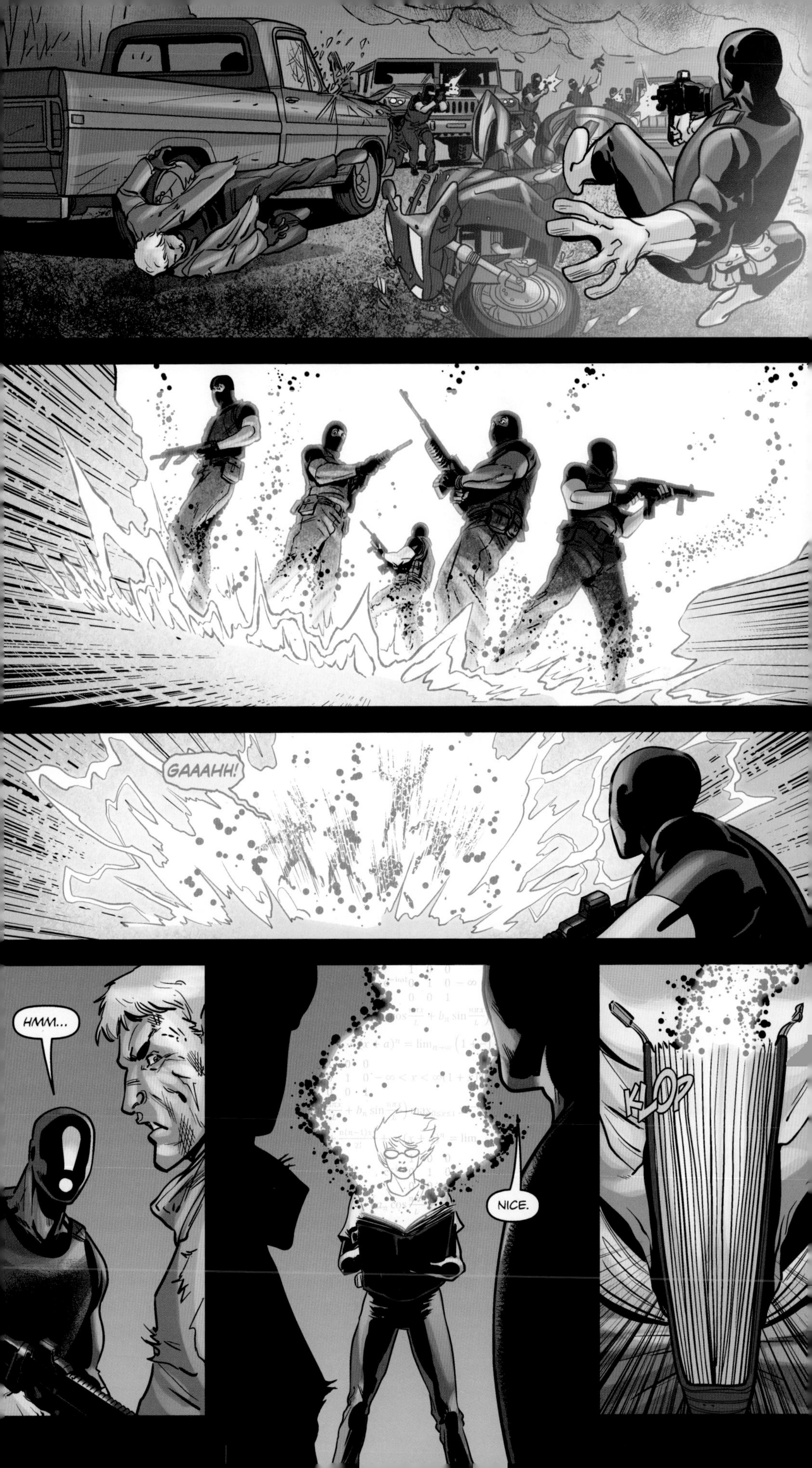
GAAAHH!
HMM...
NICE.
KLOP

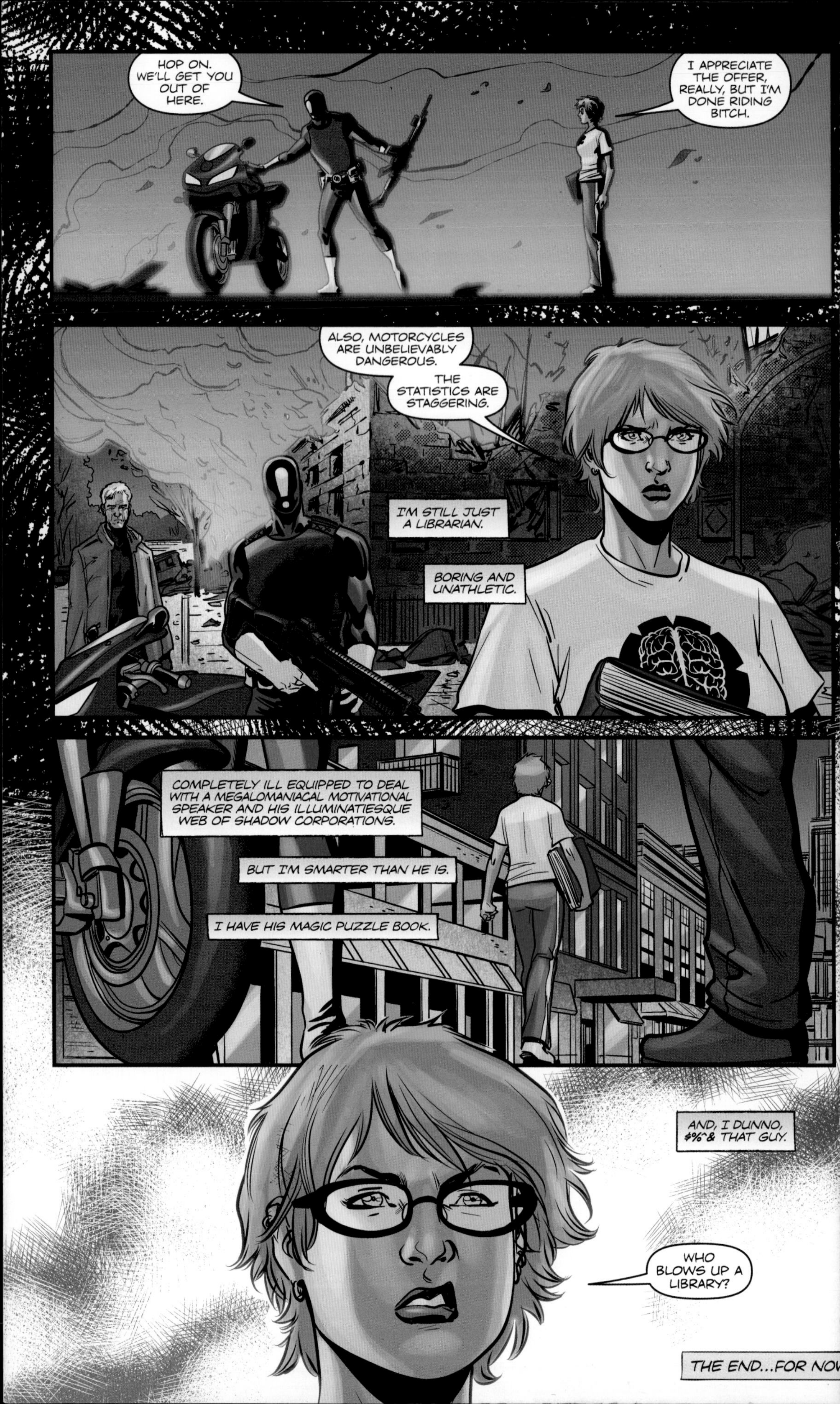
HOP ON. WE'LL GET YOU OUT OF HERE.
I APPRECIATE THE OFFER, REALLY, BUT I'M DONE RIDING BITCH.
ALSO, MOTORCYCLES ARE UNBELIEVABLY DANGEROUS.
THE STATISTICS ARE STAGGERING.
I'M STILL JUST A LIBRARIAN.
BORING AND UNATHLETIC.
COMPLETELY ILL EQUIPPED TO DEAL WITH A MEGALOMANIACAL MOTIVATIONAL SPEAKER AND HIS ILLUMINATIESQUE WEB OF SHADOW CORPORATIONS.
BUT I'M SMARTER THAN HE IS.
I HAVE HIS MAGIC PUZZLE BOOK.
AND, I DUNNO, $%^& THAT GUY.
WHO BLOWS UP A LIBRARY?
THE END...FOR NOW

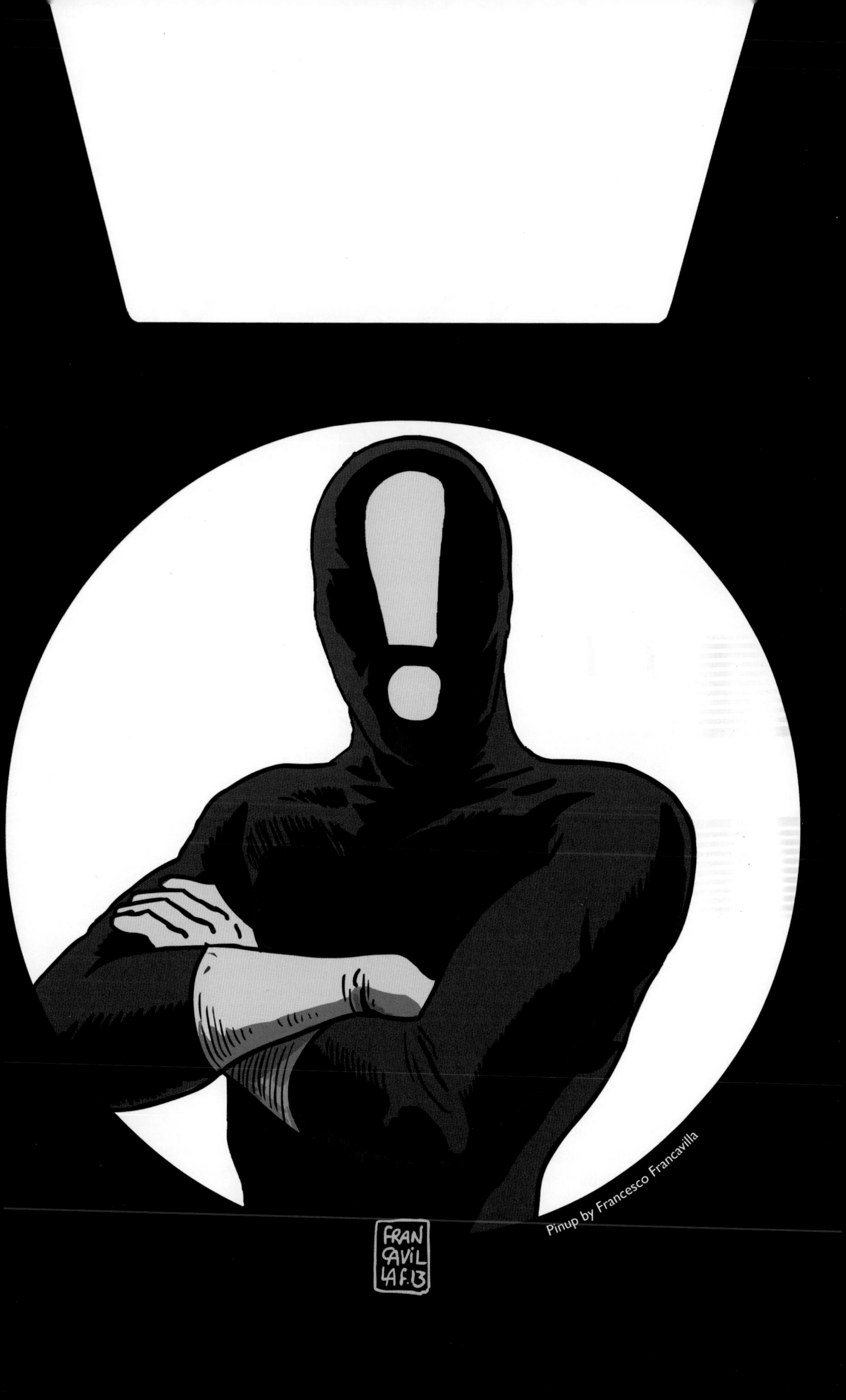
FRAN
CAVIL
LA F.13
Pinup by Francesco Francavilla